# Two Years
## OF
# Eternity
One Missionary's Experience

# TWO YEARS
## OF
# ETERNITY

One Missionary's Experience

SCOTT R. HOYT

**KS**

**Kravitz & Sons**

INNOVATORS IN PUBLISHING, MARKETING AND ADVERTISING

Kravitz and Sons LLC
1301 Farmville Blvd, Suite 104
Greenville, NC 27834

Published by Kravitz and Sons LLC.
ISBN:(sc)        979-8-89639-024-4
ISBN: (eb)       979-8-89639-023-7

Library of Congress Control Number: 2024924757

# TABLE OF CONTENTS

# INTRODUCTION

Each mission experience is unique to the individual missionary because of the diversity of each missionary, mission locations, cultures, missionary companions, the investigators, the members, and the general public a missionary encounters.

However, there are common elements and experiences to missions everywhere, including the preparation, the ups and downs, the difficulties, the spiritual experiences, and the valuable lessons learned and qualities acquired. My challenge in writing this book was to capture the mission experience with all of its spiritual and emotional highs and lows, its personal triumphs and hardships, it's fun times, it's discouraging and boring times, and its effective and creative missionary approaches and others I found to be ineffective.

My goal was to blend general experiences and in- sights, which may be helpful to those thinking about serving and those presently serving, with enough unique experiences to also interest those who have served missions. My family has heard most of the stories and seen the obligatory mission slides. They are my toughest critics and I resolved to publish this only if they thought it was interesting.

The foremost reason for me to write this book was to help my children approaching mission age to make their decision about serving a mission. I derived this book from my missionary journal, my photographs, and my letters.

A journal is indeed invaluable to a missionary who later wants to savor the details of the mission experiences and I would recommend that every missionary keep one.

# CHAPTER 1
## Deciding Whether to Go

Like most other boys raised in the Church, my parents always taught me that my goal was to go on a two-year mission at the age of nineteen. This goal was reinforced regularly in my primary-school, Sunday-school, and eventually priesthood and seminary classes. It never occurred to me to question that goal when I was younger. I eagerly raised my hand, along with the others, whenever a teacher would ask, "How many of you plan to go on a mission?" To a younger boy in the Church, nineteen-year- olds giving missionary farewells seemed like departing knights off to a glorious crusade to encounter innumerable adventures. It seemed I would never grow up to the ripe old age of nineteen in order to leave on my own adventure.

The mission's goal was accepted without question because it never occurred to me to question the truth of the gospel. In the New Testament Christ's apostles seemed confused when the Savior taught that in order to reach the Kingdom of Heaven, one had to become like a little child. In looking back at my own experience, I understand that teaching when I consider the unquestioning faith I had as a youngster, compared with the difficulties of throwing off the cynicisms of adult life. As a youth, my unwavering faith was borrowed in part from my parents' testimony and in part from the testimony of my various teachers, but was also based upon my own personal experiences. I remember, in particular, a family water skiing trip when I was maybe ten years old. We traveled through the desert toward the Colorado River but stopped along the way to use the roadside bathroom—bushes and rocks under a railroad bridge. Afterward, the car would not start. It was extremely hot and we had not seen another car in a long time. My dad, who was mechanically inclined, tinkered under the hood for quite a while until I suggested we have a word of prayer to get the car started again. He smiled at my mom, they both turned and grinned at me and agreed it was a great idea. We had prayer, my dad looked up after the prayer, turned the key, and the car started. He jumped out, shut the hood, and we took off. I had no doubts. In my mind the car would start if we had a prayer, and it did! If only I could have carried this faith through my teen years. It was not to be.

When I entered Sonora High School in Orange County, California, in 1966, I had very few Mormon friends and I began to associate with a different crowd. Although I maintained some friends at my church, as I progressed—or "digressed" may be a better term—to my teen years, my interests seemed to shift more from learning about a mission and spiritual growth through the church, to a quest for the ultimate fun of the moment. The friends I developed in high school would have preferred visiting a leper colony to going to church on Sunday. We never dis- cussed the fact that I was a Mormon, nor did we discuss my religious beliefs. Although I continued to go to church on Sundays, church was becoming less significant to me and a mission seemed less desirable.

One of our fun-seeking adventures, at the expense of others, involved my friends' and my renting of a U-haul van for general mischief on Halloween evening in 1969. We were well organized, we brought fire extinguishers filled with water, extinguishers filled with flour, eggs, and stale produce from behind the market. Loaded with this arsenal, we proceeded to smear, spray, and splatter the water, flour and eggs on numerous trick-or-treaters, including one guy and his girlfriend we had callously teased at school, who had the great misfortune of being located by us in this van with their car doors open, listening to music. Such great training for me, a future missionary! I had little regard then for feelings of others, or for the need to serve through missionary work. Halloween in 1969 culminated with all of us around the van, arms against it and legs spread with police officers patting us down and telling us they had been alerted by three different cities to look for a U-haul van that was causing havoc. When asked what all the old vegetables and fruit were doing inside the van—fortunately, we had unloaded the eggs and fire extinguishers—one of my friends sarcastically advised the policeman that we were on a picnic. In response the officer told him to start eating.[1]

In addition to focusing on general mischief and fun with friends at the expense of any spiritual progress, I also began to doubt I wanted to leave my fun-loving life for two years. My parents probably felt some measure of relief when I agreed to spend my college freshman year at Brigham Young University (BYU). They may have thought that decision was related to church activities. It wasn't. The decision was motivated primarily by my love of snow skiing and the realization that at BYU, I could take it as a PE class.

Far from taking advantage of the many opportunities BYU offered me to grow spiritually and prepare myself for a mission, I continued seeking out friends and fun, which stunted and retarded any growth I should have been experiencing. This "fun" included a number of dormitory pranks, including: filling a vacuum cleaner with flour and reversing its flow in order to shoot the white dust under the door of our floor monitor; putting a table and chairs in the elevator and playing card games as we went up and down; launching water balloons with a surgical tubing catapult into the girls' dormitories across the street; and nighttime commando expeditions up to the mental hospital above to spy on the inmates. Although I usually went to church, there were also times when I felt compelled to be on the ski slopes on Sunday, instead of attending my meetings.

When I came home for the summer, at a time when I should have been leaving on my mission—my birthday was in June—instead, I was more interested in working and going with a girl I had fallen for. My bishop tried to corner me the entire summer, but I knew what he wanted and I tried to avoid him. Unbeknownst to me, my parents had been fasting and praying all year that I would make the right decision and go on a mission. I had changed a great deal—all for the worse—from the young primary school boy who consistently raised his hand when asked if he wanted to go on a mission, and who knew that a prayer could start a stalled car. I persistently told my parents I had no

---

1. I know I will be criticized for discussing some of this mischief making, but I felt it important to show how far I came in trying to get my life in order through my mission to demonstrate, to those who have put a mission as the furthest thing from their mind, that not only is there hope, but they can change and successfully serve a mission.

desire to go and I wished to further my schooling instead—in actuality, wanting to further my pursuit of "fun."

The first time the bishop called me in—I believe he finally corralled me in Sunday school class—he asked me for my thoughts about a mission and I told him I really did not think I wanted to go. Fortunately, he was persistent and he wanted me to go pray about it and talk with him again at the end of the week. Although I had also stopped having regular prayer, I did pray off and on that week about a mission, but not with an open mind. It was always asking for confirmation of my decision not to go. I avoided the bishop for several more weeks until he finally called and scheduled an appointment on a particular Sunday. I remember that morning before I met with him, my mother asked, with earnest hopefulness in her face about my decision. Her hopefulness turned into tearfulness as I told her I still was convinced that I would not go. I arrived at the bishop's office determined to hold to my initial decision, but before he could even broach the subject, I heard myself saying, without any apparently conscious effort, "I will go on a mission." I was not convinced it was really me mouthing the words. I felt like it was an "out-of-body" experience, with the Holy Ghost taking the stubborn young man and prying the words out of him. After I spoke, I still could not believe I said I was going since a mission had been against my wishes up to that very moment.

My parents were ecstatic. I believe they tasted something of what King Mosiah and Alma must have felt at the conversion of their sons after years of hell raising amongst the church members. I am also convinced my decision was not the result of effort on my part up to that point, but rather, because of the faith, fasting and prayers of my parents. My full reconversion—getting back to that childlike faith I had had in younger years—was yet to come.

In hindsight now, I realize I was greatly disadvantaged by my delinquency in Scripture reading, prayer, and association with good church friends through my teen years. I had attended seminary regularly, but for the most part, at least in the later years, without any intent or effort to learn and I often did homework or slept during class. One teacher, having experienced my weak attitude, made a truce. "You can sleep or do homework as long as you don't disrupt the rest of the class."

I found myself woefully behind in my actual knowledge of the gospel and in spirituality and would advise the youth of the church to pick better friends and commit to regular Scripture study and prayer in order to be effective missionaries from the very beginning of their mission. As I see missionaries preparing to go, and returning now, I see many that are more prepared and more effective missionaries than I was, because of choices they made during their teenage years. However, I would still tell a youth, coming from a situation comparable to mine, to get it together and go, regardless of your state of preparation, as long as you have a testimony and a desire to serve. With these two ingredients and help from your parents and church leaders, you can spiritually recuperate and still become an effective missionary.

# CHAPTER 2
## The Call and Preparing to Go

Although I had two years of Spanish in high school, Spanish was as foreign to me as Russian and I really did not consider it much of a factor in regard to where I would go. I was directed to the Cal State Fullerton Institute to take a language aptitude test, which did not seem to make any sense at all. It consisted of make-believe languages which we—there was a group being tested—had to try to decipher and perform various grammatical functions with. I felt that an English-speaking mission was definitely on the horizon!

I had decided to work during the fall semester after my birthday, purportedly to save money for my mission, but, in actuality, to see more of a girl I was going with at the time. This was a mistake, both because it made it more difficult to leave when the time came and because I was a semester behind in my schooling when I got back. I know that for some it is hard not to get too involved with any one girl before leaving on a mission, but later I could see the wisdom of staying unattached, especially since I did not end up marrying her. Romantic involvement just makes it all the harder to leave for two years and to keep focused on missionary work while you are in the field.

Even though I knew I was going, I still did not take as much time as I should have taken to begin a study of the Scriptures in an organized manner. I did have more regular prayer and some Scripture reading. I also obtained a set of the discussions but did not pay much attention to those. It would have helped a great deal for me to have read those through and to have at least begun memorizing the first few lessons. When I finally did learn those lessons in the Language Training

Mission (LTM), they were as big a surprise to me as they were to the first investigators I taught! At that point I realized this gospel really does make sense. There is really something to it!

The day my call came in the mail, I arrived home from work and my mother eagerly held up the envelope, which she had refrained from opening, with great difficulty. She had held it up to the light in different angles, unsuccessfully attempting to read it through the envelope. We excitedly opened it together and read that I had been called to the Andes—the Peru mission. What an exotic place it seemed. It conjured up images of the Lost City of the Incas, and tracting on llama trails through the Andes, working with the Indian descendants of the Incas. That was about the extent of my superficial knowledge of Peru, gleaned from what little I had paid attention to while I was in world history and geography classes in school. I quickly went to the encyclopedia and read what I could about Peru. Later we had some friends over who had visited Peru while on their vacation and they showed us slides, some of which dispelled some of my misconceptions, particularly the slides of Lima, with its modern buildings and traffic congestion.

I was thrilled to read the signature of Prophet Joseph Fielding Smith at the bottom of my call. It was not a stamp and although it appeared a bit shaky—probably due to the prophet's advanced age—the fact that he individually signed each call showed how much concern he had for us and how involved he was in the process. Along with the call, there came a letter from the president of the Andes-Peru mission, listing some general guidelines, descriptions of climate and weather, and what to bring. The notion that I would spend my mission in the An- dean outback, visiting villages, also seemed dispelled by what I viewed then as the unfortunate requirement that I bring white shirts, suits, and ties. I had not owned or worn many suits in my life up to that point and wasn't particularly fond of them. I was even less partial to ties. I could never quite understand the purpose of a tie, especially since it seemed so inhibiting to the neck, but it was time to go shopping and I reached a compromise by purchasing several clip-on ties. I would later regret this when I was standing in a small Quonset-hut airport in the middle of the Amazon jungle with a passenger jet turning full circle in front of us, causing its jet blast to blow off my clip-on tie. The tie went flying and an Indian cholo lady went scurrying to grab it off the ground and run away with it.

We made a trip into the garment district of Los Angeles and I picked up several suits along with extra pairs of pants, since all the walking would be hard on them. We also had to buy certain garments. Although my parents had explained as much as they were allowed to about the Temple in an effort to prepare me for it, nothing could come close to preparing me for the Temple ceremony. It was far different from anything I had ever imagined, and although it seemed a bit strange the first time, it was nevertheless mentally challenging and exciting. It was more strange, however, adapting to wearing garments for the first time.

There were no two-piece garments in those days, just one-piece garments with a button-down flap in the back. I once heard that a nonmember had exclaimed: "Mormons wear strange underwear, like T-shirts with legs." Later in Peru, when my digestive system was having a hard time adapting to certain spicy Peruvian foods, one missionary friend offered sage advice concerning garments. He said, "When you are heading for the bathroom in an emergency situation, don't waste your time unbuttoning the flap, just rip the button off, because you will probably need the extra time. Sacrificing the button is better than the alternative!"

Although my mother had worked with me on cooking and I actually reached the point where I could make a pie, when I learned, I was going to Peru, I found out I would not need to worry about cooking because we would be eating with other people, or we would have maids who would prepare our meals. I had to go through a series of hepatitis, malaria, and other shots whose names I cannot even remember. I do remember that the hepatitis shot had to be taken in the rear, which seemed rather humiliating for me, at my age, not to mention their being painful. I later found out the hepatitis shot was a waste since it was given for a strain of hepatitis not prevalent in Peru. We later had to renew those shots once every six months in Peru. This became a dreaded experience, especially if you were out in the field, away from the mission home, where at least there was somebody good at injecting. Missionaries experimented with giving shots to each other or injecting themselves, neither of which seemed very desirable. Usually several puncture wounds were inflicted before the needle was accurately placed in the thigh or in the arm.

Since I was going to a foreign land, I also had to get a passport for the first time in my life. This process seemed a lot like going through the DMV, with huge lines, and a great deal of paperwork culminating in a booklet with a hard-looking mug shot inside.

It finally came time for the obligatory farewell Sacrament meeting. It was fairly typical of missionary farewells—my parents exaggerated about what a good kid I had been and what a great missionary I would make, though no one would ever have guessed it from my behavior during the several years leading up to it—and I concluded with a bit of a travelogue about Peru and what I hoped to do there. I did not offer much gospel insight since I still had a limited vision of the gospel and what a mission was. I was talking with the Stake president before being set apart, when he asked me why I decided to go on a mission. I listed a number of rather selfish reasons, when he gently reminded me of the most important one, a desire to serve others. I was still thinking mainly of the benefits I could personally derive, but I would soon focus on service and develop a desire to reach out to the Peruvian people. This purpose and vision came to me in the mission home and the language-training center.

# CHAPTER 3
## The Mission Home in Salt Lake City

The last day before I left for the mission home in Salt Lake City was surreal. It was hard for the reality to sink in: that it would be my last "normal" day for two years. My last day at home, my last day with my girlfriend—my last day to do what I wanted to do on my own schedule. I spent most of the day at the beach with my girlfriend. My last day to enjoy Corona Del Mar Beach, my last day to kiss a girl, and my last day to go in the water, although it was too cold to really enjoy it in March. I was set apart by the Stake president in the late afternoon and then my family and girlfriend and I headed for Los Angeles Airport on a Friday evening—probably the worst of all times to be at that airport. Due to the traffic, we reached the gate with about five minutes for me to board the plane. This was probably just as well since it precluded a protracted good-bye, but it left me harried and in a daze by the time I reached my seat on the plane, looking out the window and realizing that, with the exception of a brief greeting at the Salt Lake airport when I took off for Peru from the language-training mission, this would be the last time I would see any of those waving good-bye to me for two years.

I stayed with family friends in Salt Lake City for the night and awoke early to ride their dirt bike motorcycle through the sand dunes behind their house, for an hour, while trying to ponder what it meant for me to leave for two years. Later that morning they dropped me, with my luggage, at the mission home, which, in March 1972, was a converted high school near Temple Square. The place appeared more like a military barracks, with metal bunk beds in large, open dormitories. We were greeted as a group in the assembly hall by the mission home president and later that day, I was assigned to a bunk bed. We then filed through the cafeteria to eat. I can remember one elder—yes, we had to adjust to the deletion of our first names from this point forward—who was in as big a daze as I was. He asked a group of us if we were feeling as strange as he was about having left his home and his girlfriends. We all assured him we were.

The next day was Sunday, and we shared the Sacrament together in our assembly hall and had a string of general authorities speak to us. I had only attended one session of a General Conference in my life and although I was already feeling homesick, I was excited about hearing from four or five general authorities. Toward the end, I remember one stern general authority, with a powerful voice, telling us that at least 10 to 20 percent of us in the room were not worthy to serve missions and needed to clear up problems with the mission president before entering the field. That created a rather uncomfortable atmosphere, with each of us looking at the missionaries sitting next to us, wondering which of us he was talking about. After the talk ended, however, there was a line of missionaries outside the mission president's door. It appeared that his point was well taken and accepted by those listening. On Monday the mission home president suggested we fast before going to the Salt Lake Temple for a session. I hadn't felt like eating much all weekend anyway, so it was not difficult to fast, although by then I was already rather weak, in addition to being homesick. We did two sessions back-to-back and by the time I got out, I felt faint.

After the second session we had the tremendous opportunity of meeting, in the general assembly hall of the Temple, with the then president of the Quorum of the Twelve Apostles, Harold B. Lee. He seemed like a grand- fatherly figure to us and spoke in a kind and comforting manner about our responsibilities and opportunities as missionaries. He asked if we had questions. I remember how impressed I was that for every question asked, he flipped to a Scripture passage to provide the answer, showing not only his humility in deferring questions to the Lord's written word, but also his great knowledge and mastery of the Scriptures.

By the end of the fourth day, after having a little time to go over to the church's gymnasium near Temple Square, to play basketball and relax, most of us started to adjust somewhat. The next day saw those of us heading for foreign missions packed into buses and headed to Provo for the language training mission, while those going Stateside, or to English-speaking areas, headed off for airports to fly to their various mission fields. Their "boot camp" was over, but ours was only starting.

# CHAPTER 4

## The Language Training Mission

In 1972 the language training mission, or LTM, as we called it, was located on the lower BYU campus. It was a long, boxy brick structure that looked much like a large, all-enclosed school building. As we arrived, we were as- signed to districts composed of approximately twelve missionaries for each district. The districts in turn were organized into zones. This was the organizational format we would find in our mission fields. There were district leaders at the head of each district, who reported to zone leaders. In the LTM, the zone leaders were returning missionaries who reported to the LTM president. Our zone leader at the LTM, Elder Swain (nobody seemed to recall anyone's first name in the mission field or the language training mission, since everyone became a "sister" or an "elder") continually warned us that our first companions in the mission field probably would be un- willing to work hard, would like to sleep in, would read everything but church literature, and generally would flake out. Although I can understand his motivation for telling us this—he wanted to toughen us and create self-starting missionaries who would motivate flaky senior companions to do the job they had volunteered for when they went on a mission—I also believe this negative message created some problems when missionaries reached the mission field believing they truly knew how to be better missionaries than the senior companions they were assigned to.

I felt uncomfortable and less than kindly toward Elder Swain at first, but my attitude about him soon changed. I was in class one day, caught up in my homesickness and probably gazing out a window, instead of working on memorizing the discussions. Elder Swain, who had a habit of roaming the halls checking in on the classrooms, because, we thought, of his big-brother approach to intimidating us to do our job, called me out and asked me to visit with him in his office. Instead of giving me a stern lecture on why I should have been paying attention, he showed real concern and asked me why I appeared to be stressed out. I told him I had a lot on my mind, primarily my home and my girlfriend, and that it was making it difficult for me to concentrate. He expressed sympathy and told me I didn't need to worry about those things. If my relationship with the girl was right, it would last through the mission, as had his. Home would be where my heart was, especially since I was to be a representative of Jesus Christ, and He would walk with me. We talked pleasantly for a while and I began to see that he was deeply concerned about the missionaries in his zone and would do what he could to help them become mentally, emotionally, and spiritually prepared for the mission.

Each district had missionaries in it who were going either to the same country, or to countries with the same language. In the LTM, and later in the mission field, the district became like a family, providing an opportunity to develop friendships which would last through the LTM and often into the mission field and beyond. This camaraderie became an important support through times of making a difficult adjustment. The LTM was a difficult adjustment for most of us. At least sleeping arrangements were a little more civilized than at the mission home. There were four missionaries per room, two to each of two bunkbeds. There was a large cafeteria, where over a hundred missionaries could eat at the same time, and schedules were alternated, with different breakfast, lunch, and dinner times being assigned, in order to handle all of the missionaries at the mission.

We quickly settled into our daily routine, starting with the absolute rule that we were to speak only in the language we were learning, twenty-four hours a day. There was no time or place for English! The rationale was that this forced us to learn our language in order to function. We quickly learned some fundamentals, like *baño* (bathroom) and *comida* (food). Our district stayed together for the daily classes, which included lessons to memorize the seven discussions we taught in Spanish. We used a flannel board, with little cut-out figures, to help demonstrate the various gospel principles we taught. These flannel boards folded up, much like a compact umbrella. I was to find out later in Peru that they were useful not only for teaching, but also for warding off the numerous dogs that ran through the streets of Peru.

Most of our teachers were recently returned missionaries, with fresh enthusiasm, boundless testimonies, and almost an envy for us because we were just starting the greatest two-year adventure, which had recently ended for them. They envied us for the experiences we were yet to have and we in turn idolized them for the experiences they had recently returned from. One teacher—Elder Hawkins—was older and had a family. He tried to give a stern, no-nonsense appearance and approach to grinding through the discussions, but his quick wit, dry sense of humor, and insightful mission-field stories, won us over. He became a great friend and confidant.

In addition to lessons on the discussions, we had daily Spanish classes focusing on the language, the grammar, and the speech principles. Our Spanish teacher, Hermana Ortiz, was a short, rotund, always-smiling cherub from Mexico. She always seemed happy and her attitude was infectious. We looked forward to her afternoon classes. It was amazing how quickly we began to converse, albeit at a crude level, in Spanish. From speaking the language every day, memorizing discussions, which included a number of useful vocabulary words, and practicing in our Spanish classes, we progressed faster, in a matter of weeks, than high school students can even hope to come close to in two years of high school Spanish. I was convinced, though, that the primary reason for our progress was the "gift of tongues." Missionaries called to serve in foreign-speaking missions are blessed, by the Lord, with the gift of speaking many tongues, and I believe missionary work is the primary reason for receiving this gift. I can find no other way to explain how quickly I was able to speak Spanish. I had suffered through Spanish for two years in high school and could not at this time, speak a word of it. I am equally convinced that people waiting for a mission call, who are concerned about learning a foreign language, should exercise their faith and put their trust in the Lord, because they will be given this gift, especially if they are willing to work hard at picking up their new language in the mission training center.

We had regular gospel study classes, which I found very interesting since I had greatly ignored my gospel development for a number of years. In fact, one of my biggest adjustments was seeing how much gospel knowledge I was lacking when I compared myself with a number of other missionaries. Through memorizing the discussions, I was not only learning Spanish, but I also found I was learning the gospel. These discussions excited me because they made sense and the gospel became logical to me—of course it would have seemed logical all along, had I paid attention in my seminary, Sunday school, and priesthood classes. I actually became my own first investigator. I was teaching myself the gospel and I found I was thirsting for more. We had an open evening study session each day and since I was quickly picking up Spanish and easily memorizing my discussions, I was able to make use of much of this time to immerse myself in gospel study, reading the Book of Mormon, the New Testament, and Jesus the Christ. The more I read, the more I hungered for more knowledge. I was becoming excited about reaching the mission field and beginning to teach what I was learning.

We had testimony meetings at the LTM like no others I had known or felt. The Spirit was tangible and alive—filling me from head to toe, starting with the burning in my heart. I knew the gospel was true and I was in Jesus Christ's service as his representative. I felt the meaning of the testimonies in Spanish when I first arrived at the LTM, I did not need to understand each of the words, which came later as I learned the language. The spiritual highs helped ease the big adjustments we made in the LTM. The LTM was not easy, it was hard work in the face of the emotional challenges of being away from my family, my home, and my girlfriend. It proved to be a mistake to have had a steady girlfriend before I left. I had cringed every time I heard that admonition as a teenager, coming from what I thought were "know-nothing" parents, teachers, and advisors. I never thought I would give the same advice. Yet, in hindsight, I feel that steady relationships prior to the mission field become a distraction to missionary work and add more stress and anxiety to a missionary's life. They engender worries such as, "Why didn't I get a letter this week," "I wonder what he or she is doing this weekend in my absence," etc. It is not worth the headache. I could have saved myself a lot of wasted worrying and had more time to concentrate on being an effective missionary.

The pain of being away from home and being away from my girlfriend escalated for the first few weeks in the LTM and finally peaked after about two weeks. I began to feel consumed and overwhelmed by loneliness and self- pity. I could not handle it. I became homesick, lovesick, and tired of a rigorous schedule, with very little diversion except for one hour a day spent down at the BYU gym, playing basketball. The adjustment was more difficult because of the close proximity to the BYU campus. For example, we saw other guys walking on the campus with their girlfriends, enjoying the so-called normal life, while we sweated it out in a military-style training program. I called home to tell my parents I had had enough and that I could not endure this. Looking back, I think the phone call was more of a plea for sympathy than a serious surrender I intended to follow through with. My parents were distraught. They urged me to stick it out, they had my girlfriend talk to me, and she advised the same.

I am convinced that many missionaries go through a similar peak point, either at the mission training center or early in their mission, a point where they feel they cannot take any more or cannot make the adjustment. It will pass! My turning point came the next weekend during the April conference. Elder Monson spoke about hardships, using, as examples, missionary stories, and demonstrated how we can pass through hard times and endure to the end. I felt he was speaking to me personally. My attitude changed and I became committed to following through with the mission I had begun. President Monson has been one of my favorite general authorities ever since that moment and I never tire of listening to his stories and advice. To cap off my turning point, Paul Dunn, then a general authority of the LDS Church, came that weekend and spoke to us. He motivated and excited us about teaching the gospel.

My "crisis" soon passed and I am convinced that the similar "crises" of other missionaries also will pass, especially if they will focus on getting to the mission field. At my turning point, I set my sights on getting to Peru and teaching the people. I realized that once I was anxiously engaged in that service, I would lose myself in it and the adjustments to being homesick, lovesick and whatever else, would come naturally.

In looking back, I realize that it would have been the greatest mistake of my life to give up at the point when I felt like it was too difficult to go on. There were those who did quit—some for-health reasons, others simply because emotionally they were unable to handle the transition. I believe that my having spent one year away at college helped prepare me for living away from home, being independent, and making the adjustments that came with the LTM and heading for my mission abroad. There were missionaries who obviously had not experienced living away from home, or who had not been trained to be in- dependent. For them, the transition was even more difficult.

One Scripture section that helped me at the crisis stage was Doctrine and Covenants Section 122, a beautiful sermon on the value of persecution, taught by the Savior to the prophet Joseph Smith. The prophet passed through tribulations I can only imagine, and persecutions and hardships that mine could not even barely approximate. Yet, the Savior taught him that, through all he was asked to endure, he would gain great experience and blessings. He was reminded that the Savior passed through much worse and Joseph could not pretend to be greater than the Savior. I read this Scripture often and pondered the fact that my so-called hardships were insignificant and that I could endure and fulfill my mission.

One beneficial result of the difficult adjustments and perceived hardships was that my prayers became more meaningful as I pleaded for comfort and help from my Father in Heaven. I became more dependent on, and more trusting in, His spiritual guidance and comfort. Prayer became a more meaningful and regular part of my daily life, especially as I began to focus on being the best prepared missionary I could be. I realized, one night in the LTM, how important this work was. I then awoke suddenly in the middle of the night—the others in the room were asleep, with a dark, forbidding feeling of dread encircling me. I was afraid, yet I could not logically think of any reason why I should be. As my fear increased, I walked to the windows of our dorm room, which was on the second story. As I pulled the curtain aside, I looked out and envisioned numerous evil spirits surrounding the LTM, attempting to gain access. My fear escalated and I could not comfort myself, especially after seeing what I had. I climbed back into bed and quickly said a prayer and, in the process, commanded that the evil feeling and the evil spirits depart in the name of Jesus Christ. I was instantly comforted and felt secure once again and was able to drop back immediately to sleep.

In thinking about this experience the next day, I realized that our little army of young missionaries, while in training, constituted the biggest threat to Satan on the face of the Earth. As missionaries, we were taught to carry truth and light to those in darkness, those who did not yet have the truth. If he can prevent missionaries from leaving the LTM, convincing them, by fear, homesick- ness, lovesickness, etc., to quit, to go back to the comforts of home, girlfriends, boyfriends, and family, many people who otherwise might be reached by those missionaries will remain in darkness.

We all struggled, trying to balance the seriousness of our learning and preparation, with just having fun to vent pressure and anxiety. We were able to do a little of this daily through playing basketball and engaging in other forms of recreation at the gymnasium. There were also the inevitable pranks which occur anytime you get groups of teenagers together—for all of the seriousness of our mission preparation, most of us were still teenagers. These ranged from some missionaries placing a piece of plywood, used in remodeling one of the showers, across the shower entrance and filling it up with water to take a large bath, to one missionary who liked to wedge himself between the walls of the corridors with his hands and feet, and crawl up near the top of the ceiling, much like a spider coming down the hallway. Some of us posed for some rather ridiculous pictures, our suit coats turned inside out, with the silk lining on the outside, and our collars turned up, as we posed sanctimoniously with our Book of Mormon in one hand to look like an old-time prophet.

Although some of these stunts were silly, and better left undone, they caused no real harm and were simply one way of adjusting with a little humor and comic re- lief. In hindsight, I think it is important to learn early in a mission that it is not only a time of incredibly hard work and spiritual progress, but also a time for enjoyment and fun. We have the truth and should be happy people. I think many teenagers in the church are turned off by those who take everything too seriously. They need to be shown that you can live by the gospel and still have fun—"Man is that he might have joy."

Giving up my 1960s rock-and-roll music was a real sacrifice. Although I took along a cassette tape player, I had tried to pick an assortment of what I thought was appropriate music. The only pop music tapes that survived that cut were my "Moody Blues" tapes. I also had an     assortment of Mormon Tabernacle Choir music. I used to enjoy sitting on the steps of the LTM, on the crisp Utah nights, looking out over the valley, listening to a little music and pondering what I had read in Jesus the Christ, the New Testament, and the Book of Mormon. I thought about how my life had changed and would continue to change through the course of my mission.

The 1971-72 Lakers season was one of the best sea- sons ever. I had avidly followed them as they won over thirty consecutive games—a record that lasts to this day—and advanced to the playoffs, which unfortunately began while I was in the LTM. There were no TVs since we were being weaned from the things of the world. Television had never been a major part of my life—I am sure later generations have had and will have more serious "withdrawals"—but I did miss seeing my team win the NBA championship.

There was only limited access to telephones, and phoning home was discouraged as part of the process of mentally focusing us on the mission field. I made a few calls home, especially when I reached my "crisis point," but letters from home proved to be the greatest comfort. This was a time when any news or letters from home helped smooth my difficult schedule. The first months of a mission are critical for letters from home. Parents, family members, and ward members who write to their missionaries during this period, especially with uplifting letters about what the missionary is doing and how worthwhile it is, do a great service to the missionary effort. They can scarcely imagine how their letters boost a missionary's spirits and determination.

Our trip, as a district, to the newly constructed Provo Temple was a spiritual feast. The Temple meant so much more to me, after having studied the gospel seriously for several weeks, than it had the first time through, when I was less prepared. We sat together in the celestial room, soaking in the spirit, the beauty of the Lord's house, and the warmth of our love for each other.

My family came up to see me at the airport, once I had completed my training and was ready to fly to Peru. They happened to cruise by the front of the LTM on the day before we were going to fly, in the hopes they might catch my attention, and they did. I ran outside and met them in the parking lot across the street to talk for about a half hour. It seemed awkward at first, like I was a different person—and I was—yet they had stayed the same. This was a taste of what it would be like when I got back from my mission.

The big discussion among the missionaries in my district, the night before we were heading for the airport, was whether we should kiss our girlfriends or not! There was no question in my mind that I would, especially after hearing one of the more down-to-earth leaders say that it would be our last kiss in twenty-two months, so "go ahead *but keep it brief!*"

At the Salt Lake Airport, I was able to spend several hours with my parents, my brothers and sister, my girlfriend, and my grandmother. It was a time of mixed emotions. It was a time that I had been looking forward to for two months, yet it was also a time I realized, with longing would be my last visit with them for twenty-two months. The reality of that was beginning to sink in. This led to a whole new adjustment as I took off on what would be the longest flight of my life.

# CHAPTER 5
## Peru—Culture Shock

Four of us were going to the mission in Peru. We stopped in Dallas, then stopped in Tampa and then in Miami, and had four hours there in the middle of the night. Our next flight took us to Panama City, where the air-conditioning on the plane broke down and we sat sweating in the tropical sunlight for two hours while they worked on the plane, before we finally took off.

We landed in Quito, Ecuador, where I received a little flavor of what South America was like as we walked around the airport and out to the streets in front of it. I saw several grizzled little Indian ladies, wearing "bowl- er" felt hats, bright-patterned dresses, and crude sandals, stooped over, carrying large bundles on their backs and chewing what I thought was gum. I learned later they were chewing the traditional coca leaves from which cocaine is derived. Finally, we left Quito and arrived at Jorge Chavez International Airport in Lima, Peru, where the mission president, President Driggs, and his assistants—two missionaries selected to work directly with him in administering the mission—were waiting. They gave us a warm greeting and directed us to the old Volkswagen bus that was the assistant's mode of transportation.

We rode with the assistants to the mission home, where we had interviews and discussions with the mission president and dinner with his family. President Driggs, in his forties, was a bit young to be a mission president. He had an attractive wife, and children that ranged from somewhere around five or six up through teenagers. He had sacrificed a great deal to become a mission president, giving up a successful executive position with a large company in northern

California, and it was difficult for him and his family in South America, especially with some of his children being at the high school level. Through the course of my mission, I grew to love this man because of his great empathy with, and love for, the missionaries. He had served a mission in South America as well, and his obvious sincere concern and the consideration he gave to each of his missionaries were evident in associating with him at the mission home from time to time, and also at mission conferences.

When I arrived in Peru, the church there was in its infancy. There was only one stake, Central Lima. The outlying cities had only districts and branches. President Driggs was the central authority for the church in all of Peru. He had to work not only at keeping the mission running, making companion assignments and leadership calls to missionaries, but also naming certain missionaries as branch presidents in outlying areas where the depth of the membership was insufficient to provide local leadership. He also took charge of church district meetings (the equivalent of stake conferences at the district level) among the members, as well as planning for stake conferences for the one stake in Central Lima. For two years he filled a father-type role for us as we looked to him for encouragement, motivation, guidance, and support in what we were doing. I would thus encourage any missionary entering the field to develop a strong relationship with his or her president. It makes a mission more meaningful, and creates a friendship that will last eternally.

After dinner with President Driggs and his family, we were introduced to our first senior companions. My first senior companion was Elder Adsero, from Fargo, North Dakota. We grabbed a taxi—a beat up 1960s U.S.—brand automobile with peeling paint, wired on bumpers, and a smoke-belching tailpipe, and proceeded to our area, which happened to be Callao, the port city of west Lima.

Elder Adsero was everything Elder Swain had told me he would not be—hardworking and highly motivated. He wore the heck out of me for the first two weeks until I got accustomed to his rigorous pace. He was about my height, 5'10", of stocky build, with sandy blond hair, rosy cheeks, and a perpetual grin. He liked to walk through our assigned territory, from appointment to appointment, at a pace somewhere between that of a roadrunner and that of a cheetah. I thought I was in pretty good shape after doing four years of water polo, and track and field, and lifting weights on a regular basis, but it took my legs two weeks to get over their stiffness from the pace set by Elder Adsero. I could tell he had been in Peru about two years. His suit was worn thin in spots and it had a sheen from the dirt and grease filling the pores in the material. His shirt collars were ragged—up thrusting fragments of material peeking over the top—as were his ties. His slip-on shoes seemed stretched a size too big and the toes were scuffed. I saw all these signs as his badge of hard work, experience, and endurance, something to be proud of, not ashamed of.

"You will see things you have never seen before, hear things you have never heard before, and smell things you have never smelled before." This was part of the advice given to me by President Driggs, in the mission home in Lima, just before Elder Adsero arrived to take me to our assigned area in Callao. This was the president's way of describing the culture shock I would be experiencing and he was right. I got a taste of it while coming from the airport to the mission home on my first day. We passed numerous houses that appeared to me to be in a state of semi-destruction, with bricks everywhere, and empty frames on the second story. I asked the assistants in the mission minibus if people were rebuilding from the major earthquake they had had a couple of years before. They just laughed and told me that these houses were not being rebuilt from an earthquake but were being built for the first time. Because of the poverty in Peru, most people built their houses in stages when they could afford the materials. They would start with bamboo and cardboard, eventually building a brick wall here and there until they completed the first story, and then if they desired to expand, they would accumulate bricks as money permitted and slowly build the second floor.

I don't care where you are called to serve, but in every case, you are going to go through culture shock. It is probably almost as big for missionaries coming to California from Utah and Idaho to as it was for me going to a foreign country. Of course, the differences would not be the same, but there are peculiarities and differences in each mission field. For this I am grateful. These differences add a sense of adventure to the mission and broaden one's outlook on life, giving each missionary experiences he or she would not otherwise have at home. My philosophy is, enjoy the differences. Some of the differences I encountered within my first few weeks in Callao included the language, showers, food, taxi cabs, the people, dogs, and smells.

Although we made monumental efforts to "live our language" at the LTM, it was not quite the same as being out on the streets of Callao in Peru, knowing that everyone around you could not simply smile at you, acknowledge the Herculean effort you made at speaking Spanish and then resort to English to learn your true meaning. It was a case of either improving and polishing my Spanish or not communicating. My first taste of trying to understand and be understood in Spanish came almost immediately on my first full day in Peru. Elder Adsero and I went to a teaching appointment he had scheduled several days before I arrived. We walked a number of blocks from where we lived— we walked everywhere in this area—to a small mud brick home located back in a courtyard, surrounded by other small housing units, and were invited into a small living area with sparse furniture. We were teaching a third discussion, and Elder Adsero expected me to present my part of the discussion. The discussions were divided between missionaries with a lead role and those with a secondary role. I was able to present my portion of the discussion from memory and it seemed to be understood, but I was in awe at the ability of Elder Adsero to actually carry on a discussion with this lady, answering questions and clarifying where needed. I wondered if I would ever have that level of proficiency in Spanish.

I also made an effort to speak with the son of the people from whom we rented the upstairs room we lived in. He patronized me a little bit by telling me how well he thought I was doing in learning the language. A couple of days after I arrived in Callao, we joined with two of the other missionaries in our district and set up a display board in downtown Callao. This board showed pictures from the Book of Mormon that asked a question in Spanish, "Do you know the Lamanites?" Our object was to stop people on the street as they were walking by and try to interest them in their own history as Lamanites and explain that the Book of Mormon told their story and the story of ancient Peru. I was able to inartfully ask questions of people walking by, but was not too handy at providing answers, so if it appeared that someone was interested, I would ask the person to please write down the directions to their houses. I probably would not have known how to spell the words, anyway. I filled out quite a few referral cards from people I talked with, and perhaps it was a good tactic to elicit their sympathy by showing them how abysmally I spoke their language. One of the lessons I learned quickly, from this presentation, was how many Peruvians do not wish a confrontation or to appear rude. As a result, they would provide a phony address in response to a situation like our street display, or schedule appointments without any intention of ever really being there, not understanding that from our cultural perspective, it would have been better to simply tell us they were not interested. We learned this as we followed up on some of the "golden" reference cards I had solicited, ending up on dead-end streets, or at the fish-processing plant, or other places where there were obviously no residences.

Elder Adsero helped me tremendously with my Spanish. Each day after lunch, when essentially the entire country shut down for a "siesta"—the traditional rest period after lunch, which was the biggest meal of the day in Peru, as it is in all Latin American countries—we would read the Book of Mormon aloud in Spanish to each other. This helped me develop my vocabulary and my pronunciation, as well as drawing me even closer to the Book of Mormon.

The Book of Mormon took on added meaning in Peru, where I was actually teaching Lamanites. Whenever I thought that my mission to the Lamanites seemed difficult, I liked to recall the mission of the sons of Mosiah and Alma the Younger. Their conversion from being troublemakers to helping the church (much like mine, only to a much greater extent) led to a fourteen-year mission to the Lamanites, who at that time preferred to kill any Nephites they saw. I had never really stopped to think about whether the sons of Mosiah and Alma the Younger had to learn a different language, or whether the Lamanites and Nephites shared the same language during the entire Book of Mormon time period. Obviously at some point, their languages diverged, leading to the dialects spoken by the ancient civilizations of South America from the Incas to the Mayas.

Another habit we practiced, to improve our language, was to speak only Spanish while we were out on the streets. We did this not only to improve our Spanish, but also to demonstrate that we were there to be part of the culture as best we could, instead of standing out as visitors. It seemed more polite, and I think it was appreciated by the Peruvians. If there was anything we grew to hate as missionaries, it was rude American tourists acting brash, walking around with cameras, brightly colored shirts, and Bermuda shorts, with dark socks and wingtips— the typical ugly Americans. There was already a growing sentiment, among many Peruvians, against "Yankees." Part of this was a matter of simple envy, but part of it was also because of their perception that small Latin American countries had been kicked around forever by the United States, economically and sometimes militarily. We were accused, by some of the more vocal teenagers, of being everything from homosexuals to CIA agents. I found the first accusation to be both angering and humorous. The Peruvian culture, like most Latin cultures, is more touch oriented than ours and it was not unusual to see teenage boys walking arm in arm. It Deemed somewhat ironic to have teenagers walking arm in arm while accusing us of being homosexuals. Once in a while, when we were accused of being CIA spies, I would tease them by responding, that "Yes, we are spies and we have come to spy on your use of the military equipment the U.S. sold to Peru!"

As I struggled to learn Spanish in order to teach the gospel, it seemed like some of the teenagers we passed on the streets were trying to learn the filthiest English words they could in order to taunt us as we walked by. I had been a rather rowdy teenager and I was new to the mission field, so my first reaction was, "Let's pound them." The teenagers were often smaller than we were and seemed physically intimidated by us, probably because they saw mostly reruns of U.S. television shows depicting tough guys, cops, and James Bond. Fortunately, my companion was more mature and told me to simply cool down and ignore them. He gently suggested that our missionary efforts might be more fruitful if we did not beat up the people's teenagers. I struggled to control my temper, in reaction to the taunts, throughout my mission, I was mostly successful, but sometimes I let my anger show.

Showers in Peru were an ordeal, not a pleasure. Very few people knew what a gas water heater was, and our single room, with its small bathroom off to one corner, was no exception. It had a small six-inch electric coil that was plugged in. It feebly attempted to heat water as it ran through the coil and out the shower head. The tradeoff was, if you wanted the water hot, you had to let it barely trickle through the shower head, but for really rinsing off and getting any kind of a stream of water, the water ran through the coil too fast to be heated. It also seemed like risky business to attempt to plug the cord in while you were under running water. I wondered how many Peruvians were electrocuted in their showers. As a result of these miserable little showers, I itched horribly from rinsing with cold water. I also ended up shaving with cold water for the first time. Trying to get a lather with shaving cream or soap, in cold water, led to many nicks and scruffy shaves.

Walking the streets of Callao inevitably led to frequent encounters with the most dangerous animal in Peru, the taxi driver. Most of the cars they drove were not just from the 1960s but many went back to the 1950s and some to the 1940s. Many were in very rough shape and appeared to be held together with salvaged scraps, wire, or anything else that could keep them running. Typically, their paint was peeling, their mufflers hung from coat-hanger wire, and getting in required special care to avoid getting jabbed by pieces of metal protruding from the doors or seat covers. The horns on many of these cabs had stopped functioning, so the drivers disconnected the horn wires and had a wire with its bare end sticking out toward the dashboard. When they wanted to honk the horn, which was almost as often as they got behind the wheel, they would push the bare wire to the metal dash, triggering the horn. Some of the cabs had no horn. The drivers would put their left arm out the driver's window and beat on the side of the car to show their displeasure. Environmentalists would cringe if they saw these cabs take off while spewing burned black oil clouds.

Most had a "saint"—a small figure of a Catholic canonized person in church history whom they looked to for protection—glued to the dashboard. Whatever could give them protection, they in fact needed. Their passengers and the pedestrians they encountered needed even more protection! There were a number of times throughout my mission, and in particular, in my first few days in the country, when I nearly got flattened by cabs. I was under the false assumption pedestrians had the right of way in Peru, like they did in California. I was sadly mistaken. Taxi drivers seemed to have a license to kill pedestrians—at least it seemed they speeded up or veered toward them instead of braking or trying to avoid them. Years later, I would encounter a dangerous animal of the same species in New York—the New York cab driver.

Once in a while, we took a chance and rode in taxis—which was an experience to remember. Most of the seat springs were broken; you were lucky if you didn't get a jab in the rear with the sharp end of a broken spring. Most of the cabs had not been tuned up in ages and smoked and sputtered as they made their way through traffic, with the driver banging on the side of his door or honking his horn by slamming the bare wire on the dash. I can remember arriving in a dilapidated cab at the mission home on a P-day (preparation day for missionaries). This cab ran so badly, we thought we were going to stall all the way there. It was rattling and clanking in about ten different spots. The bumpers looked and sounded like they were held in place by wire, the grill rattled, the hood ornament shook, and we were leaving a cloud of smoke behind. As we pulled up to the mission home, several elders standing outside started pointing at the cab and laughing. We clattered to a stop, the cab overheated, the radiator cap exploded off the radiator with a bang, and a violent cloud of steam blew the hood up—apparently overpowering the wire used to hold it in place. The car erupted like a volcanic geyser, engulfing all of us in mist. We emerged from the smoke and hooted and howled with the other Elders until we were in tears. I suppose we should have been sympathetic to the cab driver, but it seemed so comical at the time. The heckling elders said, "Boy, you guys sure know how to pick 'em."

I was saved from disaster at least once by a cab. Elder Adsero and I ate with a family that lived in an apartment about a block and a half from our little pension, or apartment. After I had been in Peru for about a week and was still trying to adjust to the differences in the food, we walked one morning, down the steps from the apartment where we ate, after eating breakfast, and I was hit with sudden cramps and an immediate need to find a bathroom. As I was waddling, doubled over, I realized I could not walk the one block to our apartment and I grimaced and told Elder Adsero, "I know it sounds silly, but I need a taxicab." He laughed and fortunately a cab came by as he stuck up his arm. We hurried into the cab and received a dirty look from the cab driver as we told him we were only going one block. He probably thought to himself, "These spoiled and pampered Yankees." It seemed forever to travel the block. I was surely grateful for that cab as we pulled up in front of our apartment.

Prior to my mission, my mother had been fattening me up and spoiling me with three full meals a day, starting with a breakfast of scrambled eggs and toast, with sausage or bacon, and occasionally with fried potatoes. I was used to eating as much as I wanted for dinner. I also remember having three complete meals in the LTM and usually having as much as I wanted to eat. Getting used to the food in Peru at first was a shock, both because of the different types of food, and also because of the different quantities. Peruvians tend to be smaller and traditionally they have only one big meal a day—at lunch.

My first full day in Peru, Elder Adsero and I walked to the apartment where we ate breakfast and lunch with a family that we paid a modest monthly sum to. As we sat down to breakfast, I noticed two rolls on my plate along with a cup of hot chocolate. I ate the rolls and enjoyed them, with jam and butter, patiently awaiting the main part of the meal. When Elder Adsero finished his rolls, he said, "Let's go." I was stunned, and said, "That's break. fast?" He assured me that was it. By lunch I was starved. Although at lunchtime we tended to have a fairly good. sized meal, usually with some combination of rice, beans and beef, or chicken and potatoes, with a hot pepper sauce over them, I was still hungry by evening, and I was shocked to learn there was no evening meal—we were on our own for dinner. Dinner tended to be candy bars and soda pop at the local stores that were on almost every other block. Occasionally we would treat ourselves at a place called the "Chifa," a little Chinese restaurant in downtown Callao where we would order fried wontons or some other delicacy. It was nestled between other small stores on the main street of Callao. I lost ten pounds during my first two months in Peru while trying to get used to the reduced quantity of food and all the walking we did.

There were certain traditional Peruvian foods I grew to like. One was ceviche—raw fish, marinated overnight in lemon juice until it turned white. It was naturally cooked, at least on the outside, by fermenting it in the lemon juice. These small pieces of raw fish were served with chopped onions and peppers. Although it tended to be spicy and hot, I grew to love it. The Peruvians grew extremely hot orange peppers, called "aji" (aah hee), which they chopped up and put in everything. Small pieces, sometimes undetected by the human eye, could ambush you as you were pleasantly chomping on your salad and lead to an eye-watering, nose-dripping, red-faced experience. Eating aji also could lead to close calls while working out in the field, especially since in Peru there were no public bathrooms, and it was culturally taboo to ask friends or members of the church to use the bathrooms in their homes. Many of those we visited had no flush toilets. Many of the members in the suburbs, or barrios, had only a hole in the floor over which you had to strategically position yourself.

Once, during my first week in Callao, we were quite far away from our pension in a small barrio, when a wave of indigestion hit me, and I asked a not too sympathetic Elder Adsero where I might be able to use a bathroom. He chose that very inopportune moment to teach me that the Peruvian culture mandates that you do not ask to use their bathrooms. He advised me to simply wait until later that day, when we would be back near the church—easy for him to say! Finally, later that day, we ended up near the church as I was about to explode.

Peruvians eat a lot of fish, especially in Callao, which is one of the major fishing ports of the country. The fishing industry is one of the primary industries in Peru. Elder Adsero and I visited a member of the church who was a fisherman living out on the coast. He explained that in order to be successful at his trade, he needed to stay up well into the early hours of the morning, tending his nets and pulling in his catch. This led to his conclusion that the Word of Wisdom's prohibition on drinking and smoking did not apply to his use of cocaine leaves to stay awake during the early hours of the morning to work his fishing nets. He said, "The Lord understands." We assured him the Lord would probably not be understanding and that for his own good health, and because of the Word of Wisdom, he should try to sleep a little during the day. After our discussion he offered us a fish which, though gutted, had been fried completely with the head, eyes, and tail intact. I remember picking at the body of the fish, which was tasty, and leaving the head, spine, and tail. The fisherman looked at my plate and told me to go ahead and finish my meal. "Do not be embarrassed to finish it all: if you are hungry, I will give you more," he said. He actually expected me to eat the head and eyes! I assured him I was full, at which point his little son grabbed the fish off my plate, stuck the head in his mouth, and sucked out the eyeballs, while chewing off the rest of the head. I figured I had to draw the line somewhere, even if I was famished most of the time!

While in Peru, I tried many different foods I had never imagined eating. Later in my mission, I was in Iquitos, on the Amazon River in the northeastern portion of the country and had various meats from animals I could not even put a name to in English. Some of them included snakes, monkeys, giant rodents, and every fruit known to mankind. I heard one of the worst food stories from an elder who had served in a small, poor village up in the Andes. He was invited to attend a party where the purported main course was "qui," or guinea pig. I found that guinea pig was a delicacy in Peru. The pigs tended to be much larger and fatter than the guinea pigs in the United States, with some of them approaching the size of a rabbit. I still found them to consist more of bones and cartilage, rather than meat, but they were palatable when prepared with the traditional Peruvian sauces. Anyone who has seen guinea pigs knows they have no tails, only short little stubs. When the elder was given his plate, his "qui" had a long, hairless tail. At that point, even a green missionary realized it was a rat, not a guinea pig. To avoid offending his host—it was an insult to not eat what was placed in front of you—he found a way to slip it off his plate onto the ground for the stray dogs working the table for scraps.

One of the things I missed the most was fast food. There were no hamburger places with the exception of one restaurant in downtown Lima that served what they called "hamburgers." Their "hamburgers" were mixed with some kind of green barley and tasted more like grass patties. Some of the soda pops were unusual, especially the "Inca Cola," which did not taste like a cola at all. It tasted like carbonated bubble gum in a bottle. It was a form of a carbonated herb drink, with a picture of an Inca on the bottle. One delicacy I ate often consisted of the chopped and marinated beef heart pieces served on little sticks, grilled over an open fire. They were available on many street corners in Callao. At first, it seemed gross to be eating a cow's heart, but the small pieces of beef had been pounded, marinated, and grilled to perfection. To a hungry missionary who had eaten his big meal hours before, they seemed heavenly. Of course it was taking a risk to eat on the street, as we had been warned of parasites, worms, and other diseases and food poisonings, but when it came to a choice between these maladies and starvation, food won out. Although I was really sick a few times from food poisoning in Peru, I cannot recall any of those times as having resulted from eating barbecued food on the street.

One thing I stayed away from, and had no desire to try, was the fried blood sausage that was also sold on the street. Street vendors had huge blood sausages—intestine skins from cows, filled with curdled blood—that they would proceed to slice and fry in patties. They did not interest me in the least, especially after I saw how the flies congregated over the sausage both before and while it was being cooked. I also was not big on tripe—fried cow and pig intestine pieces—which also seemed to be a favorite on the street.

We occasionally saw "cholos," or Quechuan Indians who had come into the big city from the mountains, looking for work. These Indian people were dressed distinctly, with brightly embroidered skirts, sweaters, and knit caps with ear flaps. They were the literal descendants of the Incas, and it was sad to see the way the Spanish conquest had led to their degeneration from a once proud and noble civilization to, for the most part, people who were humiliated and discriminated against. They appeared to be rejected by employers and were at the lowest economic levels of society. They also seemed to have lost other vestiges of the once great Incan civilization. We saw them go by in the mornings, digging in the trash cans, looking for scraps of food. The women wore large skirts, and whenever they needed to go to the bathroom they simply squatted on the ground where they'd stood with their skirts around them. The men usually found a convenient corner and took no notice that they were in public. Unfortunately, one of the habits they carried over from the days of the Inca was the use of cocaine leaves or coca leaves. They were constantly chewing these leaves, which gave them energy without calories. This led to severe aging on the body as they were starved of protein. Many of these cholos looked like they were in their sixties when in fact they were in their thirties.

Two missionaries told us a story of their efforts to move a piano from one of the branch meeting houses to another in a city in northern

Peru. As they struggled with this piano, a small cholo man approached them and said that, for the equivalent of two U.S. dollars, he would move the piano. The elders were skeptical, but thought if he could do it, it would save them a lot of effort, so they agreed. He asked for fifteen minutes to get ready. For fifteen minutes he stuffed his mouth full of cocaine leaves, which he chewed and chewed and chewed. Once he felt like he had his maximum strength, he had the elders help him hoist the piano on his back, with one end of a big strap around its bottom, and the other hooked over his forehead. As he leaned forward, they held the piano in place on his back while he carted it several blocks to the new location.

I was fascinated by the many different people we encountered. Because we walked so much, we met many interesting people in the course of a typical day. There were interesting people right around our pension. There was a beauty salon next door, with a woman and a son there. They lived on the second floor and operated the salon out of what used to be the garage down below. From the family we rented from, we learned this woman had always run a beauty salon and had always wanted a daughter instead of a son. As her son grew up, she dressed him in girls' clothes. He had thus grown up as a transvestite working in the beauty salon. He wore gobs of makeup and frilly feminine clothes. It was an eye opener to me, a middle-class, sheltered teenager from the comfortable suburbs of Southern California. I reeled from one new "people experience" to another. For example, I was startled to see drunks lying in the park out near the head of the peninsula in Callao. I had never encountered the home- less before, and I felt tremendous sympathy for them, as I did for the Cholos I saw rummaging through the trash cans in the mornings. I began to appreciate the fact that what had seemed to me a rather modest lifestyle in the United States was quite comfortable and actually quite exceptional when compared to most lifestyles in Peru.

The Suarez family had received a few discussions from Elder Adsero and his prior companion. We went to visit them in a barrio named Frigorifico (Free-go-rifeeco), out near the fish processing plant. The plant was up the coast, one mile north of the main street and peninsula, situated near the harbor and docks. We walked out of town, across the tracks and past barrios, to get there. As we approached the plant, I recalled the admonition of President Driggs, when I'd first arrived in Peru, that I would smell things worse than I had smelled before and worse than my wildest imaginings. This was one of those occasions. The plume of fishy, greasy smoke spilling out of this plant seemed to darken the entire landscape and permeate everything, including my clothing. Because of these odors, the housing surrounding the factory belonged to squatters who had moved into vacant fields that no one else wanted to occupy.

We walked down a dirt road bordering a vacant field on our left, and a bunch of tin and cardboard shanties on our right, until we reached a small dirt pathway tucked between some of the shanty huts. We passed straggly dogs of varying shapes and playful, dirty children, and then we came to the Suarez hut. From the outside it looked like mostly a bamboo mat and cardboard, with a few pieces of wood loosely put together as a frame. Hermano Suarez greeted us at the "door," which was simply a piece of wood wired to the wood frame around it, and he let us in. He was a short man, about 5'5", with a slender build and the characteristic dark brown skin of the mestizos—the mixed race of Spanish and Indian people who made up the predominant portion of the population of Peru. As was also typical of all Peruvians, he had black hair and a warm smile and greeted us with a friendly handshake. As we proceeded into the only common room in his home, I saw that it had a dirt floor, which had been packed and stamped with water until solid. It was swept clean. There were only a few chairs, which were made with wood frames strung with rattan. Hermano Suarez offered us the chairs while he, his children, and his wife sat on a wood beam strung between two bricks. Light was provided by a kerosene lamp which flickered our silhouettes on the bamboo mat and the cardboard walls surrounding us. Hermano Suarez eagerly looked forward to these visits. He was thirsting for the gospel of Jesus Christ. He had made some progress in reading in the Book of Mormon, but his wife was illiterate, and he moved slowly through the book while attempting to read aloud to her and explain the concepts. Their two little boys were cute, round, jovial characters. They were fascinated by the missionaries, probably because of our size, our white skin, and strange accents. As we taught them a third discussion on the flannel board, attaching little characters or concepts at crucial moments in the lesson, I was overcome by the Spirit, and with joy at seeing the sincerity with which these humble, good people desired to learn the message we had come thousands of miles to bring to them. As we taught them that evening, a powerful wave of the Spirit surged through me. As we knelt in prayer, this spiritual fire caused me to shake and I unsuccessfully battled my tear ducts as Hermano Suarez prayed earnestly and sincerely, to know whether the message his friends from the north brought him was true. My eyes watered and my chest burned—I was filled with love for this humble family and their desire to learn the truth. I knew at that moment, without any doubt, why I was on a mission and why I wanted to be the best missionary I could be.

The Suarez's receptiveness to a message taught so unartfully by two gringos from North America, struggling with the language and coming from an entirely differently lifestyle, culture, and background, forcefully convinced me we were teaching the truth and that it would be received by humble, good people everywhere. I also began to realize how special the Peruvian people were, and how in tune to the Spirit they were, while being unencumbered with material interests and distractions. I can only wonder how I would have reacted, had I not grown up in the church, to missionaries from a different culture, struggling with my language while coming to my door and telling me they had the truth about religion.

In the Scriptures, it talks about how difficult it will be for the rich to inherit the Kingdom of God, and I began to realize that people's interest in the gospel at times seems proportionate to their circumstances in life, and that the proud and wealthy are a much harder "sell." I looked forward to teaching the Suarez family in their humble little home on a weekly basis. Hermano Suarez had recent trials in his life, including a crudely performed appendectomy that left non dissolvable internal stitches in his body. One by one, these stitches were working their way out through the skin, leaving welts and infections. His tremendous faith provided a testimony to me.

The most interesting part of a mission is meeting new people; companions, investigators, members, and everyday people you encounter on the street or while tracking. These encounters make up a large part of the mission experience. I was soon to learn that there was also a lot of excitement in encountering all the free-roaming dogs in Peru. Dogs seemed to proliferate everywhere. They were on the streets, in the houses, and in the alleyways. Veterinary care was beyond the economic means of most Peruvians. As a result, the dogs were not "fixed" and there were many homeless dogs on the streets. Since we lived close to the city center in Callao, we did not have as many problems with them there as I would have later in my mission. When we visited the Suarez family, near the fish processing plant, I saw many pathetic dogs. Many were hairless, some because of their breed and others because of their malnutrition. Scraggly, scruffy beasts, with protruding rib cages, stared at us with gaunt, hungry eyes. I remember one pathetic dog limping along on three legs near the railroad tracks by the fish-processing plant, with one of its front legs broken, the bone protruding. From the caked dirt and lack of blood, it appeared the leg had been broken for months, and I was amazed the dog had not died from infection.

Because there were so many dogs, they were always being hit in the street. I remember being at one investigator's house, teaching a lesson, and hearing a thud and squeal as another dog parted the veil for the Spirit World. There were so many dogs hit on the streets that street keepers would stack dead dog carcasses along the sides of the roads. Once the stacks were big enough, they were lit up and burned, emitting yet another one of those smells my mission president warned me about.

# CHAPTER 6
## First Area Experiences and Routines

Wherever you go on your mission, the first area you go to becomes very special and remains that way because it is where you make your biggest adjustments and experience bigger changes as you first begin to feel the thrills, heartbreaks, highs, and lows of being an actual missionary. In Callao I experienced the full range of missionary experiences, and I have many fond memories of it, primarily because I had a very good companion there—we worked hard, met many people, taught many people, and thoroughly immersed ourselves in missionary service.

Our day there consisted of waking up between 6:00 A.M. and 6:30 A.M., studying scriptures individually for an hour, discussing our plans for the day—going over our schedule book to discuss the people we had appointments with, whom we were going to teach, or where we were going to tract—having prayer together for individual investigators and guidance for those receptive to our message, and then going for breakfast around 8:00 A.M. After breakfast we would be out on the street by 9:00 A.M. either to teach discussions, knock on doors to try to meet new people in different areas of the city we decided to visit that day, or look up any referrals we received from members. Because the church was not yet fully developed in Peru, we did not have that many referrals from members. We looked forward to receiving any referrals since it was much more effective to have the members' fellowship and try to discuss the gospel with their friends and neighbors, rather than having the "gringo" missionaries try to make the first contact. This is true no matter where a missionary teaches the gospel. It is always more effective to have the member's assistance in missionary work.

We would stop to eat our main meal of the day—lunch—at around noon and then come back to our pension at 1:00 P.M. to read passages in the Book of Mormon together out loud in Spanish. We would take a half-hour nap before going back out on the streets at about 2:00 P.M. We would continue working until about 9:30 at night and then grab a snack and head back to our pension by 10:00 P.M., to retire for the evening. This schedule remained pretty much the same throughout my entire mission in all the areas I served in.

Elder Adsero believed in walking almost everywhere. Once I grew accustomed to the strenuous pace, it was enjoyable because we were able to immerse ourselves in all of the activities on the streets of Callao, stopping to talk with people, knocking on doors, and generally observing this new and exciting place. Callao had a small downtown section, with shops leading down the main boulevard, toward the tip of the peninsula extending out and protecting the port of Callao. Out toward the end of the downtown area was a fort and a central plaza, or square, where many streets converged. Most cities in Peru had central plazas filled with gardens, trees, and fountains. People in the city lived mostly in brick buildings built wall-to-wall, next to each other, and are generally two stories, covered with plaster, and painted bright pastel colors of blue, pink, red, or green. Usually, their front door was only about three feet off the sidewalk. In the city there usually were no backyards, but at most a little courtyard, and most of the houses had a wall around their roof section with flat roofs that could be used for clothes lines and storage.

Generally, houses in Lima and Callao did not have pitched roofs because there was no concern for water run—off—it had not rained in Lima in recorded history! This is because the Humboldt Current, a very cold current of water that plunges up along the coast of South America from Antarctica, combines with the Andes Mountain chain to create an inversion gap over Lima that keeps clouds from forming. The Humboldt Current also brings a wealth of anchovies, and all of the larger fish that feed on them, to the coast of Peru, making it one of the major fishing nations of South America. Although it did not rain, it was often very humid in Lima, especially during the warmer months, which are directly opposite from our seasons in the United States—summer in Peru falls during our winter, and vice versa. During the summer in Lima, we were able to work without our coats in short-sleeved white shirts and ties.

There were many people, such as the Suarez family, who did not have the luxury of living in brick and plaster homes. They lived in the larger barrios or areas surrounding the core of the city. The barrio dwellers lived in huts made of whatever materials they could gather, including cardboard, bamboo mats, and wood. Their huts had no running water or electricity. They used kerosene lamps for light, and collected water in large cans either directly, or via deliveries from water trucks. In contrast, there were neighborhoods of large Spanish—and Tudor—style homes out on the peninsula of Callao. They looked like Beverly Hills homes. We visited an inactive member family living in one of these homes. They had a son in the United States and enjoyed talking to us about our country, but not about the gospel.

Over 90 percent of the Peruvians are Catholic by tradition and upbringing. When the Spanish arrived in Peru they imposed Catholicism on the Incas. As part of the conversion, the Spaniards tore down the Incan temples and built cathedrals on top of them so that the Incas would come to the Catholic cathedrals to worship. This traditional Catholic influence made it difficult for us to find receptive listeners to our discussions as we walked the streets of Callao. Often it was the men that showed interest at first, since Sunday masses were attended mostly by women and children, while many of the men stayed home to watch soccer games, play soccer, or have get-togethers with their buddies.

Catholicism seemed very different in Peru, from what little I knew of it in the United States. There was a great emphasis in Peru on tangible and visible items like statues of saints; statues of Christ, crucified; and all kinds of gruesome pictures of Jesus Christ, with thorns piercing his head and hanging on the cross. The saints—those who had been canonized for performing certain miracles and becoming worthy leaders in the Catholic church in the past, had a place of great importance in the lives of many in Peru. Often prayers were directed to saints instead of our Father in Heaven, and different saints were specialists, or were sought for different types of miracles.

One day we visited the home of a family whose male leader was more interested in soccer than in Catholicism. (We usually called the man of the house "Senor," or Mister, and the lady of the house "Senora," or Mrs., unless we were familiar with them, and then we would call them "Hermano" or Brother, and "Hermana," or Sister.) On the wall his wife had hung a picture of one of the more popular saints of Peru, Saint Martin de Porras. Saint Martin, an Afro-Peruvian saint, had, several hundred years ago, been canonized for his great peace-making abilities, as demonstrated by a miracle he had performed in having a rat, a cat, and a dog drink milk from the same bowl. During our visit, the senor was watching the Peruvian national soccer team in World Cup competition on television. The leading scorer for Peru at that time was Teofilo Cubillas, another Afro-Peruvian. We pointed to the picture of Saint Martin and teased him about how much he actually must idolize Cubillas since he had a picture of him on his wall. He joined us in a good laugh and warned us not to retell the joke in the presence of his wife, who took Catholicism more seriously.

We saw TV antennas sticking up out of even the poorest hovels. It seemed that TV was a must, no matter how afflicted by poverty you happened to be. Most of the TV shows were decade-old shows that had once been seen in the United States. They appeared rather comical to me because the actors were obviously speaking English, but they were dubbed in Spanish. From time-to-time new soap operas from Venezuela or Argentina would air on TV and we could save ourselves the trouble of trying to interest anyone in what we had to say during the soap- opera hour.

Because of the heavy influence of Catholicism, and its emphasis on rote prayers in Peru, many of the people we taught were not used to spontaneous prayers. One of the most rewarding aspects of our work was teaching spontaneous prayer from the heart. At the end of the second discussion, and sometimes the first, we would ask the families if they wished to have a prayer, and often, after we demonstrated prayer on at least one prior visit, we would ask them to pray. It was always a great spiritual experience to kneel with sincere Peruvian investigators who had never before opened their hearts to our Father in Heaven, and to hear their sincere requests for blessings, especially the blessing to be able to recognize whether what we taught was true.

The national census was taken on my first Sunday in Peru. Everyone had to stay off the streets and inside their residences until they were counted. Since we could not leave to eat, we stocked up on "health" food from the local little *tienda*—store. This included candy bars, soda pop, and stale rolls. I had changed so much while at the LTM and in my first week in Peru, that I actually looked forward to time spent in our apartment, when I could study the scriptures and read about the gospel. If my family and friends could only see me then! They would not have believed the transformation.

In the afternoon we attended my first church service in Peru. I had a great time. The Peruvian members were very friendly and enthused about the missionaries. They were especially anxious to greet and introduce themselves to new missionaries. Much of what they said to me went over my head as I was struggling to learn the language, yet their spirit and warmth needed no translation. One thing I noticed about the meeting was that no one played the piano for the hymns and as a result, they were sung largely off-key, though with great gusto. I mentioned to Elder Adsero that at one time I had played the piano and perhaps could at least help by playing the melody hand. As the weeks progressed, I started out by playing just the top keys to help everybody sing on key and eventually, through practice on P-days, I worked into playing full hymns for the congregation. The members appreciated it, and so did our ears! We could all sing on key as long as I didn't play wrong notes.

Mondays were the P-day, or at least until 5:00P.M. This was our day off to prepare for the rest of the week by writing letters, running errands, and doing a little sightseeing. We spent much of my first Monday in Peru writing letters and going to the post office to get post. age and mail. While we were downtown, we walked out to the point along the coast and looked off the coast to a fog shrouded island lying about three miles off the tip of the peninsula of Callao. Elder Adsero explained that this was San Lorenzo Island and that there was a prison on the island where hardened convicts were imprisoned. In the afternoon we sat up on the roof of our apartment, looking out over the Lima skyline. The roofs of Lima did not present an attractive view. Since it never rained, they were covered with dust and dirt, and because they were flat, they were used for clotheslines and storing discarded junk. The roofs of Peru were like garages in the United States.

They received all of the unwanted items supposedly stored for use at a later date that would never arrive. Looking beyond the roofs, we saw the pretty scenery visible from our roof, the foothills of the Andes Mountains, which rose up ten miles inland. As I sat contemplating the scenery from our roof, it seemed almost like a dream that I was thousands of miles away from my country and in a foreign nation.

At 5:00 P.M. on Mondays we had a district meeting with the other missionaries in our district. In Callao there were only four of us. The other two elders covered the area next to ours. District meetings included a spiritual thought, a discussion about how the work was going, and a general sharing of creative ideas for missionary work. We were always coming up with novel ways to knock on doors and get invited in. Some of these included flashing our missionary passport, an official-looking document, which seemed to impress some of those we encountered, especially when we told them we had come all the way from the United States with a message for them. At times we tried to arouse their curiosity by asking them if they knew who the Lamanites were. When they didn't, we told them that they were Lamanites and asked them if they would like to know the ancient history of their people.

The biggest obstacle to overcome in door knocking, in areas above the lowest poverty level, was the maids. Everyone living above subsistence level in Peru had a maid since they were so inexpensive. Typically, the maids were *cholo* women, or Quechua-speaking Indian women who came down from the Andes to try to grind out a living working as a maid. Many of them did not speak much Spanish, which was the first hurdle, and even if they did, they were under strict instructions, from the lady of the house, not to invite in strangers, especially missionaries! We were thus often stymied by the maid. At times it was humorous. We knocked at one house, and we had the following dialogue with the maid:

**ELDER ADSERO:** Is the lady of the house home?

**MAID:** No she's not here.

**ELDER ADSERO:** Then would you please ask her when she will be home?

**MAID:** One moment, please. (*The maid leaves the door, goes into the interior of the house, and re- turns in about two minutes.*)

**MAID:** She says she won't be back until about 6:00 P.M.

**ELDER ADSERO:** Well then, would you ask her if we can come and see her when she does get home?

**MAID:** One moment, please. (*Maid leaves the door and returns again in about two minutes.*)

**MAID:** She says she is not interested in seeing you when she gets home.

I did not blame the people for trying to avoid us. I could recall how annoying it seemed to me when Jehovah's Witnesses made the rounds of our neighborhood while I was growing up. From knocking on doors in Peru, I gained a lot of empathy for those, of whatever faith, who circulate through neighborhoods attempting to talk to people. I became much more tolerant of missionaries of other faiths when I returned from my mission. I was more receptive to talking to them and exchanging ideas, even though they were not Mormons.

With certain "creative" door approaches, we went to extremes that probably would have gotten us arrested in the United States. We got good at sticking our foot in the door so that the maid could not close the door, and had to go get the lady of the house. Usually this just got them mad, but once in a while, after we got past the maid, we were able to converse with the lady or the man of the house. At times they admired our tenacity and were curious about the United States. In our view, whatever got us in the door was a significant first step as unless we got that far, we could not talk our way into teaching opportunities.

We had fun teasing the maids. The typical doorbell in middle-to-upper-class Peruvian homes was a two-way switch on the wall near the door. It pivoted in the middle and was spring mounted so that it could be pushed and held down. One day after being rebuffed by several maids, I folded up a referral card and wedged it between the door button and its socket. This held the buzzer button down and left it running continuously. We then walked back toward the front gate and waited until the maid came out and saw what had happened. She pulled the card out. We played this game a couple more times until we had the maid so flustered she did not know what to do. We finally left laughing.

After I'd been in Callao a short time, we had a mission conference at the church, about five miles from where we lived. There were only a couple of actual church buildings in Lima, and one stake chapel. Now there are numerous stakes just in Lima, but when I was there, there was just one stake in the entire country. The mission conference was a great motivator. President Driggs spoke to us, and we had numerous demonstrations on door approaches and creative ideas for "mini expositions." Mission conferences became something to look forward to, both to hear from our mission president and to hear testimony strengthening experiences as well as creative approach- es. It was also great to see all the missionaries within Lima and the outlying areas, and to renew acquaintances with missionaries who had been companions or friends.

Once a month we exchanged companions for the day when our zone leaders came to work individually with us. This would give us a chance to see different areas and to work with different elders. After one of these exchanges, I was working in an area between Callao and Central Lima with one of the zone leaders. We were sitting in a house talking to a lady we met while knocking on doors, when we heard a loud crash. We went running out and saw a man standing next to his flatbed truck, virtually shaking his head with a dumb expression on his face as he looked at the damage, he had just inflicted on the house next to his truck. He had parked his truck in a lot adjoining the house, which was typical of houses in Lima with adobe bricks and painted plaster. As he attempted to pull out of the lot, he cut the corner too sharply, catching the edge of the flatbed on the front wall of the house and pulling down the entire front wall with all its windows and its doorway! The front of the house was in pieces on the sidewalk!

Part of the adventure of my mission was seeing the unusual sights which came daily while we traveled through our area. One morning we tried to set up an appointment with an investigator who worked at a meat company located by the fish-processing plant—another chance to experience unique smells. As we approached the plant, I thought I was hallucinating, but it looked like giant pigs were walking on two legs. As we walked closer, I realized what I was seeing—workers with leather hoods and capes were carrying large, gutted pigs on their backs and heads. In order to support the weight of the pigs, the workers covered their heads with the leather hoods and stuck their heads up inside the carcass. The pigs were draped over their backs and heads as they lugged the pigs from inside the plant, up ramps, and into trucks.

Teenage girls in Callao—and everywhere else in Peru—loved to talk to Americans about America. Once, a couple of *brazen chicas* strolled up to us and pinched our cheeks. It was hard to tell whether they were more interested in us or where we came from. For the sake of our egos, we assumed it was because we were such macho hunks! Occasionally teenage chicas would follow us, giggling and spying on us to see what we did with our time. I even had a few written letters handed to me, saying they wished to meet with us. The girls weren't the only ones that followed us. We started teaching a young man who, we soon realized, was mentally unbalanced. Once we had him interested, we could not shake him. He would come to church and laugh out loud during the meetings, and follow us around like a dog, not accepting the hints we threw out that perhaps he should go home.

There were several members who quickly gained a reputation with the missionaries for providing "good eats." Hermana Rios had such a reputation. She was a robust, friendly lady whose husband was not a member. She lived in another area, but Elder Adsero knew her from his prior assignment in that area. She was always eager to have the missionaries visit, especially those with whom she had become acquainted through their earlier service. Although the members were always anxious to have the missionaries eat with them, usually we were uncomfortable doing so because they would often spend far more than they should have spent, far beyond their means, to provide a meal to the missionaries. In the case of Hermana Rios, however, we were not so concerned because she and her husband made a good living as foot doctors. On one memorable P-day we arrived at her house at a quarter to seven in the morning and she continued to assault us with wave after wave of different foods. It was heavenly! We started with hot chocolate and hot cereal, proceeded to pancakes, eggs, and steak, then finished gorging with a round of fruit, bread, and orange juice. I ate more that one morning than I had for the whole week.

After bloating ourselves on breakfast, we went to the church and met Hermano Cartwright, his son, and their jeep. Cartwright was an appropriate last name for this combination—they seemed a lot like Ben and Hoss Cartwright from my favorite Western. They were kindly, outgoing, and the son was barrel-chested and beefy, just like Hoss. Generally, we were much larger than the Peruvians, but Brother Cartwright and his son were very large and robust. They took us by jeep to a large ancient city outside Lima, called Pacchucamac. It was spectacular. It was surrounded by a huge plaster-covered wall. In the middle of the walled-in ruins was a large central pyramid and a temple with baptismal fonts! This city had been used until the conquest of Peru by the Spaniards, and dated back to well before the conquest, probably to the time of Christ. There, inside the ancient city, I had my first look at llamas and alpacas. Llamas are about the size of camels, but they have white fur and no hump. Alpacas are a miniature variation of the same. I was warned not to get too close to them or make them angry—they spit a slimy green cud when mad. The highest part of the ancient city was the Temple of the Sun. It was a huge, terraced pyramid. We played futbol—soccer—at the ruins. Everyone in Peru, from the age of one's first steps to the age of using canes, plays soccer. On our way to and from the ancient city we traveled in the Cartwrights' jeep along the beach. Although in California it is unheard of to drive a vehicle on the beach, except maybe at Pismo Beach, in Peru, there are no regulations or anything else stopping you from driving on the beach. It was a blast—ocean spray all over us and cool air in our faces.

It is very rare to own a car in Peru. We only knew two members in the entire branch that had automobiles and they both had very steady, well-paid jobs. For the most part, unless you drove a taxi in Peru, you did not own a car, but instead traveled by bicycle, bus, or taxi, or by walking.

One of the adjustments a missionary has to make, no matter where one is called to serve involves the ups and downs of the mission field. One day you are on a high after teaching a great discussion and having an investigator come to church, and the very next day you might be on a down because all your appointments fell through or you were feeling sick. One of my periods of ups and downs was documented in the following contrasting journal entries:

June 17, 1972: We gave a second discussion to a Japanese

architect and his family today. His wife is really sharp. When we told them about people being on this continent at the time of Christ, she said, "Oh, is that what Christ is referring to, when he said, 'Other sheep I have which are not of this fold." She was right on. We gave a fifth discussion to Suarez. As usual, he understood pretty well, and the hermana was starting to answer a few questions on her own this time. The fifth discussion was really cool to give to them because they had never heard of the plan of salvation before.

June 21, 1972: We didn't do much teaching today, most of our discussions fell through. I was really getting discouraged today. My cold is really bad, and I am so sick of walking, I can hardly stand it. I guess it was just a bad day.

One thing that always seemed to get us in better spirits was a trip for Chinese food. We celebrated my twentieth birthday by going out to a *chifa*, Chinese restaurant, after working for the day. The next day I switched companions and worked with Elder Stevenson, one of the other missionaries in our district. He treated me that night to a late birthday dinner of roasted chicken. There seemed to be quite a few rotisserie chicken barbecue restaurants in Peru.

One of the advantages of trading companions while Elder Adsero, our district leader, worked with other missionaries, was the opportunity to meet and associate with other missionaries. It was fun to trade off and see how other missionaries worked. I enjoyed working with Elder Stevenson. He was somewhat of an imp. He had a toothy, sly grin, large "bottle bottom" glasses, and sandy, bushy hair. Although he enjoyed his mission, he did not hesitate reminding other missionaries, especially those of us who were "green," or newly arrived, that he was leaving to go home in just four weeks. With his impish grin, he was quick to remind us that he would be thinking of us as he returned to dating, swimming, and sleeping in. We had a word for Elder Stevenson's condition, it was called "trunky." It meant having your trunk mentally packed and ready to leave. It seemed to be a phenomenon that hit all missionaries who were within six months of leaving for home. It was fine to look forward to going home, as long as it did not interfere with your missionary work. Unfortunately, there were some missionaries who seemed to be "trunky" from the day they arrived in Peru. These missionaries never achieved a vision of why they were there to begin with.

Elder Adsero and Elder Stevenson often talked about several of these missionaries—one, in particular, who went on his mission solely because he was in love with a girl who told him she would never marry someone unless he were a returning missionary. While this encouragement is generally good, it did not work in his case. He never had a testimony, he went solely because of her. As it turned out, she dumped him while he was in the LTM. His "Dear John" letter came within two months, and in anguish, he arrived in Peru still reeling. He then was determined to treat his mission as one big vacation to a foreign country. His companions struggled with how to deal with him. After getting home from being dragged out to work on the streets for the day by senior companions, who were determined to get him to work, he would change into his gym shorts and without a shirt, would invite the teenage girls in the neighborhood to join him in listening to rock-and-roll music on the stereo downstairs in his apartment. Things were worse when he became a senior companion. He told one of his junior companions he intended to take a "weeklong" trip up north in Peru since he had never been there. He advised his junior companion he was free to come with him or to stay—either way, he did not care. The junior companion made a frantic call to the mission home and the assistant to the president arrived before the senior companion took off and convinced him to come to the mission home to stay for a while. Although this missionary made it to within a month of finishing his mission, he was ultimately sent home, not for anything grievous but simply because he refused to be a missionary.

I describe this elder to show the emphasis that must be placed on gaining a testimony before hitting the mission field. Otherwise, the experience will bring only grief to the missionary, his or her companions, the mission president, and loved ones back home. It is a devastating experience to parents who rejoice in the knowledge that their son or daughter is in the mission field, but who then see the person return under less-than-honorable circumstances.

I later saw this same elder again on Peruvian TV. He had returned to play basketball on the Peruvian national team—we were startled one day as they announced the team before a game with Chile and there in the middle of the very Latin-looking group was one big, blond gringo we had known in the mission months before!

Elder Stevenson's "trunkiness" did not affect me, although a certain amount of envy crept in when I thought about how satisfying it must be to have carried out a fruitful and successful mission and to be getting ready for a "triumphant" return to one's family and friends.

One day Elder Adsero decided we should set up a mini-exposition down in Callao, by the open air market. place. This was one of the best areas to find large groups of people coming and going. Marketplaces in Peru were an eye opener. They typically lined a small back street or alleyway, with stalls and booths on both sides, which were constructed out of wood frames, with brightly colored plastic over the top to keep the sun out. Within the booths various food items were set out or hung up. These included whole ducks and chickens, plucked, featherless and hanging in naked glory with flies swarming all over the doughy skin. As I entered the "stall lane," I felt surrounded by cow tongues, cow hearts, cow and pig intestines; pig feet hanging or pickled in jars; mounds of brightly colored orange, red, and yellow chili peppers, and other assortments of vegetables; large smelly fish being chopped before my eyes, blood and slime everywhere; large blood sausage being sliced and fried; people pushing, elbowing, crowding. In the morning the marketplace was filled with women carrying large bags on their arms, which were loaded with the day's meals. Many Peruvians at that time had no refrigerators and, as a result, made their trek to the open-air market daily to get fresh vegetables and foods to cook for their main meal at midday.

We captured the interest of several people, as they were going to and from the market, with our exposition on the Book of Mormon and how it pertained to them as Peruvians. We filled out several reference cards to follow up on their interest in the days that followed.

I was interested in history and archeology before I arrived in Peru. It did not take long for me to gain a heightened interest in archeology and ancient history of Peru. We traveled up the coast to one of our areas that was isolated from Callao by a stretch of highway and sand dunes. We received a reference card for a family there and intended to teach them a discussion. Before we started the discussion, we became fascinated with the senor's collection of little sculptured heads and wooden artifacts. He also had a skull and a mummified foot and leg, preserved with toenails and dried leathery skin. There were many ruins just on the outskirts of Lima. It was impossible to protect them all from looting and digging. This man told us you could walk through a number of the old pyramids and archeological sites and find bits and pieces of pottery and mummies that had exposed by the looters and grave robbers. This is how he had obtained his collection. The discussion that day bombed, but my interest in ancient Peru caught fire and eventually became the focus of my P-days. Gaining an interest in the history and culture of the area enhanced my love and appreciation for the people and helped me to be a more effective missionary.

Every missionary will encounter bizarre philosophies and peculiar views when meeting various people in the mission field. In any given day we talked with people ranging from a Catholic priest who assured us the church wasn't placing emphasis on the saints and other "idol"-like objects, to a man claimed that Jesus Christ was the first communist because he taught that everyone was equal and should share. Then there were those who acted interested and engaged us in discussion until an odor from their breath came our way and we realized they were drunk and out to have a good time by entertaining a few Yankees. I learned it was unproductive to try to argue against the different philosophies, or to "bash" the scriptures. Though Elder Adsero and I spent hours studying and becoming fairly proficient at finding scriptures that "disproved" all of the major religions we usually encountered, I never once saw anything positive come from a "Bible bashing" session. We had a few of these, with efforts being made by both sides to prove a position or point via the scriptures, almost like lawyers with case authorities in a court of law. I enjoyed these situations from the standpoint of my

51

personal ego and pride, and they influenced my professional choice-a trial lawyer. However, I soon realized that satisfying my personal pride and ego, by demonstrating proficiency in arguing with the support of scriptures, did nothing to actually teach the people.

We engaged in a few bashing sessions with a Catholic priest and a Seventh-day Adventist preacher. They had spent years studying the scriptures, and although we could confuse them with references to scriptures such as the one in Corinthians discussing baptism for the dead, in the end it was a losing effort to try and keep pace with them. It was especially futile when contrasted to true teaching situations where we bore simple testimonies to the truthfulness of Joseph Smith's first vision, the restoration of the gospel, the Plan of Salvation, and the Book of Mormon, then taught people the true manner of prayer. Through testimony and teaching with humility, we could feel the Spirit. It wasn't there when we attempted to "bash."

Missionary life provided ample exercise for the legs, but without regularly planned exercise, the rest of my body was heading downhill. My second evening in Peru, I saw how quickly you could get out of shape as a missionary. Elder Adsero had a spring exerciser—a contraption with four springs and a handle on each end. He would stretch it across his chest and do curls by hooking one handle under his foot and flexing his biceps with the other end. He looked stocky and strong, and I assumed, in watching him grunt and groan in red-faced fury as he tried to curl this spring trap, that the springs were very tight. He invited me to try it and stood there crushed as I easily punched out twenty curls without a single heavy breath. My only fear was that the handle would slip from under my foot or one of the springs would break, causing the whole thing to smack me in the face. I decided to regularly work out on the roof of our apartment so that I would not return home as a 180-pound weakling. I felt more alert and less tired after exercising and was able to study more and concentrate effectively on the work.

We had one investigator, a short, cheerful guy, Hermano Sifuentes, who was more interested in talking basketball than the gospel. He assumed that anyone from the United States was an excellent basketball player, and he kept pressing us to meet him at his club to play a group of young Peruvian men he coached on a basket-ball team. We finally agreed and, one P-day, met at the club as a district to play four on four with members of his team. They ran us to death. We were totally blown out of the water and, after the game, were too tired to do anything but go back to our apartments and take a nap. We then bought a gallon of ice cream each and a large bottle of Inca Cola and tried to consume the whole thing by making and eating Inca Cola floats, until we felt like throwing up. My exercising now took on added intensity, starting the day after our basketball game. After seeing how out of shape I was and how stiff I was after the basketball game, I became more determined. Of course, you never knew if you were stiff from physical activities or from the uncomfortable beds that were typical in the mission field—the bed I had was more like a hammock; it sunk in the middle until it almost touched the ground.

On my P-day, in the evening after our game, we got word that Joseph Fielding Smith died the night before, meaning that Harold B. Lee, whom I was so impressed with in the Solemn Assembly room of the temple, while I was in the mission home, would become the next prophet. He seemed young to fill that role.

The day after we played basketball against Hermano Sifuentes's team, we gave the "basketball nut" a discussion. All he wanted to talk about were basketball rules and maneuvers. As he talked, he was dribbling an imaginary basketball through his house. We burst out laughing.

Unfortunately, our most consistent investigator who was attending church, and following through with discussion meetings we'd planned, was the "crazy" young man. Not only was he still laughing during the Sacrament meeting, but he also started singing during a discussion when Elder Adsero was bearing his testimony. At times, though, he seemed halfway sane as compared to some of the people we met on the street at our mini expositions. One man came up and asked us, "If the twelve apostles who live today have the power of Christ, why don't they stop the war in Vietnam?" Another old guy, who had unusual blond hair and pants up to his armpits, told us he did not need religion because he had a paper from the pope, telling him he was saved.

At our Zone Conference in July 1972, President Driggs told us about a few experiences of our fellow missionaries in Peru that demonstrated how protected we were as missionaries. The week before, one of the elders stepped out into the street and was hit by a Big Mac truck. The truck launched him for thirty feet. He should have been dead but instead, after thirty-seven stitches to close a cut, he was back to work within a week. A few weeks before this, two of the sister missionaries were coming home late one night in Lima, when a guy followed them and started shooting at them. They ran to a new housing development. One of the sisters ran into one of the empty houses and the shooter followed and fired a few more shots at her. A carload of guys pulled up, and the sisters felt relieved until they saw, with horror, that those in the car were friends of the shooter. The other sister ran into the empty house to join her companion but saw yet another car pull up. She went running to this car to try to get help. The man in the car told her to go get her companion, while he waited. The sisters jumped in the car and the stranger took them to their home. On the way there, he said, "You know, you were hiding in the new house I am building. I was home in bed when, all of a sudden, I felt that I should go and check out my new house. I sensed something was happening there, although I had no particular reason to think that."

A few days after the conference we had our first baptism, that of the Ojeda family. Elder Adsero and his prior companion had taught them before I arrived, but they had to wait for their baptism until they were formally divorced from their prior spouses and then officially married. Because of the bureaucracy Peru had inherited from the Spaniards, it was particularly difficult to obtain divorces—many people waited ten to twelve years for divorces. The result was that many began living with their next spouse-to-be. This created difficulties for the missionaries because we could not baptize anyone who was living with another but not properly married. It was great finally to see the Ojedas join the church, after being so faithful in attending meetings, listening to the discussions, paying tithing, and following every other aspect of the gospel.

The police in Peru were different from what we were used to in the United States. They wore military green uniforms and typically carried submachine guns. It was not unusual to find them standing near banks with sub. machine guns or in Lima patrolling on horseback with riot-type helmets and assault guns. It was also not unusual in downtown Lima to see "live traffic signals." These were policemen standing in a box, under an umbrella, elevated about six feet off the ground on stilts and lit up at night. With movements of their white-gloved hands, they would direct traffic from these crow's nests. This "cop in the box" seemed precarious, especially with all the cab drivers racing by on both sides! There did not seem to be many policemen for the broad density of the population, due probably to the inability to afford more police presence.

One day in Callao, as we were attempting to locate an address in Frigorifico, down by the fish processing plant, we stopped at the local police station to try to get directions. One of the officers told us the address was downtown and said for us to get in his car and he would take us there. He drove us to the address and dropped us off. It beats a cab ride, or a walk and we received some interesting looks from the people, who probably thought we were CIA agents working with the police, or that we had been arrested. On the way out to Frigorifico we saw an old dump truck loaded with fish that had been thrown in the back and left uncovered. As the truck went down the road away from us, it was covered with swarming pelicans and seagulls of all sizes. They formed a cloud of white flying above it, around it, and on it, pecking at the fish, screeching, squawking, fighting over the fish. The whole scene became a moving mass of noise and a stink as the truck wafted a strong fish odor along the street, which mixed with spewing plumes of diesel fog from the truck's stack.

A trait common to most missionaries, especially those of us in South America who we were not getting fed the same quality of food as in other places, was overindulgence in eating when the opportunity to gorge presented itself. We had one of these rare opportunities when an investigator who worked at the Mott chocolate factory, just out of town, invited us to tour the plant on a P-day. We went through the plant and the next day, when we went to teach him, he gave us two large boxes filled with assorted candies, sweetbreads and pastries, and other delicious items, all packaged for us at the plant. We scarfed most of the box down in one night. We were perpetually hungry. Not surprisingly, I woke up sick and tried to make it through the day with a sour stomach. I was in a bad mood all day. We were walking down a street as a teenager and his friend came toward us, pinching girls. As we passed them, they made an abrupt U-turn and followed us, imitating us. Instead of just ignoring them, as Elder Adsero had the wisdom to do, I told them to "get lost," at which point they bumped me and I shoved them, just about knocking them over. They started yelling, "What do you want? What do you want?" I finally followed my companion's advice and simply ignored them until they left. It was a harsh lesson in not allowing myself to get provoked and to have patience in the face of antagonism. As missionaries, we were ambassadors of goodwill for our church, culture, and country. By not acting accordingly, I was doing more harm to the work than good for it. Missionaries who had failed to see the importance of acting as ambassadors, and worthy representatives of Jesus Christ, left harmful legacies. One such missionary in Peru a couple of years before me was an expert in martial arts. Instead of showing patience, he sometimes got physical with teenagers and others who harassed the missionaries. Once, as he was walking down a street with his companion, only a few feet off the sidewalk, a teenager started yelling foul words at them in English. As this elder approached, the teenager quickly slammed the door, which did not provide him with the refuge he expected, because the elder reared back on one leg and landed a karate blow with his foot to the door, completely caving in the door frame and sending the teenager behind it back onto the floor. The door landed on top of the teenager in a pile of plaster dust, splintered wood, and adobe fragments. It may have been a humorous sight but it landed this elder and his companion in jail. It made a negative impact on those who witnessed it since many Latin Americans already consider the United States, and Americans in general, to be "imperialist" bullies. It also had a negative impact on the police who processed the arrest and called to ask the mission president to send an assistant to bail the elders out. Learning to turn the other cheek and become more Christ-like was certainly one of my greatest challenges in the mission field. Although it is probably one of the greater challenges of most missionaries, it is absolutely essential to success in the mission field.

My patience was also sorely tried by the progress or lack of progress of our investigators. Because we heard so much in the United States about the thousands of baptisms in Mexico each month, I had very high expectations about the baptism rate in South America. For the first few months of my mission, however, we did not have the opportunity to see anyone we had taught get baptized. The work seemed to be plodding along slowly. I was aware there were missions in the world where a missionary would be fortunate to see a single baptism, but I expected more in South America. We were always instructed to keep a positive outlook because if we did not have the opportunity to baptize, we would at the very least lay seeds for the missionaries who followed. Our good work and efforts, through the inspiration of the Holy Ghost, would pay off, if not while we were on our mission, then later. We were seeing great progress by the Suarez family, whose members were sincerely receiving the discussions and praying. The *hermano* was also reading to the *hermana* out of the Book of Mormon.

A few times in Callao we rode the buses. Elder Adsero must have had sore feet! These bus rides were an adventure. Usually, we squeezed on amid a number of *cholo* ladies loaded to the gills with fresh fruits and vegetables and other purchases from the open-air market. The bus was filled with pungent smells of onions, hot chilies, and other vegetables, and most of the open space was consumed by huge mounds of lettuce, live chickens flapping their wings and throwing feathers, and other debris. Often there was at least one drunk in the back of the bus, yelling to himself or trying to sing a slurred song while the people around him laughed at the "entertainment." It was also not unusual to have to stand up during the ordeal, holding on wherever you could while the driver slammed on the brakes or stepped on the accelerator— there seemed to be no in-between—spinning us down the aisle into the *cholos*, the groceries, or the poultry and drunks. The rolling clouds of diesel emitted by these buses made me sick to my stomach. The architecture downtown was covered by black dust from the bus traffic.

In Callao I got scalped by a barber who gave me the shortest haircut I had seen since I was probably three years old. As you are preparing for a mission, you get what you think is a short haircut to start with, and then you realize, when you reach the mission home, or now the mission training center, that it was only halfway there. On your first P-day in the mission training center, you get it taken up another notch. Once in the mission field, where you have to pay for your haircuts out of your precious monthly allotment, any pride you ever had in your hair goes out the window and you realize the shorter it's cut, the longer you can go without paying for another haircut. Besides, who were we going to impress, girls? What I did not realize at the time was how ridiculous my hair looked in pictures and slides I would show, after my mission, to girls I really did want to impress!

The Suarez family was indeed progressing well during my entire stay in Callao. I learned the true meaning of "line upon line and precept upon precept" while teaching people who often were illiterate and thus were not prepared to accept a challenge to read the Book of Mor-mon. Instead, we proceeded to spoon-feed them, teaching a concept or a principle, or reading out loud to them, or using the flannel board with the little cartoon characters to demonstrate the Book of Mormon and gospel stories. It was time consuming and slow, but very rewarding to feel like we were helping humble people truly interested in learning about the Savior and his gospel.

Hermano Suarez gave us some insight into how strong his faith was even before he learned of the gospel. He told us that before he met the missionaries, he was very sick, so sick that he was unable to go to work, which is disastrous for most Peruvians since in Peru there is no equivalent of workmen's compensation or any other benefits or disability insurance. He went to the doctor, who told him to buy this and that medicine. Hermano Suarez could not afford the medicine, so he went home and prayed and prayed about his illness and asked that he might be healed. Within a matter of days he felt better and was able to go to work again.

One thing I grew to appreciate quickly while in Peru was the quality of medical care in the United States. We met many people who had nearly died from something as simple as an appendicitis attack. Many others had relatives or family members who had died from such things. It seemed rather common among the people of limited finances, probably because of their poor diets and living conditions. Once the appendix was infected, many just learned to live with the pain. They could not afford a doctor. Once the appendix became ruptured, they did not have much chance of living since most medical care was inadequate to deal with the resulting infection. Even if they were lucky enough to have the appendix removed before it became ruptured, complications often set in, like those experienced by Hermano Suarez.

Each day in Callao brought its unexpected ups and downs. Many days were spent knocking on doors and wearing ourselves out, trying to meet people after having scheduled discussions fall through. Yet toward the end of a couple of these days people came up to us, stopped us right there on the street, and asked if we were Mormons. They were curious about the church and wanted to learn more. These were times when you looked at your companion, shrugged your shoulders, smiled, and realized the Lord would touch people's hearts in spite of us. We would have the blessing of meeting such people if we worked hard. If we were not putting in the effort, if we had not been on the street, we would not have met these "golden" contacts. We learned the value of working hard, praying hard, and leaving the rest to the Lord.

When we taught third discussions on the Word of wisdom, it was always interesting to see whether the investigators would give us the "ingredients" of their vices. If they drank coffee, we asked them to give us their coffee grounds. If they smoked, we asked for all their cigarettes; if they drank, we asked for all their booze. When we were successful in carrying these away, outside observers must have wondered what these crazy Mormon missionaries were up to while carrying around whiskey, cigarettes, and coffee. We did the same with their "saint" statuettes and gruesome pictures of Christ. There were times when we could be seen carrying these out of houses. We generally tried to find the nearest large dumpster or trash can to dispose of these items, but we had to be discreet when it came to religious relics, or we would raise the ire of any staunch Catholic who happened to see us discarding them.

On one of our P-days we went to downtown Lima to tour the catacombs underneath the large cathedral. The cathedral, one of the largest on the continent, had immense fifty-foot plank doors with big high metal ring knockers that only giants could use. Inside, the vaulted ceiling soared over one hundred feet above, and hundreds of candles flickered at the far end, over two hundred feet away. Behind the candlelit altar, ornate dignitary seats, carved in wood, lined the walls underneath pulpits floating above spiral stairwells. The body of the Spaniards who "discovered" Peru Francisco Pizarro, lay encased in a musty glass case off to one side. He looked like a skeleton wrapped in parched leather and wigged hair. We followed a tour guide down a small staircase outside the cathedral, descending through dark, dusty passages. We walked by rows and rows of bones and skulls laid out along the walls. Our guide told us these were the bones of those who had paid for the privilege of being buried underneath the church. I had read books on Peruvian history, however, and knew that most of the bones in the catacombs were of people that had been killed in the "Holy" Inquisition, which Spain brought to its colonies, including Peru. They were often secretly executed, and their bodies were hidden in these catacombs. In the garden above the tunnels, I was appalled to see a statue of Saint Francisco, along with all of the signs of Jesus Christ, including nails in his hands and a wound in his side. The guide said Christ came down and made the wounds on this saint and then he went and preached for three years. It was as if one Christ were not enough; they had patterned another saint after Christ's mission.

It didn't take long for me to realize I had taken much of my former life for granted. Simple things like litter gave me pause to consider and compare. There were no public trash cans in most of Callao. It seemed like everyone threw their trash in the street when they were done with it. Later it was haphazardly picked up by cleaning men carting brooms, dustpans, and trash cans with wheels.

Friday became a day of great anticipation in the mission field because that was when we received our package from the mission home. Because we never knew when we were going to get a change of areas, most of us gave those at home the mission home's address to write to. The mission home would collect all of the letters received during the course of a week, put them into a package, and deliver it to the district leaders in all of the areas in Peru. Also included in the package sent to the district leader were any notices of change of assignments to different areas for missionaries in the district. The packages became inflictors of happiness or sadness on Friday evenings as we learned whether we had received any letters for the week or a change to a different area and companion.

Since as a missionary, I felt like I had stepped out of my family life and into a completely different life apart from the world and its events, I greatly looked forward to correspondence from home to update me on what was happening in the lives of my family, friends, and girlfriend. I got on an emotional high and could not be happier when the package included letters from my family and my girlfriend. I got on an emotional low and was completely glum when the package did not contain letters for me. My inclination was to rummage through the package, asking Elder Adsero whether he was sure there was nothing else in there for me. Letters were the one thing that kept us in contact with our support groups back home and gave us a great deal of encouragement and motivation to keep our spirits high and continue with new determination for the next week. Letters were the biggest morale boosters, often making the difference between an upbeat, positive and effective missionary and one who was too absorbed in self-pity and homesickness to do the job.

One of the interesting members we met, in the course of our daily missionary exploits, was Hermano Soto, a small, quiet, timid man with an easygoing disposition, who owned a jewelry shop that opened onto the street from the back side of his own home in the downtown section of Callao. He was on one of the narrow cobblestone streets that ran through a section of Callao just off the main street. The homes in that section of town shared common walls fronting the street. The only way to tell where one house ended and the other began were the colors on the walls, usually vivid pastels. These colors approximated where one house inside the wall ended, and another started. Everyone was supposed to put a new coat of paint on the front of their house by Peruvian In-dependence Day, as a matter of national pride. Hermano Soto worked studiously in his jewelry shop each day. He gave us a tour of his equipment and showed us some of the items he was fastening. I had him work on a few pieces of jewelry I wanted to send home. Hermana Soto was always feeding us when we visited, which was a welcome relief from the usual hunger I experienced as we were out walking the streets. I enjoyed just about everything she prepared until the day she gave us large, oily olives, or *acetunas*. They were fixed traditionally, which made no difference to me. The oil seemed so rancid, I could not eliminate the taste from my mouth. Rather than appearing rude, I slipped the pit out of my mouth and into my napkin and put up with the overpowering bitterness until we could get back to our pension and drink some milk.

As we arrived home, we passed by a party in full gear next door. There were several drunks talking boisterously with glazed-over eyes. Elder Adsero and I joked that, with the lack of success we had been having, about the only way we were going to see someone in the waters of baptism was if we could convince one of these drunks to listen to us, give him the discussions, then dunk him in the bathtub afterward. Although we sometimes felt frustrated by the lack of actual baptisms, more frustrating yet was the attrition rate of those who had been taught and baptized without adequate preparation or testimony. This was probably a universal problem for most mission fields. There were missionaries who, because of their own ego and pride in compiling statistics, whipped people through the discussions, primarily focusing on chalking up baptisms, as opposed to diligently taking the time to teach with patience and compassion until an investigator was truly rooted in the gospel, with a solid testimony that would carry him or her through the years of challenges ahead. At least we had the satisfaction of knowing we were trying to teach with the spirit and trying to truly convert. Our efforts were paying off with the Suarez family. They continued to come to church, to pray with us after the discussions, and to slowly work their way through the Book of Mormon.

We occasionally encountered some very superstitious people, including a young man who came from a village up in the Andes where, he told us, Black Magic was practiced. He told us many of the villagers went to a certain place up on the mountain at midnight to enter a covenant with the Devil. After making this covenant they would practice Voodooism, by cursing people and chanting. He finally quit the practice because he said he could not sleep at night. I was later told there were colonies of witches in certain areas of Peru, including a town up north—Chiclayo. According to this young man, a cult of those practicing White Magic had banded together to try and combat the evil effects of Black Magic. Some of these "white" witches had healed people he knew with the use of herbs and other natural medicines and enchantments. Apparently some of these superstitious people had great faith, enough to be healed of physical ailments. This faith needed to be channeled into the gospel and Jesus Christ. That was where we came in.

We had one memorable zone outing while I was in Callao. The entire zone went to the beach to play football on P-day. It was a nice white, sandy beach that stretched for several miles around a bay. We played football for a couple of hours and then roasted hot dogs and had root beer. I remember that several of the "slacker" elders managed to get themselves in the surf, supposedly because of overthrown footballs. While collecting the balls, they just happened to lose their grip while in the water and had to swim out to grab the elusive footballs. Then of course they had to catch a couple of waves in order to help them—poor swimmers that they were—back to the shore. One elder managed to step on a stingray and get a spine lodged in his foot. When he went to the mission home to get directed to proper medical care, he could not quite satisfactorily explain to President Driggs what he had been doing in the surf. Mission rules really do have a purpose, and whether the power of Satan over the water includes power over stingrays, I do not know. I only know that had that missionary been obeying the rules, he would not have had such a painful experience.

Our helplessness concerning anything related to food—we all ate at different pensions and had maids—was demonstrated by the root beer we made at zone conferences. We put too much extract and sugar into it. Even though we put dry ice in it to give it *pizzazz*, it still tasted like pancake syrup! The day finished on a high note as we visited with a family being friendshiped by some of the members. They had a son who had been sick for quite some time with swollen glands. They were made aware of the church through their friends and were also aware of priesthood blessings. Being humble people with great faith, though not yet focused on our church, they asked for a blessing for their son. We gave him a blessing, and he quickly healed, leading to a greater interest on their part in having the discussions. We eagerly obliged.

The week of July 25 was marked by a series of in-dependence celebrations commemorating Peru's achievement of independence from Argentina in 1821. The actual main Independence Festival occurred on Friday and Saturday. Leading up to the festival, everybody with a plaster-fronted house, and even those who had only cardboard or wood, repainted their house. This was the custom, tradition, and government requirement for the independence festival. They all used poster like paint in pastel colors. Since it never rained, there did not seem to be a problem, although if it had rained, there would have been colors running all over the place. As it was, many of those painting their houses slopped the paint all over the sidewalk. They carefully folded up newspaper hats to wear while they painted, to keep the paint out of their hair. They looked quite comical. It reminded me of some of the children's primary parties where we made newspaper pirate and revolutionary-war-type hats. As we walked past the painters, toward the port, I also noticed a dead dog lying by one of the houses. Most dead dogs and dead pelicans were left to bloat and rot in the sun.

I seemed to perpetually have a cold in Callao, perhaps because of the fog which seemed to hang near the coast. The people had many farfetched explanations for why I caught the "grip," as in the grip of the jaws of death. One of the theories was that I should not be drinking cold soda pop. Most Peruvians drink their soda pop warm—yuck!

In July I worked one last time with Elder Stevenson before he was scheduled to go home. I enjoyed his personality and his sense of humor but he was not exactly pushing missionary work, since he was only days from going home. I made a resolution that I was going to end on a hardworking high note. I was not critical of Elder Stevenson, though, since he did take time to enjoy what he was doing, which was more than can be said for a lot of missionaries who worked without enjoyment. This went back to my belief that missionaries determined to impress with statistics like numbers of baptisms, hours, and numbers of lessons taught missed all the fun. It might look good to fill out the weekly time sheets with many hours taught, many discussions taught, and many baptisms; but with-out taking the time to actually befriend the people and love them and teach them in the true spirit of Christ, the statistics were worthless and brought no real enjoyment.

Elder Stevenson and I worked in an area called "La Perla"—the Pearl—which was down by the beach. We could hear the surf crashing and smell the salt air, which started to take my mind from Peru back to Southern California and the beach, something I really missed. There are moments on a mission where you suddenly get lost in your thoughts of home, but you pull yourself back to reality and get back to work. We visited a young man and his aunt that evening. The aunt was a divorcée whom we called a "dolly" lady because she seemed unusually interested in the missionaries. She got a charge out of trying to get the missionaries to take a drink of liquor. She got about six phone calls from men while we were there. I concluded she was "bad news." We finally left and went to our favorite place—the Chifa—for Chinese food. After being in the mission field for close to two months, I felt pretty well adjusted.

One of the exciting things about being in South America on a mission was working some of the territory that Christ had visited after his resurrection. His visit left many lingering legends. I was intrigued by all the legends that came from his visit. Elder Adsero and I learned enough about the legends of the visit of the Great White God to the Incas' forefathers, who had called him "Viracocha," to put together an exposition downtown to try to interest people in the Book of Mormon. We presented it with legends from the other ancient civilizations that corresponded, such as the whitebearded God of the pre-Aztecs people who called him "Quetzalcoatl," and of the Mayas, who called him "Kukulcan." Anyone in Peru who was really familiar with the Incas was well aware of this legend of the visit of the Great White God and the expectation that he would return. So prevalent was the legend that at the time Francisco Pizarro and his men landed on the coast of Peru, the Incan ruler in the men lam territory—Atahualpa—allowed Pizarro and his men to proceed, unhindered and unharmed, up through the valley to the northern Incan capital of Cajamarca. Atahualpa could have killed the Spaniards in the valley, but he let them pass solely because of his knowledge of the legend of the visit of the Great White bearded God to his ancestors and this god's promised return. Atahualpa was curious to see whether the white bearded men came from the Great White God. The result for him and his kingdom was disastrous.

From time to time we would show investigators film-strips with the use of a little projector combined with my tape recorder. The tape that provided the music and narration would ding a little to let you know when to turn to the next slide on the transcript. One of the filmstrips was titled "Was Christ in America?" It told of Christ's visit in the Book of Mormon and some of the corresponding legends, including that of the Great White God among the ancient civilizations. It depicted the welcome Captain Cook had received in the Hawaiian Islands because the people there also had the legend of the Great White God. This filmstrip and our discussion of the legends interested a number of the Peruvians. Later in my mission, one of my companions and I were shocked to see, on the front page of the daily newspaper, an article that had the headline "Did Christ Visit Ancient Peru?" It was authored by the head curator of the Inca museum in Lima. He theorized it was possible Christ had visited the ancient civilizations in Peru before the time of the Incas. He based his theory on the legends of the Incas, such as those I described, and on accounts, by some of the Spanish historians who had arrived with the conquistadors, of a large statue of a man with a beard, and a tunic that went down to his feet, in one of the temples outside Cuzco—the ancient capital of the Incan Empire. It was well known, according to the curator, that the Incas could not grow beards; they had no facial hair, as with most Indian people, and their tunics were more in the Roman style, going down to the knee, not to the feet, as on the statue cited. The early Spaniards concluded it was a statue of one of the apostles of Christ who had come to visit the Americas, after having been with Christ in Palestine.

As we were attempting to give our exposition down-town on the legends of Christ in America, there were a number of drunks lying around the plaza. One came over and lay down against the building near our exposition. His hands and legs were coated with so much dirt and grease, we could hardly see his skin. His face was partially covered by a greasy black beard. His clothes were ragged; tattered pants so dirty, they were stiff. He was smoking an old cigarette he had found on the street and he just let the cigarette butt fall on his pants. He decided to take a nap, so he rolled over and laid his head on the dirty sidewalk next to our exposition. We decided to pick it up and move it because it seemed a little incongruous to have him lying there right next to our discussion board as we were attempting to gain people's interest.

We were teaching a man, Hermano Garcia, who was an inactive member. He got strange ideas from his friends. One evening he was trying to prove to us that reincarnation is true. I asked him, "If reincarnation is true, why does the Bible reference baptisms for the dead? If the dead come back, why don't they do the ordinances themselves?" That puzzled him a little bit.

I became more aware of other religions while in Callao. Because we were out discussing religion each day with people, we often were pulled into discussions about their beliefs as well as ours. Some of these discussions involved antagonistic people callously defending their own religions and putting ours down, while others were with more open-minded people desirous of exchanging ideas. We met a Catholic priest from Spain who worked on the peninsula in Callao. He was friendly and interesting to talk to. He wanted to hear about the Book of Mormon, so we gave him a discussion on it and he in turn told us some of the beliefs of the Catholic Church and gave us a pamphlet on Catholicism. We went to give him some pamphlets on our church, but he said, "No, thanks, I already have most of them." Elder Adsero believed he got the pamphlets from people in his parish whom we had talked to. These people in turn gave the pamphlets to their priest at confession for having entertained the Mormon missionaries. We also had discussions with Jehovah's Witnesses and with Seventh Day Adventists. They both carried on aggressive missionary efforts in Peru. They were more hostile than the Catholics. It was more difficult to have a friendly discussion with them. I remember telling one Jehovah's Witness about the Book of Mormon and Christ's visit to America, at an outdoor exposition. He listened for a while and suddenly blurted out loudly for all to hear, "Christ never came to America, you're just giving an interpretation."

As Elder Adsero got to within four weeks of the end of his mission, we spent one P-day on a "souvenir outing" to some of the shops in downtown Lima. To try to avoid the "special deal" the shop owners gave us as "wealthy" gringos, we took along one of the member ladies, Hermana Vargas. She volunteered to go with us to bargain with the shop owners. This avoided the 50 percent markup that went with the American faces we presented. We looked like a couple of silly, ugly Americans as we tried on cholo hats with flaps with dangling bells that hung over our ears and swooping points sticking up above our heads. We also tried on fur hats that looked like they were designed by Eskimos. We looked at alpaca rugs with patch-work patterns of mountain motifs that featured cholos, Incas, llamas, and other designs. I bought a number of small trinkets to send home with a lady who was going back to the States after visiting in Peru with her sister. One of my favorite memories of that day was of Elder Adsero and a little old cholo man selling cholo hats. Elder Adsero stood arm in arm with the little Inca. Both had on woven cholo hats, of many bright colors, that were fitted tightly to their skulls. The points of the hats swooped up about a foot above their heads, while multicolored flaps draped over their ears and framed their big toothy grins.

About three months into my stay in Callao, on P-day, Elder Adsero and I were in a book store browsing through documentary books on Callao. I told Elder Adsero I should probably buy the book I was looking at and read it, so I would know more about Callao while I was still in it. Elder Adsero said, "Well, you had better read it tonight, because you are leaving tomorrow!" He had received a phone call from the mission home that morning, advising him I would be changing areas and companions. A missionary's first change is a little traumatic when you realize you are leaving the area you first became familiar with in the mission field and changing companions. Per-haps if I had had a bad experience with my first companion, it would not have been so traumatic. But I had had a special relationship with my first companion. With a sense of adventure I began speculating on where I would go next, and who my companion would be. I started going over all the "glamour" spots in the mission. Perhaps relented to a little bit of unrighteous desire, acting more like a tourist than a missionary. Iquitos came to mind. It was the one spot in our mission field on the Amazon River and in the jungle. My speculation was heightened because Elder Adsero had come to Callao from Iquitos and he thought one of the junior companions had been there quite a long time. We went to a number of the areas in Callao that I wanted to take pictures of that day and we visited with people I wanted to see before I took off. We went out by the river and saw a shantytown near the airport. I had never seen such squalid living conditions. A row of wood and cardboard shanties on stilts leaned out over a river from a hillside. The huts were all different colors of dusty, dirty gray, black, and brown, with rubbish strewn around after being thrown out of the windows and doors and into the river. There were dirty children running around barefoot, with equally dirty dogs with greasy, matted fur, or missing fur, yapping. Barrels of water delivered by trucks sat in front of the shanties. The trash and sewage in the river contributed to the fetid, stagnant odors coming from the opaque water. Though I would not miss sights such as this, I would miss the good people I had met in my first area, primarily the Suarez family. I would move on without seeing them get baptized. After working with them for so many months and painstakingly helping Elder Adsero explain the gospel to them, I wanted to stay for the "reward." This was the fate of many missionaries. We had to become accustomed to change. We were not always present to see the fruits of our labors, but I had seen the fruits with the Suarez family—the changes in their lives and the growth of their testimonies gave me reward enough.

I learned that evening that I would not be going to one of the "glamour" spots such as Iquitos or Cuzco, but instead would be transferring to El Augustino, a suburb of Lima, to be the junior companion to Elder Hepworth from Clearfield, Utah. I met him at the mission home. He was a tall, thin, blond elder whom I would grow to know as humorous, easygoing, and a fierce competitor on the basketball court. Our area was on the other side of Lima from Callao, up by the foothills. It was a small community nestled in between dusty beige hills devoid of vegetation. We lived in the back room of a home on a square park, several blocks from where the barren foothills began. In looking toward the hills from our pension, I could observe many cholo-Indian people walking footpaths all over the foothills, going to and from marketplaces in the city and shantytown communities nestled up higher in the hills and mountains.

My first change worked out well. I went from one good companion to another good companion and one interesting area to another. Most missionaries get a com-bination of what they perceive to be both favorable and unfavorable changes. I learned that you adapt to the changes and that they end up giving you experience in patience, empathy, and adjusting to other people, other places, and in other approaches to missionary work. The changes thus give a missionary the chance to meet different companions, different members of the church, different investigators, and to see different areas of the mission field. It is also a way to make sure missionaries do not get too entrenched in their area and too familiar with the members, especially their daughters or sons.

My second evening in El Augustino, we met a man who did not understand a word we said. We had a word for this lack of understanding "foggy," as in having a layer of fog over the mind and being unable to comprehend what we were teaching. Perhaps the fog was induced by our inability to explain ourselves well in Spanish! Elder Hepworth was much less of a take-charge person than Elder Adsero, which enabled me to improve my Spanish by speaking more to those we met, and to gain more confidence in my ability to teach. I took more of a role in the discussions and hoped to dissipate any "fog" which kept the people from understanding our message. In my new area I was able to eat three meals a day, which helped me regain some of the weight that my family and girlfriend had found missing in looking at my first set of pictures delivered from Callao.

We lived in the home of a lady who had been wearing black for two years since her husband died. Most of the traditional Catholics in Peru seemed to wear black for years instead of a matter of a few days. The house was large, by Peruvian standards—three bedrooms, a living room, and a small but adequate kitchen. The house was built out of baked adobe bricks plastered over and was painted bright green.

One unsettling aspect of living near the coast of Peru was the frequency of earthquakes. Three times in my first couple of months, I felt a rattle, often at night or in the early morning. In fact, shortly after I arrived in El Augustino, we felt a shaker and heard there had been a serious earthquake south of Lima in Ayacucho. It had killed many people and destroyed sections of the city. We had no concern about our missionaries because they had been run out of Ayacucho months before by people convinced that the missionaries were an evil influence. One similar story of mission lore that circulated was about missionaries run out of Huancayo, a small town in the Andes, north of Lima, shortly before a major earthquake. The people in this town circulated a petition signed by those who wanted the missionaries out. A small group opposed the petition and wrote their own supporting freedom of religion and allowing the two missionaries to stay. Theirs was a lost cause, however, and under a threat of violence, and after consulting with the mission president, it was decided the missionaries should leave. They went down the valley to the next town to work. A few weeks later, an 8.2 earthquake struck just off the coast of northern Peru, at about the same latitude as Huancayo. This massive earthquake caused a section of a huge peak standing over twenty thousand feet, just up the valley from Huancayo, to sheer off with all of its glacial ice and snow and other debris and come careening down the canyon. This event was captured on film by members of a Japanese climbing team. A few members of the team, with a camera, had gone on ahead of the rest of the group and were out of harm's way when the face of the mountain came rolling past. They watched and filmed in horror as it engulfed, buried, and swept past the rest of their climbing team and continued down the valley.

The slide completely buried the town of Huancayo—only the top of the church steeple and some palm trees could be seen above the debris. It reached the town below where the missionaries had retreated, causing destruction, deaths, and injuries there as well. Everybody, including our two missionaries, abandoned the town in the face of the disaster. When the missionaries awoke the next morning in a makeshift tent, they were surrounded by *santitos*—figurines of various saints. After the destruction, the people were convinced the missionaries were the cause of this great disaster that had befallen them. They placed the *santitos* as a Voodoo-like ritual to threaten and curse the missionaries. The missionaries began to fear for their lives. Later in the day, a relief helicopter, flown by a Vietnam veteran from the United States, landed, after flying in from a military base in northern Peru. The pilot and one of the missionaries recognized each other from having served together in Vietnam. When it became apparent to the pilot that the missionaries were in danger, he evacuated them.

In following up on the disaster in Huancayo, the mission home learned that the only people from Huancayo who survived the disaster were those who had signed the petition to keep the missionaries in the town!

There was more mission lore about the Vietnam vet/missionary whose pilot buddy flew them out. He had served as a Green Beret in Vietnam, and he went through companions fairly fast. They soon became intimidated and actually terrified since he often had bad nightmares and would get up kicking and screaming in various martial arts poses during the middle of the night. He was serving up north in a little town when a drunk accosted him. He tried to shrug off the drunk, but he kept grabbing at the missionaries until finally Elder Green Beret picked him up, twirled him around, and set him back down. This drunk was sober enough to run away, once he hit the ground. Elder Green Beret could not quite leave his military experience behind. He became a district leader up in the mountain town of Cajamarca and organized a militarylike P-day "expedition." So they would not violate the Sabbath, he told his district to re-port at one minute past midnight to take off on their P-day exercise. They took off into the foothills at the base of the Andes and hiked up into areas where the cholos had never seen white faces.

When the sun came up they were suddenly surrounded in a cornfield by machete wielding cholos dressed in traditional quechuan garb—alpaca ponchos in brightly woven colors, pointed-top cholo hats with ear-flaps, also of alpaca, knee-length pants, and sandals. Much of this garb carried over from the days of the Inca. These particular cholos were not happy at having their fields invaded by strange white men, especially since their oral tradition and legends graphically depicted the death and destruction that came with the Spaniards when they conquered their forefathers, the Incas. Elder Green Beret lost his cool and started going through his martial-arts routine, smacking cholos in the chest, and the side of the head, with his feet in various spin moves they had never seen before. For a moment they were awestruck, but when the whirling dervish stopped to catch his breath, he noticed the cholos had captured several of the other missionaries and were menacingly holding their machetes at their necks, threatening to slit their throats if he did not stop the Bruce Lee routine. He surrendered and they were led, at machete point, to a crude adobe hut that would serve as their jail. The missionaries began to worry whether they would see the light of day again, especially since they could not communicate with these cholos, who spoke only Quechua. They did start communicating with their Father in Heaven, though, praying for a way out. Their prayers were answered. After a day passed, one member of the national police force in a village down below the mountain, heard a rumor, in one of the small corner bars, that the cholos in the mountains had captured a group of white missionaries and were holding them as prisoners. Although the entire mountain region was within his jurisdiction, the policeman seldom ventured up where the cholos lived. Fortunately for the missionaries, he decided to pursue the rumor and traveled up into the mountain that day, found where the missionaries were being held, and convinced the cholos to let them go.

Their adventure was only partly, over, however, as they had to find a way to get back to the city. As they were stumbling their way down the mountain, following a river gorge, they attempted to cross a river swollen with glacial runoff, and one of the missionaries tripped into the water and plunged over a twelve-foot cascade, fortunately landing in a pool of ice water, instead of hitting a rock. His camera was ruined, destroying whatever photographic evidence of their little adventure he might otherwise have preserved. They finally reached a dirt road down below and hitched a ride with a flatbed truck. When they reached the city, another elder lost his camera, forgetting to remove it from the truck when they got off. In the end, it was a graphic lesson for every missionary involved, on the propriety of marching into uncharted territories in the highlands of Peru. The miracle of their rescue by the national policeman, in response to their prayerful pleas, also did not escape their attention.

Elder Hepworth and I had matching senses of humor and always appreciated funny daily incidents. One amusing custom he and I encountered, as we went about our daily missionary activities, unfolded whenever we met a lady who had been washing clothes. She would offer us a sudsy forearm to shake or an elbow. It seemed comical for us to be grabbing someone's forearm or elbow to shake it like a chicken wing. They would do the same if they had something in their hands. Elder Hepworth was definitely a missionary who knew how to have fun. We held a Family Home Evening one night with a member family and one of our investigators who had a little clothes factory in his house up on the hill. The father of the member family gave the lesson and afterward we had refreshments and clowned around. Elder Hepworth became "Joseph F. Hepworth," posing with the collar of his shirt turned up, nineteenth-century style, holding his Book of Mormon, with a serious chin-out facial expression, imitating the pose shown in the church paintings of Joseph F. Smith and Hyrum Smith. We took pictures after I transformed myself into "Hyrum Hoyt," with a similar pose. The family then demanded that Elder Hepworth do his *borracho*—imitation of a drunkard—which he did in hilarious fashion with disheveled hair, a cross-eyed expression, a stumbling gait, and slurred speech.

The humor and good time lasted only until we reached our pension, where we found that the married daughter of the lady we lived with had been rushed to the hospital earlier in the day, with serious burns from an exploding gas water heater. She died that night. Those fortunate enough to have a gas water heater in their house had a small tank, three feet high by two feet in diameter, sitting in close proximity to the shower in the bathroom, so that if you had a problem while you were in the shower, it became a very dangerous situation. The senora we lived with was already wearing black as a result of the death of her husband two years earlier and was practically carried into the house by her friends in a distraught condition.

The next day, we really did not know what to say and felt out of place simply being there. We tried to express our condolences as best we could in Spanish. I had never experienced much incidence of death, except for the passing of my grandparents when I was young. It caused us to reflect on the importance of our message about the Plan of Salvation. After asking for comfort for the senora, I expressed deep gratitude that night in my prayers for the gospel, the Plan of Salvation, and my strengthened testimony of the truth. Prayer was indeed my one sure source of comfort and solace in the mission field. I prayed often during the day for teaching opportunities, progress for investigators, help with depression, and protection for my loved ones at home. Sweet peace and soothing thoughts usually enveloped me after these prayers.

It seemed that every area in Peru had at least one problem dog. In El Augustino, ours lived right next door. This beady-eyed mongrel would wait until we passed by, then would pop up with his head just over the wall, viciously growling and scaring the heck out of us. We devised a plan to solve the problem. We stood by the wall and whistled. When he popped up, we smacked him on the head with our folded-up flannel board. After a few pops on the head over the course of a couple days, he never pulled his "jack-in-the-box" routine on us again.

There was another, more amusing dog in our area and we called him "Baby Rhino"—short for rhinoceros. He was a small, black, corpulent dog without hair. I burst out laughing whenever I saw him. He had one tassel of frizzed hair sticking up between his ears like a rhinoceros's horn. As the weather grew cold, his owners greased him up with something like Vaseline to keep him warm.

I ran into the same frustration in this area as in Callao—our appointments seemed to have the lowest priority of any activities in the people's lives. They would set up appointments, then not worry much if it turned out they had something else to do after scheduling with us. We heard many, many excuses and this was one of the frustrations that I know every missionary must confront, no matter where he or she serves. We received very few references in this area. To break the monotony of knocking on doors every day, I suggested to Elder Hepworth that we make a "mini-expo," like those we used in Callao. We went into Lima and bought a big piece of cardboard and brightly colored paper. We put bright blue paper as a background on the cardboard and I cut letters out of bright orange paper, which spelled "Lamanitas," meaning "Lamanites," and put that across the top. We then cut up newspapers and church magazines, gluing on colored pictures of a couple of Peruvians; of Lehi in the boat with his family; of Machu Picchu, the Lost City of the Incas; of Christ in America; and of Moroni with the Gold Plates. We took the display downtown and set it up beside a bus stop. We stirred up some interest among people walking by, and those waiting for the bus, that led to references. Unfortunately for us, all of the references were for areas outside our own. At least we could provide references for other missionaries.

We talked with an older couple for about a half hour one day, discussing the church, its organization, and Christ's visit to the Americas. We felt like we were very effective teachers making some real progress until we reached the end of the discussion and they asked us, "Are you guys Catholics, or what religion are you?" I guess my Spanish still wasn't quite ready for these and the old fog was still lingering in the minds of some of those we met.

We watched the start of the Summer Olympics along with the people we ate with and felt proud as we saw our team parade by on the television set. On our way home, a bunch of little kids swarmed us, begging for money—a frequent occurrence whenever they saw the gringos. Being in an Olympics, competitive mood, we set up a race with these kids and gave the winner a dollar, second place a half dollar, and third place a quarter—all in soles, Peruvian money.

With winter there came a heavy misty fog, as close to rain as we ever saw in Lima. The dirt roads and dust-covered asphalt roads became muddy as we knocked at one house that had a big dog lying in the muck out front. I started to pet the dog, when he jovially jumped up on me, with both of his big muddy paws right on the front of my suit coat—what a mess! I washed it off as best I could since we risked destroying a suit by sending it to an unknown dry cleaner.

On August 30, I saw my first Saint Day celebration. It was "Dia de Santa Rosa de Lima," or Saint Rose Day. We witnessed processions—parades led by fully costumed people marching up and down the streets. Some were dressed in large outfits, imitating Saint Rose, while others carried statues of the Virgin Mary on poles. Still others crawled on their knees to inflict pain upon themselves, in the hopes they would more fully receive penitence, while some sang as they walked—it was quite a spectacle. It looked like a cross between a Mardi Gras celebration and a funeral march.

It was always a great feeling to have investigators show up at our church. My second Sunday in El Augustino, we had two investigator families attend, the Zapatas and the Vegas. If we could get them to church and involve the other members in friendshiping them, there was a fighting chance that they would fully embrace the gospel and be baptized. We met and taught a first discussion to a family headed by a man who had lost his sight at the age of sixteen. He studied Braille, went through high school, the university, and law school and became the first blind lawyer in Peru. He showed me some of his books in Braille and how well he could read them. I admired his perseverance in the face of adversity. Elder Hepworth wrote to his mother to see if she would send him a Book of Mormon in Braille.

My favorite discussion was the fifth, where we taught the Plan of Salvation. With an attentive, open-minded family, we always felt the Spirit in giving this discussion because they had never heard a logical explanation for where we came from, why we are here, and where we are going. It was a very spiritual experience to explain to them the preexistence, the trials and tests we are here to pass, the spirit world, the possibility of receiving the gospel after this life, and progression in the hereafter to the degrees of glory. Many had been steeped in the belief that unless you accepted Christ's gospel in this life, you were condemned in the hereafter, just as little children who were not baptized would not reach any degree of glory. The fairness of God's actual plan was very appealing to the people we taught, since it put life in a fairer perspective. One of the single most powerful precepts in this discussion was that children are innocent before God and go to him when they die, even if they have not yet been baptized. Because of the poor standard of living there, poor health care, and other problems many people we encountered were burdened with—many either had lost a child or knew someone who had—this part of the Plan of Salvation touched them deeply, especially those who listened with an open mind and an open heart. It emotionally affected me to see the suffering many of the Peruvians had grown up with. I felt the gospel could bring hope to lives that had previously seemed more like nightmares. Being able to provide hope to parents who had lost little children gave me Spirit-induced "goose bumps." We shed many tears with our investigators as we taught these beautiful precepts.

The youth in El Augustino did not seem as intent on heckling or smart-mouthing us. They were more curious than obnoxious. Three times in one day a bunch of little kids started following us around. One time, about thirty little girls, who had just finished school for the day, followed us, laughing and giggling. As a joke I jumped around with a scary expression and yelled at them in English. They scattered, laughing and squealing.

On September 5, 1972, as I was hobbling around with a sprained ankle from playing basketball on our P-day, we heard the tragic news, on the radio that the Palestinian guerrillas had captured and killed members of the Israeli team at the Olympics in Munich. We also heard the bad news from President Driggs: that he was thinking of closing down our area since it had pretty much been tracted out. We did not hear about where he would move us, or when we would leave. I felt like we had failed since we had been unable to interest many people in the gospel and had only a few investigators. I now realize these low points must be endured by missionaries everywhere. Baptisms are the crowning glory for every missionary, and without them, it is common to lapse into a depression, thinking you are not living by the Spirit or teaching by the Spirit, or somehow not a worthy missionary. The only way to pull out of these blues is to work your hardest, put in the time, pray, and work with the Spirit and realize that you cannot control people's faith or openness. If you do your job as a missionary, the rest is up to the Lord and the people. I was reminded that even Jesus Christ could perform no miracles in certain parts of Palestine because of the lack of faith there.

To prepare for the eventuality that our area would be closed, I provided all of the addresses of our good investigators to Hermana Terreros—the mother of the member family that we had Family Home Evenings with and had introduced to a number of our investigators. She promised to visit them in case we were pulled out.

As we neared the end of our stay in El Augustino, we had a Stake Conference at the one Lima Stake. We traveled by bus, with a couple of the member families, to central Lima for the conference. We always looked forward to the Stake Conference because it was a chance to see members we had known in other areas of Lima, investi-gators we had taught in other areas who had joined the church, and other missionaries we had served with, or were friends with. This Stake Conference was no exception. I visited with many of the missionaries I had known in the LTM.

After we got word that they might close our area, we gave our investigators a concentrated discussion, squeezing many lessons into one so that we could advance them in the gospel as quickly as we could. The Zapata family, whom we had been teaching since I arrived, committed to a baptism within one to two weeks. To our delight, the Zapata and Vega families both came to church several weeks in a row. We reached another low, however, when Hermano Zapata told us he would not be able to pay tithing if he became a member. This was a real problem in Peru because most people were already barely living at survival levels as it was. In addition, as they approached baptism, it seemed that investigators were subjected to more temptations and more influences to try and distract them from their goal. We tried to stress the importance of tithing to Hermano Zapata, but in the end, we lost him. We also lost the struggle to get the Vega family to baptism. They remained interested, but uncommitted—the principle of tithing was just too much for them to commit to. We were upset by this development. They had been golden families, families we had grown to love, and families we wanted to see share the full blessings of the gospel.

We had a revitalizing district meeting on September 11, with each of us revealing our testimonies about the work and the love we had for the people and each other. These weekly district meetings became a real source of motivation and spiritual fortification for the week ahead. We were like a family and a mutual support group giving a lift to each other. We had two sister missionaries in our district. They were both really cool and fit in well. They were hard workers who were able to come in and teach people who were not receptive to the elders. There were always those who felt more comfortable learning the gospel from the sisters—they had a gentler touch.

Shortly after the district meeting, we found out that Elder Bendickson was leaving the area and that Elder Hepworth was to be the new district leader. We picked up half of Elder Bendickson's old area along with ours, which excited us because we had seen just about every door in our old area. Instead of closing our area, we were able to consolidate it with another, larger area. We moved into Elder Bendickson's apartment/pension, where we had a phone and a more central location.

At first I missed living in our old area because of the family we ate with, and some of the kids that we used to play soccer with at night after work. Being a couple of gringos, we thought we were playing pretty well, although the kids we played with were much more adept and skilled soccer players, and often let us move through and score because they were afraid we might bowl them over with our size and awkwardness.

We took over one of the investigators Elder Bendick-son had been teaching at the pension. I told Elder Hep-worth to set up all of our appointments for our pension as if we had office hours with appointments run back-to-back like a doctor's! It was rumored that the missionaries in Mexico operated this way since they had so many investigators and so many baptisms. We saw a whole different lifestyle in our new pension. These people seemed to have plenty of money. The maid would answer to a little bell the senora would ring. They also had a buzzer in the bedroom to summon the maid. It was a two-story house with big, spacious rooms lit up with chandeliers, and a huge sun deck up above.

As the district leader, Elder Hepworth had the responsibility of seeing that the mail got out to all the missionaries in our district. On our way out to the sisters' pension to deliver the mail, we got lost. Elder Hepworth called a taxi and when the driver pulled up, he hit a puddle and splashed dirty water all over Elder Hepworth. It was funny but I knew that I risked his wrath by laughing. We later laughed about it, once he cleaned off his suit.

There was a wild open-air market in our new area, called "La Parada." It was a small street lined with wood-framed booths covered with different pieces of bright plastic or cloth. These booths contained everything from vegetables to hanging, defeathered chickens and assorted meats out for the flies to dance on. It smelled of rotten fruit and vegetables. Tons of cheap jewelry and other trinkets also were set out, for sale by gypsies wearing brightly colored bandanas and various layers of differently colored clothes. People streamed down between the booths, making it difficult to even make your way through. We were bombarded by noise, clucking chickens waiting to have their necks wrung, arguments over prices, and hawkers yelling their prices. We were warned not to spend time there since some of the worst people in Lima could be found at the market, looking for victims. We walked through with a firm grip on our cameras.

Mendicito was another section of our new area that we were advised, by the mission home and police, to stay away from. Even the police did not venture in. It was inhabited by criminals. On our way to visit a member family one night, we were walking a block or so away from this area when we heard a scream and we saw a teenager running across the street with a lady's purse. We started running after him but he ran down a narrow, dark alley on his way back into Mendicito, and caution got the better part of valor as we let him go.

On September 17, Elder Hepworth told me I had to be in the office the next night and that I would board a plane Wednesday morning to go to another area. My curiosity was aroused since I would obviously be leaving Lima. We went around and said good-bye to the members and investigators. Changes were always a source of excitement but also of sadness as you said good-bye to members and friends. I had just unpacked from moving pensions, and now I was back at packing up again. The day I got the news of my change, I again sprained my ankle playing basketball. I guess my ankles were not made for basketball. It was making me a cripple as I seemed to be hobbling around more often than not.

I had my interview with the president and he told me I was going to Iquitos. I could not believe it! Elder Adsero had told me all about it. It was on the Amazon River. Most of the missionaries had hopes of either going to Cuzco—the ancient city of the Incas—or Iquitos. Iquitos was the area farthest from the mission office, so the president told me he only sent elders there he could trust. I later learned why. Four elders who had been stationed there six months before had decided they were going to take a jungle expedition. They prepared their weekly reports before leaving and told one of the members to mail the reports to the mission office, as if they had been there working all week. They took off for the jungle, rafting down the Amazon River in a rented boat. The member sent in the weekly reports before the week was up. The president became suspicious when he saw reports on missionary activities—discussions taught and hours logged—for days that had not yet come. He sent the assistants up to Iquitos and they were there waiting for the elders when they got back from their adventure. They came back to Lima and spent time working under close supervision by the assistants.

# CHAPTER 7
## Iquitos-the Amazon Area

I was excited about going to Iquitos, but I was not thrilled about flying there. I had doubts about the quality of the aircraft, how well it was maintained, and who was flying it. Stories about one of the Peruvian airlines—Lancet—did not help my confidence. This airline had gone out of business after losing three of its six aircraft in crashes, one of them on the way to Iquitos! That particular plane had been a Lockheed Electra that had been banned in the United States because of its tendency to electrically short out in the wings near the gas tanks and blow up in midair. The doomed flight to Iquitos blew up in midair somewhere near a jungle town called Puculpa. The lone survivor was a teenage girl who was blown clear out of the aircraft while still strapped in her seat. She descended upright, landing first in a huge tree and then dropping into the bushes underneath. When she regained consciousness the next day, she unbuckled her seat belt and stepped out of the chair unhurt. She survived alone in the Amazon jungle for two weeks, wandering until some of the jungle tribes found her and took her to Puculpa to safety.

After losing two other aircraft, Lanset Airlines became the cheapest, but also the most dreaded airline to fly. It was probably just pure rumor, but I heard that as people stood watching their relatives board Lancet planes, they used to hum the equivalent of one of the funeral marches.

I felt a little better as I boarded my plane. It appeared to be a 737, like those I had flown in the United States, and everything seemed in order. I finally sat back and enjoyed the flight, which took us over the Andes. As we crested the mountains, we could see glaciers and glacier formations creeping down the mountain and gouging out glacial lakes and ravines. After we crossed the tops of the Andes, the jungle started immediately on the eastern side. Everywhere I looked, I saw a vast carpet of greenery with no interruption except for glittering rivers meandering in different directions. These were the tributaries that fed the Amazon River from all of the rainfall on the eastern side of the Andes. We made one stop, in Pulculpa. The airport there looked like what I would have expected for Pappy Boyington and his Black Sheep, flying in World War II in the South Pacific—there were World War II—era aircraft sitting around the terminal, which was a half-circle Quonset hut of corrugated metal, abutted by wood shacks with thatched leaf roofs. As we got out of the plane to stretch our legs, the heat and humidity hit us like a coal furnace—welcome to the jungle!

The last leg of our trip took us in to Iquitos, right over the main channel of the Amazon River. The river appeared huge, over two miles wide. Our pilot announced that the river widened to two-hundred miles wide at its mouth on the coast of Brazil! I later learned that the Amazon moves more water than any other river in the world and that all by itself, could drain an area three-fourths the size of the United States. The river was muddy in color and as we crossed over it and from the air, Iquitos looked like a small town completely surrounded by jungle and the river.

I met my new companion, Elder Brooks, from St. George, Utah, at the airport. We took a taxi to our pension, which was only one block from the Amazon. As we drove toward the town, we passed outlying barrio houses, mostly built out of wood with thatched roofs. They looked like what I had imagined of native huts in a tropical jungle. As we approached the town, the homes were a variety of wood with thatched or corrugated tin roofs, and adobe brick and plaster with corrugated tin roofs. Roofs were important in Iquitos because it rained hard at least once a day. There was one main street, which we walked down after I unpacked. It fronted the Amazon River. Even in the town, if there was an empty lot, the jungle sprouted up in it almost overnight. Due to the heat, we did not have to wear suit coats. I did not have to worry about the lack of hot water here; water in the shower was lukewarm and hardly refreshing. The high humidity was op-pressive. I began to notice sweat from places where I had never sweated before, like the knuckles of my fingers.

The people in Iquitos were extremely friendly. Because of the heat, their windows and doors were always open, so as we walked down the street we could talk to them without knocking on doors, just by leaning in their windows. Almost always we were invited in to talk. There were many more motorcycles and bicycles there than cars and it was often noisy as the motorcycles went up and down the streets scattering large black vultures, which seemed to be everywhere, into the wind. Many people owned pigs and let them run in and out of the houses. As we were talking to a family on my first day, pigs went squealing through the house and out. My grin turned to laughter at this sight.

My first few days I got a flavor of some of the Amazon animal life. Elder Brooks took me to a house down by the river where an investigator lived who owned a tigrillo—a baby ocelot. It was the most beautiful cat I had ever seen. It was about two feet long and about a foot and a half high, spotted, with large blue eyes and big paws—a perfect miniature tiger. This cat's owner told us they had just killed a fifty-foot-long anaconda snake in the jungle! That same night, we arrived home to find a bat flying around our room, causing us to undress quickly and dive under the covers! The next day, we went to work in an area toward the outskirts of town, where there was a tropical fish hatchery. They had vast fields of water with varieties of tropical fish, guppies, angelfish, zebra fish, and tiger fish. The owners shipped their fish to Miami, Florida, for sale in the United States.

Although the people were friendly, most were more interested in idle chitchat about us and about the United States than they were in learning about the gospel. I soon learned that Iquitos was an exotic "glamour" spot to visit as a tourist, but it was a tough and challenging area for missionary work. Because of the friendly attitudes, we were able to hand out hundreds of pamphlets and set up many discussions, but we did not seem to have anybody really heading anywhere serious.

Fruit trees growing everywhere dropped large, thinly covered seeds called "aquajes." They cluttered the streets. More than once, we had to duck as one of these seeds whizzed by like a bullet after being squirted off the road by the tire of a passing car or truck. As we walked down the street we would hear a bang as one of these seeds slammed into a house adjoining the road. These seeds often came in handy if we were being followed by pestering dogs or pigs. I became skilled at picking up the seeds and nailing the dog or pig with a thump. One time, I felt bad after I chucked one at a pig, hitting it in the hind end and caused it to jump, with a start, into the hind of a passing truck. We watched in horror as the pig palled underneath the truck and out the tail end, squealing. It got up relatively unhurt and ran away. The fruit seeds attracted large black buzzards that congregated everywhere.

I dreaded our first church meeting because of the heat and the lack of any air conditioning. Our church was a two-story apartment building with a large room on the ground floor, where we held all of our joint Sunday school, priesthood, and Sacrament meetings, and classrooms upstairs on the second level. It was not built as a chapel but was rented by the church for the branch in Iquitos. The meetings went well. About twenty-five people attended. There was a large ceiling fan that gave the room a "Casablanca" look. It kept it fairly cool in the main room. We also had our Sunday school and priesthood meetings early in the day and our Sacrament meeting at seven in the evening, which helped with the heat. The members were very friendly, but there was such a lack of leadership experience—most were recent converts—that they relied a lot on the missionaries for the administration of the branch. I taught the investigator class and played the piano for the meetings. I enjoyed teaching, it helped my Spanish and my ability to explain the gospel. I felt like I was finally reaching a high level of comprehension, both in listening and speaking—the "fog" was evaporating.

My first P-day in Iquitos gave me an introduction to the jungle. The assistants to the mission president—two missionaries called to serve in the mission home with the president—were visiting and they wanted to explore. We walked out to the edge of town and hitched a ride with the driver of a flatbed truck carrying supplies out to the    construction site for an international airport. The springs in the truck had expired years before. It probably had never had any shock absorbers to begin with. We were pounded by the bumpy dirt road leading through the jungle. The driver dropped us off by a lake in the middle of the vast green forest. It was a beautiful spot, with jungle foliage of various layers, from scrub up through tall bushes and ultimately large rainforest-type trees everywhere, completely encircling the lake. There were large ponds near the lake, where people living in the area were breeding large sturgeon to sell for food. As we walked through the forest, we could hear innumerable birds calling and squealing. We saw brightly colored parrots flitting through the treetops.

After hitchhiking back into town, I bought a mounted piranha for a souvenir. I heard they had no trouble with piranha attacks in the main river because it flowed too fast, but they did have attacks in the backwaters where the water stagnated.

As we walked by the marketplace along the main street and the river, later in the week, we saw a few teenagers trying to get Brahman bulls into stalls. At first the bulls were going where they wanted and pulling the teenagers behind them as they tried to hang on to the ropes. One of the bulls charged out into the street toward a taxicab, and got loose. It was hilarious. The teenagers went running after the loose bull and finally got ahold of the rope. After being dragged twenty feet, they finally brought the bull to a stop but then the bull turned around and charged the teenagers. They dropped the rope and scrambled for cover!

When we were fortunate enough to run into a truly "golden" investigator, we were dumbfounded. It happened to us shortly after I arrived in Iquitos while we were out knocking on doors. In Iquitos we did not really knock on doors since everybody's doors and windows. were open. We just passed by and started up a conversation through open windows until we were invited in. We met a lady who told us she had read the Book of Mormon three times and that she knew it was the true word of God. She had never yet had a discussion from the missionaries and we were excited to begin them with her. We taught her for many weeks. It was so refreshing to teach someone who was serious about the gospel and thirsting for more knowledge. We looked forward to our visits with her. Not only was she a golden investigator, but she was also a nurse and she gave me a pill she said would get rid of the rash on my arms, which I was experiencing from the heat. I took the pill at her house—and it made me groggy for the rest of the evening.

In contrast to our golden investigator, the next day we met a lady who seemed only half there. In the middle of our discussion, she interrupted with a whole string of phony praising about how blessed she was to have us in her home, to have us show her the way, to have us tell her how it should be, and how privileged she was to have visitors from the United States, and on and on. She would not stop her litany of contrived praisings long enough to let us finish. While she was in the middle of her tirade, a big, fat, muddy pig came through the open door. It walked through the house toward the back, and plopped down on the kitchen floor. I was startled at first, but I then realized this was the family pet. Many times after that I would see muddy pigs running through the houses. It seemed perfectly acceptable to the homeowners.

I decided to start a bug collection, because there were plenty of bugs in a great variety. One of the other missionaries, Elder Caldwell— there were four of us living in the two-bedroom apartment—decided it was a good idea and tried to catch a large bug in the backroom, but it flew up his garments! I was rolling in tearful laughter on the ground as we saw him do an Irish jig and set a speed re-cord for stripping out of his garments.

About two weeks after I arrived in Iquitos, we thought we had scored a real victory when we were invited to give a discussion to the head of the Secret Police in Iquitos. His department was in charge of monitoring foreigners. We should have been suspicious when, instead of listening, all he wanted to do was ask us questions. He prayed at the end of the discussion but as we tried to set up another appointment and opened up our schedule book to write it down, he got very curious and wanted to look through our appointment book. He asked us who gave us permission to write down addresses, and told us that within the next few days, he wanted to see our visas. We ran into this man again at the café where we ate. It was a small barnlike café with vinyl chairs. It offered a limited selection, and sometimes the meats had mysterious names and origins, like "dog of the mountain." I could guess what this animal was, but preferred not to. Maybe an anteater, or maybe a sloth, or maybe a monkey. At least the café was clean and so far the missionaries had not had a bad experience with it. As we were eating, our "friend" came over and told us we had better come by his office and show him our visas, or else he would send somebody after us. We would later regret telling him, almost as a challenge, to go ahead and send someone for us. We were angry because it was obvious he had been inviting us to give him discussions only to satisfy his suspicions about what we were up to.

Well, I apparently had the first bad experience with the café. I woke up after our fast day—fasting was a challenge in the jungle since you nearly died of thirst after going twenty-four hours without any liquid—sicker than I ever remembered being in my entire life. I was going to the bathroom all night long and into our P-day. All I did, all day, was lie in bed and moan in-between trips to the bathroom. I wore a path to that bathroom on what must have been at least forty trips, and lost five to ten pounds in one day. day. I was still feeling a little sick when Tuesday came, and especially weak, but decided to try to go out and work for a while. We left to go ask questions at the plaza where the then president of Peru, Presidente Velasco, was going to speak on Wednesday. There were banners forty feet tall, with painted pictures of miners and farmworkers. They looked like the propaganda you would expect to see in a communist country. These massive work-scene pictures were where the president would speak. We asked the head of the guards at the plaza if we could take a picture of the area and he told us, "Why not?" so we took a picture of the plaza, with all of its decorations. Suddenly the head of the Secret Police, who had suckered us into giving him several discussions, showed up and ordered the policeman, whom we had asked about the picture, to prod us along at the point of a machine gun, as we followed him. He hustled us into a jeep and took us to an office building downtown. He told us he would be back in a little while, which turned into four and a half hours. We were simmering in anger the whole time, until he finally showed up and told us he would take care of us in the afternoon. They then moved us by car to another office building, where we had to wait until five in the evening before the "dink," as we began calling him, showed up. In the meantime we saw that at least we were better treated than a number of the other prisoners. About every hour they would herd a bunch of Colombians out of a holding cell where there was no bathroom and very little air movement. They hosed them down, since they had to go to the bathroom in the corners of that cell and fester in the humid stench that was emitted from the door they opened every hour. They fed them "stuff" that looked suspiciously like dog food. Their "crime" was they'd crossed the border of Colombia into Peru, without official paperwork. One of the other men they were holding was from Ecuador. His "crime" had been to come in and ask for a permit to remain in the country. Instead of giving him a permit, they were holding him indefinitely since he, too, did not have the proper paperwork. Finally the "dink" showed up and interviewed Elder Brooks and me separately. He asked more questions. Elder Brooks handled his questioning much better than I did, ultimately laughing with the "dink" at how angry I was getting. My disposition was not helped by my lingering weakness from my bout with food poisoning. I had had very little to eat or drink for two days. While Elder Brooks patiently explained our missionary service and what we were about, I could only get sarcastic with the "dink" and tell him, "Yes, our appointment book is a list of the houses that we have spied on and found to have sufficient valuables to warrant burglary," or, "Yes, we are spies from the CIA and have come down here to see what you are doing with all of our old military hardware from the 1950s that we gave to Peru." Thanks to Elder Brooks, but no thanks to my smart mouth, we finally got out of there, after being held for eleven hours as suspicious foreigners who had not shown the "dink" our proper paperwork for being in the country. I left with the voiced invitation, to the head "dink," that I hoped he would come to the United States and look me up sometime, so I could show him equal hospitality. In hindsight, I later realized how my loss of self-control and my anger could have led us to a very dangerous situation, possibly incarceration or injury. Once again, while a mature senior companion smoothed over my inexperience and arrogance, I proceeded to demonstrate an example of the "ugly American" instead of being a representative of Jesus Christ. Fortunately, I mellowed" over time in the mission field, but it did not come easy.

Several investigators persisted in coming to church, which gave us a rewarding feeling. Church attendance was a true test of whether they were sincerely interested in what we were teaching. The contrast between Iquitos and Lima was striking. In Lima we worked hard just to get in the door to present a discussion. In Iquitos it was easy to get in and teach, but more difficult to really capture their interest and get a commitment. The jungle mentality seemed to be one of being laid back. We taught one lady a discussion and got to the point where, on the flannel board, you put up two pictures that made it obvious what the difference between the true church of Christ and the other churches was the church—of-Christ picture had a foundation of apostles and prophets. In response to our question about the difference, she pointed to the picture without apostles and prophets and as we eagerly awaited the correct response, she said, "This one does not have the tree." We had to stifle our giggling to finish the discussion. She was right—the one picture did not have a tree on it—but it was not the answer we were waiting for.

The power in different sections of Iquitos seemed to go off at least once a day, almost with as much regularity as the rainfall. We were trying to show a filmstrip to a family on the outskirts of town, when in the middle of the movie the electricity went down and we sat in darkness. We had a rewarding Family Home Evening anyway, with the family and their non-member niece, Lita. She was sincerely interested in the discussions and had the full support of her aunt and uncle and cousins, who were already members. Fellowshiping by the members was a rare commodity in Iquitos, but one which definitely paid off, as it does in every mission field. The best chance of success with investigators was when they were befriended by relatives or friends.

Due to the humidity and heat, we had to drink constantly. I was still suffering some dehydration from my food poisoning, and I probably averaged four soda pops just in the morning, before it got hot. Fortunately, there were little corner tiendas, or stores, everywhere.

I began looking forward to the rain once a day, because it cooled everything down. I had never seen rain come down as hard as it did in tropical downpours in Iquitos. It came down in solid sheets, instead of individual drops. After one of these deluges we traveled way out into the sticks toward the jungle, to a reference we had for a house we reached by crossing over a large swamp, via a little log bridge. We left the people a pamphlet and a bulletin on the General Conference broadcast that was coming up. When we arrived home, there were two guys with backpacks on our porch, one from Provo and one from Switzerland. They had asked for a room down by the church where the missionaries lived, and since the motel was full, they asked if they could sleep outside our doorway. We had them come in and we gave them an extra mattress we had. The one from Provo had hitchhiked all the way down through Central America and into South America. He was going to take the Amazon River all the way into Brazil. We shared an interesting evening listening to these adventurers' travel stories.

The next day, another unusual event—huge army ants, two inches or longer, were swarming all over. The people were gathering them up to fry and eat. They told us this flying horde descended upon the town once a year and everyone took advantage of collecting the "delicacy" like manna from Heaven.

We had a large *paseo*, or party, with the entire branch on our first P-day in October of 1972. The branch people traveled to an area along the Amazon, outside the town and deep in the jungle. We played soccer and baseball and made sandwiches. The members went swimming in the river, which looked very inviting because of the heat, but we maintained our missionary dignity and abided by the mission rule that we not swim. We were there until the late afternoon, enjoying conversation with the members and drinking "Inca Cola," a gold-colored soda pop made from herbs that tasted like liquid bubble gum.

I had another unfortunate experience with getting investigators to the brink of baptism, only to have them drop out. We had been teaching a family—the Roldans—up to the point of baptism, but it all unwound as the man of the family told us he did not think he could keep the Sabbath day holy, and wondered why it was a requirement, when the Catholic church does not make a big deal about Sunday activities. He was grasping for excuses, which showed us he was not spiritually ready. To ease our depression, that same evening we had another spirit-filled discussion with Lita. She had set her sights on her baptism after seeing the example set by her aunt and uncle and cousins.

Iquitos was the only place on my mission where I showered three times a day and looked forward to each and every one. Because my pores were opened from so much sweating, I never itched when I got out of the shower, and a shower was the only way to cool down. I took a shower when we came in from lunch, a shower when we left for the day, and a shower when we got home in the evening.

There were some bizarre people walking around this town. One of them was called the "puppet man." He was certifiably insane and shuffled around wearing a plastic fireman's hat and carrying a little stool and a bag full of puppets. He kept company with himself, talking with all of his puppets and putting on a little show, supposedly for the kids, but primarily for himself. There was another lady whom everyone called "Teresa, the rag lady," who continually collected rags of different colors and then wound them around her arms, legs, and head. She walked down the street like a rainbow mummy. There was another loony, a girl about seventeen, who thought she was a little kid. She painted her face in all different colors and played with the little kids, who followed her around like the Pied Piper. All of these "unique" characters were harmless and the people liked them. I must admit they added a certain flavor to the city and pity on them was misplaced because they really seemed to enjoy themselves.

I soon found that the moral standards in Iquitos were lower than in other parts of Peru. We were walking toward the outskirts of town, toward military housing and farms, and came upon a group of women washing their clothes, underneath little thatched roofs on stilts, in pits dug into the sandy soil. The water percolated in the bottom of the pits. These women were completely naked, bathing themselves as they washed the clothes. A few of them casually tried to hold the clothes up to cover themselves but others simply proceeded with business as usual, without any concern. This eye-opening experience was followed by a couple of girls following us around that night, saying words in English like, "Let's go," "Let's go out on a date." They followed us for blocks. Shortly after this experience, we knocked on the wall of a house—the door was already open—and an attractive teenage girl, wrapped only in a towel, came out with her hair wet, obviously having just gotten out of the bath or shower. I managed to blurt out a question, asking if her mom or dad was home, and her response in Spanish was that they were not home, but that we could come in anyway. We told her we had better wait until her parents came home, and she said, "Please don't go, at least let him stay," as she grabbed my arm and tried to pull me into the house! Elder Brooks grabbed my other arm and pulled me away telling the girl, "No, he can't stay." It would have been re-ally difficult to try to stay morally prepared for a mission, had I grown up in this area. We ran into many children who did not know who their father was, since either their mother was never married, to begin with, or their father left them while they were young.

Iquitos was a jumping-off point at that time for oil exploration in the jungle. Various companies and employees from different parts of the world congregated in Iquitos before heading into the wild for weeks at a time. We kept running into Texans in Iquitos who were involved in the oil trade. It was very strange to knock on a door and have somebody come out and say, in a western drawl, "Howdy, you all come on in." One afternoon, we ran into a man from Texas, and his wife. He told us it wouldn't do us any good to talk to him because he was a Baptist, but his wife, who had only been in Iquitos for one month and didn't speak any Spanish, came running out and told us she would be happy to talk to us. She was probably hungry to find anyone who spoke English. We became good friends with this family over the next couple of months. Although they really were not interested in the gospel, they did feed us from time to time, and pro-vided a nice conversation. On our way back from talking with them, we came to a swamp where the oil had seeped up and polluted the surrounding water and mud. As we were crossing a little wooden bridge over it, Elder Brooks hit a weak spot in the wood. The wood bowed, he slipped, and his foot and ankle went into the goo. I had a good laugh, but when we reached home, Elder Brooks got the last laugh because the big parrot Elder Caldwell bought had escaped from the backroom and pooped on my bed! Elder Caldwell worked with that dumb bird for weeks, trying to teach it to talk, without much success. While Elder Caldwell was in the shower each morning I would sneak into the backroom and spend several minutes trying to teach the parrot to say "Elder Caldwell is a dink, Caldwell is a dink. Caldwell is a dink!" My hope was that that would be the only sentence the parrot would remember, and if Elder Caldwell successfully passed the bird through customs, it would be the bird's first statement to Elder Caldwell's family.

Elder Brooks was the second senior companion with whom I spent his last days in the mission field. As we got within one week of Elder Brooks' departure, he was walking around on cloud nine. Nothing aggravated him, nothing concerned him, it was like he was Alice in wonderland. Fortunately, he was still there to see Lita baptized. Elder Caldwell interviewed her and she was ready. She had a strong testimony and was baptized on the Saturday before Elder Brooks left. It was my first baptism in the mission field and was very special. All the members of the branch, including Lita's aunt and uncle and cousins, were there to witness the great occasion. It was very rewarding for me, having taught her the discussions from beginning to end, having seen her testimony grow, and having witnessed her following through on her testimony with baptism. She bore a beautiful testimony at the meeting. I was touched by her sincerity and contrasted her fervor with how little I had valued the gospel when I was her age. She was miles ahead of where I had been, as were many who were converted to the gospel, instead of being born into it.

The next to the last day for Elder Brooks arrived and I put this entry in my diary:

> Elder Brooks had to pick up his suit from the dry cleaner at the hotel and he wanted to look at the river for a while. Oh well, I imagine my last week I'll be kind of off on a cloud too.

During his "countdown," Elder Brooks kept telling me, "Cool, my last workday." At that point in my mission, I kept thinking I would never see that day myself because it was so far away. We took some fabulous pictures the day before Elder Brooks left, including pictures of the Moon, with its reflection over the Amazon River, and then we went to the Chifa to celebrate his last night. We arrived at the airport at 7:30 in the morning, with Elder Brooks breezily exclaiming, "It is wonderful, it is wonderful." He took off, and that afternoon, my new companion flew in, Elder Bernsten, from Salt Lake City. I remembered him from a class at BYU. He was a large, well-muscled blond who had played on the BYU football team in his freshman year, but who was losing some of his muscle and size because of the Peruvian food. The necks of his shirts seemed about three inches too big as they hung down toward his chest because of the weight he had lost. He was an outgoing ever-smiling, gentle giant whom I grew to love like a brother. He was like a kid in a candy store about Iquitos, impressed with how friendly the people were, how "cool" it was to be in the jungle, beside the Amazon River, and on and on.

There was a contrast in attitudes between a newly arrived senior companion, like Elder Bernsten, and one who was ready to go home. Everything was new and exciting and we were anxiously knocking on doors and meeting good people. A few days after Elder Bernsten arrived, we had to go back out to the airport to see Elder Redd, Elder Caldwell's companion, fly back to Lima for a change. We were standing in the Quonset-hut, open-air terminal watching the jet turn around, and as its tail came in our direction, the jet blast blew off my clip-on tie and sent it halfway across the terminal. Before I could reach it, a little Indian cholo lady picked it up and scampered away. I yelled and went running after her, finally caught up with her, and got it back. What would a cholo lady have done with a clip-on tie? Maybe she would have worn it with her best bowler hat.

Elder Caldwell, Elder Bernsten, and I worked as a threesome for a couple of days until Elder Lower arrived to fill Elder Redd's spot. It was easy to find fault with people who fell through on our appointments, or people that responded negatively to our baptismal challenge—"If you found that Christ's church was restored again on the Earth, would you want to join it through baptism?" Yet I wonder now, if I had been in their shoes, how receptive I would have been to a couple of foreigners coming to my country to tell me that the church I had grown up in was false and that I should join their church through baptism.

Our suit pants took a real beating—we didn't wear the coats because of the many sudden downpours we got caught in while out tracting. Little shoeshine boys near our apartment were always anxious to clean our shoes, scraping the mud off and polishing for a nominal fee. There was not much we could do about the suit pants, though. One elder actually thought that the little lady who came to get our clothes to clean them would understand the difference between something that needed to be dry cleaned and something that simply could be washed. When he got his suit pants and coat back—he had decided to send the coat out to be dry cleaned, even though he didn't wear it—he found they had been beaten in one of the wash pits in the ground. They were all rumpled, shrunken, and ruined. I do not know what this little laundry lady thought about our garments, but I do know she was awfully rough on them. I sent several new pair with her and they came back with holes all over from the beating she had administered with rocks in one of the wash pits.

Not many vegetables grew in the jungle, only fruits, so when we went to have roasted chicken for dinner, in-stead of French fries, we got fried banana chips, which really did not satisfy me, but it was all they had. One night after leaving the roast chicken at the corner café and walking down by the river, we heard all kinds of commotion on the embankment leading from the sidewalk between the buildings, down to the water. It looked like the entire surface of the bank was moving. As we leaned over the railing to get a closer look, we saw a mass of thousands of three-inch-plus cockroaches swarming over rubbish and food scraps that had been thrown over the embankment from the roadway. We found cockroaches up to four inches long in the apartment, and that is why we did not mind the iguanas that also frequented the screens on the windows, inside and outside our rooms—they kept the bugs under control. As we worked evenings outside the city, where the foliage was denser, I was intrigued by my first viewing of fireflies—I had never seen them before. They made quite a sight with their flickering lights appearing here, and then there, suddenly against the backdrop of the dark jungle foliage and night sky. Iquitos was a very mysterious and adventurous place to be, but the missionary work went very slowly. It made for great P-days when we ventured out of the city and into the jungle, looking for bugs, taking spectacular pictures, and getting lost in the foliage during some fabulous hikes. Fortunately, we never ran into any large snakes, or even small ones, for that matter, while we were out on these hikes, although we saw multicolored parrots, a few monkeys, numerous other birds, and of course all kinds of different insects.

The month of October was called the "Senor de los Milagros"—Lord of the Miracles—month. All of the devout Catholics wore purple for the entire month, and on the last three days they held processions with large lit-up images on poles. They filed past, following the images with burning candles. It was an eerie sight—huge macabre heads flickering in candlelight and masses of people mumbling chants. In purple, they expected their own miracle during the month. Somehow, we wanted to convince these people that their miracle for that month was having us come to them to tell them about the true restored gospel!

After a district meeting we went to the Chifa, a small hole-in-the-wall Chinese restaurant we found in Iquitos, which, at least to our tastes, was pretty good, and as we were eating, a teenage girl on her way out put a note written on a napkin in front of me, which said she wanted us to come by her house and "explain something to her in the Bible." Elder Bernsten and I pretty well figured out what she wanted explained, and it certainly wasn't part of our agenda.

Elder Bernsten liked to work out in the sticks, past the end of town. Not only was it kind of adventurous to be out tracting in the actual jungle, but also, we were able to meet people who had not been contacted before because of the distances involved. One day we went out on the same dirt road that we had taken as a branch to go on our party down by the Amazon, and we gave a discussion to a monkey trader and his wife. His home was a large open-air wood structure on stilts in the jungle, with a corrugated tin roof. His home was surrounded by cages containing monkeys of different sizes, ranging from six-inch little squealers to large chimpanzee-like apes. Although they appeared cute, when you approached the cage, they bared their fangs and acted vicious. I knew they could be vicious. One evening, we had been teaching a discussion to a family that had a pet monkey. It escaped and was leaping all over the house, jumping, from stacks of books, up to countertops, through the eating area, up on top of the dressers, and basically doing a whirling dervish around the room. We all scrambled to try to grab him. Fortunately, I did not catch him. The little girl of the family grabbed him and the monkey bit her on the wrist, causing blood to squirt all over from a rather severe bite.

The monkey trader told us he bought his monkeys from the Indians out in the jungle. They would drop the monkeys out of the trees by using six-foot blowguns with nerve poison on the tips of their darts. The nerve poison was made from a chemical found in the skin of jungle frogs. The poison would stun the monkeys temporarily until they were revived with a sugar-water mixture. It seemed like a cruel trade to me. Most of the monkeys were fully grown, and didn't appear to have any chance of becoming domesticated. I imagined that their meat and skins were more useful than the live monkey for trading purposes.

I had yet another "fake tie" problem. We were on our way out of town and I was standing in the door of a bus—they packed the buses to the point where if you were the last on, as I was this time, you were hanging outside the bus holding on to the handles, hoping nothing on the road came by too close—and as a cholo lady and her baby went out the door, they brushed against my chest, pulling my fake tie off and landing it in a mud puddle. I angrily stepped out the door to get it and the bus driver took off. At least that day ended on a humorous note. As we came back into town and passed a store, a drunk came out and called out to us. He claimed he knew Elder Bernsten from Lima. To celebrate, he bought us two soda pops. We told him we wanted to leave him with something and we gave him a Word of Wisdom pamphlet. We were just about done for the evening but we knocked on one last door. A lady came to the door in her nightgown, and we thought we had better leave, but her husband came to the door with half of his pajamas on and invited us in! We sat down at the table as he finished dressing and we talked for most of an hour about the gospel. They did not seem the least bit disturbed that we had interrupted them at bedtime and they were quite interested in our discussion.

You just never knew when you were going to get a friendly reception or be viewed as a nuisance. In contrast, the next day, we knocked on a door, talked to a young lady and asked her to get her father. When he reached the door, he started screaming and jumping around, telling us to "get out, leave my yard, don't bother us." He slammed the door in our faces. I had always heard about having doors slammed in my face, but this was the first time it actually happened to me in the mission field.

One thing I was not sorry to miss was the Vietnam War, which was winding down while I was on my mission. Initially, I had a college deferment as I was attending BYU, and then when the system went to the lottery—numbers that were drawn at random for each day of the year representing the birthday of each individual—my birthday drew a 69, a fairly low number. The war wound down that year, though, and they did not reach my number. I bought a copy of Time magazine in Iquitos to read a little bit about the end of the war. We did not do much on our mission to keep up on events in the world. We were spending our time focusing on missionary work, but occasionally we read a newspaper, or a news magazine, or, while at a member's house, we watched the *noticias* (evening news).

I got sick again in Iquitos, running a high temperature, aching in my back, feeling dizzy and weak. It took me two days to recover. While

I was lying in bed, it was hard to keep my thoughts on the mission field as opposed to thinking of home, loved ones, friends, and experiences leading up to the mission. Getting sick again was just what I needed to lose more weight. I worried that I was going back to the United States as a 120-pound weakling. I had already dropped from 180 to 160.

Some days, we just could not seem to run into anyone who wanted to listen or understand. Shortly after I recovered from my sickness, we spent one whole day talking to old people that could hardly hear what we were saying. We knocked on the door, asked for the senora of the house, the maid ran to get her, and out came an eighty-year-old walking skeleton with wrinkled skin and a wisp of gray hair. She stood there saying, "¿Como, como?" —"What, what?" She turned out to be very friendly and had us come back to teach her daughter and her.

One P-day, Elder Caldwell bought a package of firecrackers. In the afternoon we made paper airplanes, strapped fireworks to them, and attached several of the large cockroaches we found in our apartment. We ignited the fuse and sent the cockroaches on their very own rock-et flight! It was amazing what missionaries can think of for a good laugh on their P-day.

There were times when we dropped in on people to try to teach them a discussion and instead they used us as sympathetic ears for their problems. One morning, a lady invited us in and proceeded to tell us her troubles with her two sons. She had gone to visit the one in Lima, and before she left to fly home, he stole the jewelry out of her luggage. She didn't realize it until she arrived back in Iquitos. The other son liked to drink until all hours of the morning. We did not get much teaching done, but I think she felt better after we left.

Through occasional visits on our P-day, and by switching companions and working in Elder Caldwell's area, I became familiar with the floating village called "Belen"—Spanish for Bethlehem. It was quite a sight—wooden huts, with thatched roofs, built upon balsa wood logs spread out as far as the eye could see from the backwaters of the Amazon, where they approached the town, out into a huge lagoon. These houses floated between poles driven into the mud—one for each corner of the house. Each corner of the house was tethered to a pole by a leather thong, so when the water rose or receded, the house would float up or down between the poles, instead of drifting down the river. The sewage system for this village consisted of holes in the floors of the houses. This led to rampant dysentery and other diseases floating among the houses. Yet, naked splashing, swimming children were a common sight between the houses, and clothes were washed right there in the river. The river provided for bathing, washing, and sewage—all in one.

Transportation to and from the floating houses consisted of half a log boat, hollowed out, or, in rare instances, a more elaborate boat with a small outboard. We saw people coming and going to their floating houses and the grocery stores in town, carrying supplies in their boat. You could hire a water taxi—a cholo with a paddle or, in some instances, a cholo with a small outboard motorized boat—to transport you to and from the floating village and town. Some of the houses between the villages and town were built on stilts, instead of floating logs, but the downstairs was not used because for half the year the water rose up and covered the lower story. Some of the streets toward the edge of town, leading to the floating village, ended in the water.

There was a sprawling marketplace on the edge of town, near the beginning of the floating village. There were hundreds of open-air stalls, with every imaginable fruit hanging or stacked in them: guavas, passion fruit, papaya, at least twenty different types of bananas— orange ones, green ones, yellow ones, small ones for frying, large ones for baking—and innumerable other fruits whose names I learned in Spanish, but whose names I could not equate to any fruit I had ever heard of in English. The marketplace was surrounded by large gray wooden warehouses with corrugated tin roofs, usually covered with large black buzzards silhouetted against the gray sky. It was unusual to see a clear blue sky in the morning or evening. The water-saturated morning and evening skies created a brilliant canvas for the sun. We saw spectacular sunrises and sunsets, with brilliant oranges, reds, and pinks painted across the light cloud cover. The stalls in the marketplace were covered with brilliantly colored plastics to keep the goods dry from the daily downpour. The bright plastics and multicolored fruits provided a backdrop for fabulous photo opportunities. The colors reflected off the damp cement and tin roofs, wet from the downpour of the day before. We found people working in the booths with unusual pets, including monkeys, ocelots, boa constrictor snakes, tree sloths, parrots, and toucans. Many stalls had unusual meats hanging in them, meats from animals I had never heard of, and could only imagine, including one unusual beast that yielded steak we ate many times at the café, which was simply called the "Dog of the Mountain." Whether this was a sloth, a wild boar, a cavi—the world's largest rodent, which also frequented the jungle—or something else, we never found out. It was not too bad to eat, but I was always a little reluctant, not knowing what kind of animal I was plunging my fork into. In the open-air market most of the meat, regardless of the beast involved, was hanging there crawling with flies. It was not appetizing. I felt like strangling one of the parrots. As I was sitting there talking to its owner, the yellow and green feathered culprit bit my thumb and drew blood!

Elder Caldwell, the good sport that he was, always seemed to be the butt of our jokes, including sailing firecrackers through the grillwork into the bathroom while he was showering. These jokes helped us unwind at the end of a hard day of knocking on doors. In the morning we usually talked to ladies who, at most, could set up an appointment for us to come back when their husbands got home from work. Typically, we had at least one discussion in the evening after a lunch and a siesta, with scripture reading in the afternoon, but usually we had many more discussion appointments fall through. When we were discouraged, we also enjoyed visiting with the Texas oil man's family. They usually fed us. What better way to overcome discouragement! One night, they fed us each two T-bone steaks. We were in heaven! Although we felt a little bit like "leaches" when going over there, we continued to go and they seemed to enjoy our visits. We managed to teach them several discussions in the process and showed them church movies including "Christ in America" and "Man's Search for Happiness."

We had to be careful about visiting and eating with the members. Unlike the areas that my companions and I had come from in the United States, where there was ample food and it was routine to eat with the members, in Peru, the standard of living of many was far below what we were used to. The members were so generous, though, that unless we used discretion, members would spend a week's salary in giving us dinner. In fact, we usually avoided dinner invitations except with members we knew could afford it.

We got used to walking in the mud in Iquitos. Our shoes took a beating, since after every rainfall, the streets filled with mud and we mucked through it to continue our daily work. Most Iquitans avoided getting caught in the rain and when the downpours dropped the temperature from eight-five to seventy-five degrees, they started to shiver and called us crazy for walking in the rain and getting wet. They warned us that we were going to catch cold, yet we looked forward to getting caught in the rain—it cooled us down. When Elder Bernsten and I came back one night, we were drenched to the bone—water dripping from our heads, our shirts, our ties, and our pants. We were happy as sponges—our "coolness" felt good, instead of feeling the usual hot, steamy humidity. When it reached seventy-five degrees, we were warned not to drink soda pops cold because it would lead to serious throat bronchitis—the grippe!

A missionary's first big holiday in the mission field can be a little trying as you keep thinking about what your family is up to at home, and you remember past holidays. My first Thanksgiving in the mission field was spent in Iquitos, and I admit it was difficult to keep my mind on the work that day. The day seemed especially dreary because I did not get any mail in the package before Thanksgiving. It had been two weeks since I had received a letter from home. Holidays in the mission field can be made or broken with letters from home. As we walked around trying to work that day, my mind kept drifting to pumpkin pie and football games. As our own little celebration, we treated ourselves to two chicken sandwiches, two glasses of natural fruit juice, and a piece of lemon pie. At least our stomachs were full, even if mentally we were a little homesick.

Sometimes when we really got frustrated, we took any little challenge to make the day more interesting. We knocked on one door and the lady saw us through the crack in the window, so she scrambled to hide in the back, and sent her three-year-old son to tell us there was nobody home. I yelled back through the window to the back room, "Why don't you answer the door?" Then she yelled from the back room, "Nobody's here." We went across the street to knock on a few doors and I told Elder Bernsten that one way or the other, I was going to get into that door. After knocking on a few doors, we crossed the road and I knocked on the elusive lady's door again, then hid off to the side. When she looked through her window, she could not see anyone. As she came to the door, I said "Good morning," with a silly grin on my face. She gave me a disgusted look and said, "Come on in," with an expression that said, "Now that you've caught me, you might as well come in."

It was often difficult to get those we were teaching to pray at the end of a discussion. We reached the end of a discussion with one man and when we asked him to pray, he refused and said, "I pray in my own way," the Catholic way. I told him that he would not find any prayer in the Catholic prayer book that asked God if the Book of Mormon was true, which caused a puzzled look and a nod of agreement. He agreed to give it a try and as we knelt side by side, he offered a beautiful, sincere prayer asking if what we were teaching him was true. I started to choke up and strained to control the tears as the Spirit flooded over us. As he ended, I testified that the Spirit we all felt at that moment was an answer to his request and he readily agreed. The challenge was one of keeping investigators on these spiritual peaks until they were baptized and received the constant companionship of the Holy Ghost. Until that time, they were subject to wavering and hesitation as much as Peter had been in denying the Savior until the Day of Pentecost.

Elder Bernsten and I got tired of Elder Caldwell's annoying us with his small firecrackers when we were in the bathroom, or otherwise trying to get a moment of peace, so we bought a package of firecrackers the size of the cardboard roll in the middle of toilet paper. We realized we would probably deafen ourselves in the process, but it seemed worthwhile. We did not have to wait long to try out our experiment. We arrived home after a tiring day and tried to shower. Elder Caldwell started lighting his little firecrackers, so I snuck up behind him, lit the bomb, and placed it on the floor behind him. He did not see it until it was too late. The flash and explosion deafened all of us and momentarily blinded us in the darkness. We died laughing as Elder Caldwell ran around like he had had a heart attack and complained about where we had managed to buy dynamite.

Our choices of how to do the work in Iquitos seemed to have narrowed down to whether we would simply go out and knock on doors, or whether we would knock on doors! So, we chose to go out and knock on doors! Once in a while, our day was brightened by somebody that really appeared interested. We met an older couple and their aunt who were not only pleasant and interested in what we had to say, but seemed sincere. After we gave them a brief overview of the church and what we were doing, I noticed there was a mandolin in the corner and I talked the old lady into playing it for us. I loved to listen to the mandolin. While she was playing, the aunt brought out a little rasp board that she played along with the mandolin music. After the entertainment they brought out bottles of cold soda pop.

For Elder Caldwell's birthday we ordered him a cake and I bought him a little Catholic saint statue of Saint Martin de Porras—the saint who looked like Peru's favorite professional soccer player. I stuck the saint in the frosting on top of the cake and after work we lit the candles and brought it out while we sang the Peruvian equivalent of "Happy Birthday"—"Por tu santito."

When the work was slow, as it often was in Iquitos, it was easy to get discouraged. My typical journal entry in Iquitos read:

> I really got feeling down today. There are times when you can really get discouraged in this work. I felt like not working and I felt like I had made a mistake even coming on a mission. I guess it is because we don't have much of a program going yet and also I think our mail has been getting lost or stolen. I haven't yet received a letter from my girlfriend telling me she got the roses I had sent to her for her birthday.

In contrast, the very next night, we had an excellent baptismal service for a family that was being baptized by Elder Caldwell and Elder Lower, his junior companion. They were the first complete family to get baptized in Iquitos in the past six months. We had an investigator family show up to see the baptismal service. I played the piano for the meeting, and I was feeling much better than I had the night before. Missionary work indeed has its ups and downs.

The day after the baptism, we ran into a drunk on the street who told us his name was Ruiz. He was friendly but in a semi-coma. We accompanied him home as he staggered around, looking like he was a danger to himself and everybody else on the road. We were surprised when he opened his wallet and pulled out a picture of one of the elders in our mission. He also expressed quite a bit of knowledge about the church. We told him we would come back to his house the next day, after he sobered up. We learned he had been scheduled to get baptized several months earlier, along with his entire family, but instead he got drunk on the night of his baptism and did not show up.

Elder Bernsten and I were embarrassed while knocking on doors one day early in December 1972. We knocked on a door, the people told us to enter, and when we stepped inside, we found ourselves surrounded by women's bras. They were hanging from racks all around the room and were stacked in bundles on the tables, and on the floors. The house had been converted into a clothing factory, with numerous sewing machines and other equipment being used to put together women's bras. As we stepped in, Berni—Elder Bernsten and I had become close friends and I affectionately called him Bernie—looked around sheepishly and then really crammed his foot into his mouth as he asked the guy, "What do you do for a living?" When the man of the house said, "I make women's underwear," the ladies sitting at the sewing machines and I started giggling. We learned that everyone in the house was a Jehovah's Witness and once we got past the humor of the situation, they showed they knew something about Mormons when they asked us how we could prove the Book of Mormon was true. I turned it around on them by asking how they could prove the Bible was true. We explained that we could prove nothing to them, but that they could arrive at their own conclusion about the truth if they were sincere, if they wanted to read and pray about what they had read.

One evening, we ran into a group of Seventh-day Adventists, and though our discussion started out amiably enough, they soon got into trying to "Bible bash" with us, pointing out that Mormonism must be false because of this, that, or the other scripture they threw at us. We tried to stay pleasant and discuss the scriptures with them, but they soon worked themselves up into an angry frenzy, especially after one particularly contentious man came through the door to join the discussion and started accusing us of being liars and of spreading falsehoods about Joseph Smith. He kept taunting us and telling us to prove to them that Joseph Smith was a prophet and that he had really seen an angel. Bernie and I explained that we could prove nothing to them, but rather, they would have to read Joseph Smith's works, including his translation of the plates into the Book of Mormon, and then pray about it to receive their own testimony. They all scoffed and laughed at that, and the contentious one kept demanding a sign. Finally Bernie referred him to Matthew 16:4, where Christ told the Pharisees and Sadducees, who had demanded a sign, that it was "a wicked and adulterous generation that looks for a miraculous sign." Bernie then looked at this man and told him, "I can only assume, because of your constant demand for signs, that, as Christ said, you are an adulterer." That really set him off. Everybody frothed and brimmed with more anger and the contentious one got to the point of physically trying to throw us out, except he was intimidated by Bernie's size. We left and the next day learned, from others who knew this man, that he was publicly known to be an adulterer.

To give my family a taste of my actual missionary work in Iquitos, I took my tape recorder with us and taped door knockings and discussions with the people. I also taped the sounds of the jungle at night as we walked along the outskirts of town. This tape preserved some fond memories—a live journal for a day. My family appreciated the insights. They also hungrily digested all my letters—at least that's what they told me. Missionaries must remember to keep the support group at home in-formed and feeling like they are part of the mission experience. It was a two-way street. The more often I wrote insightful letters, the more enjoyable were the letters I received in return.

We talked with a member on the edge of town who worked at the tanning warehouse in town, where they skinned large snakes and alligators and tanned the hides. They treated these and other animal skins and exported them. He took us to the factory and we saw skins up on the wall. At least one of the huge anaconda skins was forty feet long and about eight feet wide! After we toured the plant, he took us out to his house, where he had a live boa constrictor in a bag. He wanted us to pull it out of the bag and hold it up to take photographs. Neither Bernie nor I was too excited about that, but he reached in the bag and grabbed it by the head and pulled it out. He told us that as long as we held the head, we would be okay. Boas are known for constricting and strangling their prey, but they also have large teeth you have to watch out for. We took pictures of each other as we held this boa constrictor up close to our head. As we pulled it out of the bag, it instinctively started to coil around our arms. Fortunately, it was only a four-footer; if it had been bigger it might have been a real problem.

Toward the end of my stay in Iquitos, we had finally pulled together a good program. On the second Sunday in December 1972, we had an all-time record—twelve investigators came to Sunday school, including four complete families and several youths. We were teaching discussions daily and loving it. It was a high to be teaching complete families who were readily praying and coming to church.

We played football early one morning for our P-day in Iquitos, but it was a mistake. Even before the sun came up, the high humidity and heat sapped us and we were tired and lethargic the rest of the day. We laid around and drank fruit juice until the time for district meeting. After the district meeting, we went out for our traditional Chinese meal. I regretted it the next morning. As we traveled to an area away from our apartment, dinner from the night before hit me hard and we had to take off quickly for the church—the nearest bathroom. I started out walking at a fast pace and by the time I could see the church, I was running. I would never take public bathrooms for granted again in the United States.

My accuracy in throwing aquaje seeds hit an all-time high on the day I managed to hit one of the large black buzzards with a fruit pit at a distance of fifty yards! On one of the hottest days we had experienced, with beads of sweat pooling on our upper lips and forehead, we ran into a lady while knocking on doors who started telling us how hard her life was. She proceeded from this into five minutes of complaints. I was frustrated on that particular morning, so I started telling her how tired and hot we were, and I proceeded to air my own complaints for about five minutes, really hamming it up and escalating until I worked my way up to phony tears. She thought I was serious and told me that I had better pray for help.

On Sunday, December 17, 1972, after church, Bernie told me to read a passage in his Doctrine and Covenants. It talked about the rewards we can get as missionaries. I then noticed a card that mentioned the "Callused Rear Award" and told me, "Look in your passport." I went to my passport, which was in the dresser. Elder Bernsten had put my change in it. I was being transferred back to Lima to become a senior companion. The prospect of becoming a senior companion was intimidating and exciting, but I was disappointed to be leaving Iquitos, especially on the eve of Christmas. The Texas oil man and his family were going to the States for Christmas and had asked us to live in their mansion for two weeks so as to take care of it. Bernie and I were greatly looking forward to that. We also had plans to start putting together Christmas care packages for some of the poorer children in our area. Being changed on the eve of Christmas meant my Christmas mail would not reach me until after Christmas. At least I knew that with President Driggs making the changes, although they might not seem convenient to my schedule, they did come from the Lord, through our mission president. Scheduling needs also arose, including the arrival of new missionaries from the United States.

All missionaries receiving changes from Iquitos planned an immediate souvenir expedition to purchase jungle artifacts and take pictures. On my last P-day in Iquitos, I snapped several rolls of pictures of the jungle and the Amazon and bought everything from a six-foot blowgun, which I packed in a plastic pipe, to a tigrillo—an ocelot skin. They were not illegal then. I took pictures of all the members as I made the rounds to say my goodbyes. One last disappointment was that one of the American oilmen who had a ham radio had promised to use his radio to get through to home for the holidays. We spent several hours on his radio and found we could not get past Panama because of a sunspot that was causing radiation that interfered with the radio waves.

As we left for the airport, I looked like the classical tourist. I had so much junk stuffed under my arms, I could only waddle to the plane. I had bought an old briefcase and stuffed it with an alligator skin, a stuffed piranha and a stuffed iguana, and I had my camera and tape recorder in the other hand. My blowgun was loaded on the plane. We had a close call while taking off, narrowly missing one of the stray pigs that ran across the runway just in front of the landing gear. The week before, one of the planes blew out its tires on its takeoff, hitting a pig. I can only imagine the bacon grease that flew everywhere from that impact!

Changes gave us the opportunity to see President Driggs and his wife again. They were happy to see me—they thought I was coming in the day before and had got. ten a little worried. I had a brief reunion with the elders working in the office and we showed some of my slides, against the wall in one of the assistant's offices-they were always interested in jungle pictures. I was made a senior companion and I received a junior who had come down a month ago. Elder Perry was from Torrance, California, not too far from my hometown. My new area was Maranga, right next to Callao. It abutted Callao to the south on the coast.

I was going to miss Iquitos, with its exotic sights, feel, and smells. I would miss the easygoing lifestyle; the ever-open doors and windows; the feeling that we were only a few blocks from the Amazon jungle, no matter where we went in the town; the encounters with all kinds of unusual animals and unusual fruit juices; and, most importantly of all, Bernie and our new investigators. Elder Bernsten and I had become very close friends and, as seemed typical, the work had really started rolling just before I was leaving. I would also miss throwing fruit seeds at wandering pigs, dogs, and buzzards, but I could imagine I would need my accuracy at some point in the future as many of the areas in Peru were infested with stray dogs.

# CHAPTER 8
## A New Senior Companion in Maranga

My new area had a mix of both upper-middle class and poor areas. We lived in a home with some people who by Peruvian standards, would have been considered wealthy at that time. It was a two-story house. Our house fronted a parklike plaza where kids were often playing soccer. We had a bedroom on the top floor with our own bathroom and stairway access to the roof, where the clotheslines ran. It was a brick-and-plaster home with a fairly large living room and dining room downstairs. The couple we lived with were in their sixties and retired. They lived well, having one maid for the cooking and another for general housecleaning. We ate with them, and ate better than I had eaten during my entire mission up to this point. They were very friendly and enjoyed discussing the United States with us. Their only fault was, they snored like phlegmatic grizzly bears at night with their bedroom door open. The loud raucous snores blasted down the hall and made it difficult for us to sleep. As a joke, one night, Elder Perry and I snuck down the hall with our tape recorder and taped a couple of minutes of the racket. We got quite a laugh out of it later in our room, but chose not to offend our gracious hosts by playing the tape so loud that they could hear it.

We grew quite fond of the "duke" of the house—our hosts' large German shepherd dog that lived up on the roof. Once in a while, we would take snacks up on the roof for him. He became our buddy. There was also a little dog on the roof next door that began to keep us up at night with his yapping. I soon found the cure. In Iquitos I had purchased some toy souvenir like blow guns with hard-wood darts. I took those up on the roof, and each time the little dog started yapping,

I nailed him with a little dart. He learned to stop barking as soon as he heard our door to the roof open.

Elder Perry had a four-week advantage on me in knowing the area. It was his first area in Peru. He showed me around for our first couple of days. One family, the Sanchez family, was just about ready for its baptism. Stepping into this family seemed to me like justice for being changed from Callao, after teaching the Suarez family up to the point of its baptism. It was a satisfying change to step into a family ready to be baptized.

We started out by working very hard. I was determined to have a good program as a new senior companion. We knocked on a lot of doors, but found that in the rich area the people were reluctant to let us in. Similar to my experiences in Callao, many had their maids tell us nobody was home.

The family ready for its baptism ran into a problem common to many families progressing through the discussions—tithing. The Sanchez family was in debt and wanted to wait until January to get baptized so they could get further out of debt before paying tithing. We asked them to pray about what they should do, but we feared that their financial preoccupation and debt would overpower their ability to listen to an answer to their prayers.

We spent time after lunch in our apartment, working through the discussions until Elder Perry had them all memorized. His first senior companion had not studied with him, which was unfair to him and set him back a ways. Fortunately, Elder Adsero had worked with me from the beginning to involve me with discussions, and to study the Book of Mormon in Spanish.

I enjoyed the location of my new area, along the coast. To get from the southern end to the northern end of our area, or vice versa, we would walk along the coast. The coast was fronted by a large cliff with a roadway and a sidewalk that snaked along its crest. From the coastal cliff, we could see all the way to the point of Callao and the island off the tip of Callao. December marked the beginning of summer in Lima—the seasons are just the opposite of those in California since Lima is about the same distance from the Equator to the south as California is to the north. As I started my sojourn in Maranga, the weather was warm and clear. The coastline was partially spoiled, due to people using it for dumping old furniture, mattresses, and trash. Rats scurried all over the garbage as we walked along the sidewalk above the cliff. Once in a while, we stopped and threw rocks at the rats.

We never knew what we might see on the beach or the cliffs overlooking the ocean. We saw several old cars that we enjoyed throwing rocks at as we passed by, and one day we saw a tractor lying on a beach. The driver got too close to the edge while pushing garbage around with the blade, and he tumbled the tractor down onto the beach.

Elder Perry was now going through some of the same adjustments I had in my first month, especially trying to reconcile his digestive system to the food. The poor guy was plagued with a huge case of indigestion—a gas problem. As we were walking to one of our appointments, he doubled over in cramps and grimaced in pain. He could walk no further for the moment, and as he doubled over, emitted a loud nonstop stream of gas that caused him great embarrassment and started me laughing and looking around to see if anyone else had noticed. He could only grimace in pain and get angry at me for laughing at his misery. Fortunately, it was just gas, and after a couple of minutes, he was able to unwind his body, straighten up, and continue walking to our appointment.

Our area was just to the south of the main highway leading from Callao, passing by the airport and then going into central Lima. We worked into the Christmas spirit by crossing the road and entering a large department store to find some little gifts for the Sanchez family for Christmas. It seemed hard to believe it was the eve of Christmas—my first Christmas in Peru. We had Christmas programs at church on Sunday, Christmas Eve, 1972. The ward we were in, the Lima fourth Ward, met in the Magdalena Chapel, where we also held mission conferences. After church we headed home to eat, had a little nap, then went out to work on Christmas Eve—an unusual but appropriate way to spend the eve of the day commemorating our Savior's birth. It was hard for me to mentally focus on the work, knowing how much I had enjoyed the Christmas season at home. We had a district meeting at the chapel for our district's missionaries on Christmas Eve. We conducted our own Christmas pro-gram reading out of the Book of Mormon and the Bible, about Christ's birth.

Christmas in 1972 conveniently fell on our P-day. It surely did not seem like Christmas. We rose early and tracked down our mail—my Christmas mail had not arrived since I had changed areas. We played basketball at the church, journeyed downtown for ice cream, then on to the office for a party. I played a piano solo and we had vocal solos, then ate the hams I'd brought from Iquitos at the request of President Driggs and Sister Driggs. We mingled with a lot of our friends and then a group of us went downtown to see the movie "Scrooge," which we truly enjoyed. That evening we visited the Sanchez family, gave them their little gifts, and enjoyed eating cake together with them. Overall, it was an enjoyable Christmas, although I wished I could be transported home just for the day.

The dogs on the roof started to get annoying. We passed by a house when, all of a sudden, a dog leaned over the roof, slobbering on me as he growled loudly, causing me to jump out of my shoes. I was determined to find an equalizer. We went to the department store and I bought a little squirt bottle and some ammonia. I mixed up a solution of ammonia in this bottle to carry with me. The next time we went back to the house with the obnoxious dog, when he bent over to growl at us, I let him have it with a stream of ammonia water in his face. This sent him squealing and running to the back of the house, with his ears down and his tail between his legs. Dogs seemed to remember my squirt bottle after one blast. This was evident the next time we passed this area and the "roof rover" was now off the roof, playing with the teenagers of the house, on the front lawn. The teenagers started to smart-mouth us as we approached. They warned us that if we came too close, they would order their dog to attack us. I told them their dog was a wimp and did not scare me a bit. They instructed him to get me, but when I reached for my pocket, the dog recognized me and remembered my squirt bottle as I pulled it out of my coat pocket At the sight of that little bottle, his ears drooped, his tail went between his legs, and he dashed for the front door and sailed into the house. The teenagers were in shock—their ferocious guard dog had been scared silly by a menacing stare from a gringo. The joke between their dog and me passed right over their heads. I "calmed" many more dogs in our area with my little squirt bottle.

It was harder to get in the door in Maranga than it had been in Iquitos. I was back to having to get through the muchachas—the maids first, which was no easy task. Maranga provided a real contrast to the lush green foliage of the jungle. Everywhere I looked in Maranga, I saw painted plaster, brick, concrete, or dirt. In the wealthier areas it was mostly two-story plaster-covered houses with flat roofs, with dogs on top, that were built around neighborhood central plazas—parks with very little grass and no trees. Even in the more upper-class areas, watering grass and trees was a luxury that few people indulged. A few blocks from the wealthier area, the barrios were built adjacent to dirt roads on lots surrounded by adobe walls, with a single doorway. These doorways opened into numerous little shanties built around dirt paths within the interior lots. These shanties were built primarily of adobe bricks. They had either corrugated tin or wooden roofs.

It was in this area that we met Hermana Ofelia and her little blue-eyed son, Raphael. She lived in a little two-room adobe hut that was always warm and cozy inside and as clean as you could make dirt floors and dirt walls by constantly brushing and by spreading water on them. She had a kerosene lamp and a small stove and eked out a living for Raphael and herself by doing people's laundry. She was always happy to see the missionaries and always offered us herb tea or hot chocolate. She and Raphael came faithfully each week to church. Raphael looked forward with glee to a visit from the missionaries, who traditionally—and we continued the tradition—would hold him on one knee and tell him stories from the Book of Mormon, and whatever else they could manage to tell him in Spanish that would capture the interest and imagination of a five-year-old.

Just down the road from the cluster of huts where Hermana Ofelia lived was the small *tienda* (store) of Hugo Lee and his elderly parents. Hugo was a six-foot, three-hundred-pound, jovial Chinaman who had come to Peru as a child with his parents, fleeing from mainland China to Hong Kong and then to Peru, in the wake of the Japanese invasion of China. He had a big grin and was a double-chinned, gentle giant who startled me when I first heard him call out to us in a thick Queen's English accent, which he'd acquired while growing up in Hong Kong. It seemed strange to be greeted in English, especially a British-accented English, by an effervescent, large Chinaman in Peru.

Hugo's store became a favorite resting spot for us in the middle of our door knocking and visiting. He always provided us with soft drinks and great conversation. He was interested in art, which was one of my hobbies, and shared with us many of his sketches. The store had two large old wooden doors that swung open like the entrance to a small barn, leading to the dark interior—there were no windows. As we walked in, we faced a wooden counter that stretched across the middle of the store. Hugo rested his huge arms on this counter, smiling and asking those who entered what he could do for them. It wasn't particularly well stocked, but it had basic food items and household needs for people in the neighborhood. Hugo was also a regular at church on Sundays. He had been a member for some years, but his parents were not interested.

We worked hard in Maranga. We spent about ten hours on the street, knocking on doors and talking with the people, and for three to four hours we studied in the morning and after lunch. Although we were not yet close to a baptism with any of the families we were teaching, we were teaching many discussions. I was convinced that if we worked hard and taught as much as we could with the Spirit, we would be doing our part and the Lord would do his by touching the hearts of those who truly were open. minded and interested. Especially effective was the use of the Book of Mormon, along with testimonies and pictures of families from the United States. Many of those we encountered were touched to realize that a family in the United States would care enough to send them a book with a picture and tell them about the gospel, which was so important in their own lives. We taught discussions to the family we lived with. The man of the family had just returned from a trip to Spain and showed us some of his slides of Spain, after one of our discussions.

We were also teaching a young man named Cesar, who had progressed well and had accepted the baptismal challenge midway through the discussions.

On New Year's Eve we visited with the Hermana Ofelia and Raphael and listened to some of her records. We lit off a few firecrackers, and then I treated her, Raphael, her brother, Elder Perry, and me to the Chifa. After we stuffed ourselves, we ventured to the street market and bought a huge package of skyrockets and other fireworks, which we fired down the street and over the razor-wire-adorned wall adjoining the prison.

Fortunately, New Year's Day in 1973 fell on our P-day, because we were so tired after staying out late with the members that we slept until 9:00 A.M. After finally beginning our day, we took a cab to Callao and I showed Elder Perry around my first area. We stopped at Hermano Soto's little jewelry shop and Elder Perry bought a silver ring to send home. We continued out to the point and finally ended up at the Suarez's house. They had been baptized shortly after I left Callao, and were very happy to see me. It was a warm reunion—plenty of hugs and fond remembrances of Elder Adsero, the discussions, and their baptism. They glowed with contentment and I knew they had solid testimonies that were bringing blessings of happiness to them. They were so grateful to me for my small part in their conversion. This reunion helped ease the pain of the times my mind wandered home on that day to my favorite armchair, chips and dip, and USC in the Rose Bowl.

While knocking on doors in the upper-class area, I was troubled by the poor example shown by some of the adults to their children about telling the truth. At times we would knock on a door after looking through the window and seeing that the man or the lady of the house was home, but after we knocked, the children opened the door to tell us that no one was home. It set a poor example of integrity. I am sure people do the same in the United States to Jehovah's Witnesses and our own missionaries. After seeing it firsthand, I decided I would never do it. I knew that after my mission, I would have more tolerance for missionaries from other faiths who might be knocking on my door. Since then I have made a practice of opening the door and chatting briefly before telling them to get lost! I am joking—actually, I have been cordial with all missionaries, no matter what their message might be. My mission experience taught me great tolerance for those sacrificing their time in the sincere belief they are teaching the truth.

We continued to have trouble convincing Hermano Sanchez to get baptized. He persisted in putting it off until after January, since he was not close to getting out of debt and did not like the prospect of paying

10 percent for tithing instead of the debt. Our bright spot was Cesar, who was closing in on his baptismal interview and would be baptized shortly.

We attended a Zone Conference shortly after New Year's Day at our Magdalena Church, which was built like most chapels in the United States. It was a large brick chapel with a regular podium, an inclined seating area behind it and a large congregation area with wooden pews that seated approximately two hundred. The Zone Conference focused on companion study and what we regarded as golden questions. The zone leaders conducted a "clinic," which ended with all of us traveling in groups to downtown Lima to ask golden questions. We tried a few novel questions we'd learned from the assistants in the conference. After asking questions downtown, we met again at a nearby park and then returned to the chapel. Later that evening we changed companions—I worked with Elder Donaldson, our district leader, so he could interview Cesar for his baptism. I was crushed to find out after the interview that Cesar had some problems he confessed to Elder Donaldson, which required us to postpone his baptism. These were more of the ups and downs of missionary life. At least he had been honest in the interview and now started to remedy these problems, working toward a new date.

Elder Donaldson lived with an American family—the Hubers— who were very "cool." They were in their early thirties, and she was a vivacious, outgoing blonde, always eager to talk to the missionaries and lend a sympathetic ear to discussions about girlfriends, homesickness, and the United States. She was bored by being surrounded by Spanish speakers and loved to feed the missionaries and talk with them. We started visiting regularly on our P-days, as did quite a few of the other missionaries in our district.

Cesar's situation had another upside. His entire family became interested in learning about the gospel, so although we had to postpone his baptism, we began teaching the whole family.

On our first Sunday in 1973, nine investigators came to church. Our hard work was paying rich spiritual dividends. I taught the investigator class and played the piano during the meetings. I was relearning the reading of piano music and seemed to be getting smoother at playing the hymns.

There was an athletes' country club in a canyon outside Lima, toward the Andes, called "El Bosque," or "The Forest." Somehow, the mission home made arrangements for all the missionaries in Lima to spend a P-day there. We met early and traveled to it by bus, converging on the country club. Its staff had never seen so many gringos at one time. We played football for several hours on a large field, then moved on to basketball and weight lifting. We wore ourselves out having a good time. We ended the day after district meeting at a place called "Todos," in down-town Lima. It was as close to an American hamburger-type restaurant as we could find. In fact, we never did find a real American hamburger in Peru. They liked to grind up different herbs with their meat, probably as a filler. The end result was a patty tasting like something cattle would graze on.

It was hard to tell whether the teenagers in Maranga hated us, or simply yelled obscenities at us to get our attention because they were curious about us and the United States. While we were teaching a discussion, a group of teenagers started yelling obscenities in English. I told the people we were teaching, and Elder Perry, to hold on just a minute. I got up, walked out the door and over to the group of teenagers, and told them politely that they had better be careful because I was about to wring their necks. This intimidated them, and they posed no more problems, yet after the discussion they followed us home, expressing interest in talking about the United States. We gladly conversed with them, excited about their new. found politeness. I am sure we often underestimated our ability to meet good families, by simply brushing off teenagers or little kids. I learned this lesson when we befriended a little boy at the corner store while drinking soda pop. We started talking to him and answering his questions about the United States, and as we were nearing the end of our discussion, he told us that his dad was home. He led us to his house and we gave him and his dad a second discussion.

We had another downer with Cesar: His family could not read and they worked on Sundays, making it next to impossible for them to become serious investigators.

A few evenings during the summer brought a dismal evening fog with a dampness that creeped through every part of our clothing. I enjoyed the cool air, as compared to the heat we had experienced for several months. We had our patience tried not only by the weather, but also by the reaction of many people we met in the upper-class areas of Maranga. It was not unusual to knock on a door and have the man of the house come to the door yelling, "What do you want?" and then, "Get lost." I worked hard to control my inclination to be sarcastic and angry in my response, which would have been counterproductive.

One evening, as we walked along the coast heading into the barrio at the southern end of our area, we ran into a group of kids playing soccer. We conversed for a while, then played a little soccer. I scored a few goals, then played goalie for a while and blocked a few shots. This gave a charge to the kids who assumed gringos could not play soccer. We began the discussions with the family we met through their little son, Martin, at the corner store. They looked "golden"—very sincere and very interested. From there we ran into another "friendly" man. We started talking with him and his wife in front of his house when for seemingly no reason he got real snotty and started walking into the house while I was talking. I said, "Hmm, real friendly, aren't you," in Spanish and he walked back and pushed his chest into me and said, "Why did you insult me?" I pushed him away from me and he started getting worked up until his wife came and grabbed him and walked him into the house. I still have a ways to go with my own patience and I should not have made the remark, but sometimes out in the field, the frustration level was greater than a nineteen- or twenty-year-old could cope with.

Going to the dentist in Peru could be a scary experience. Fortunately, it was not me that needed dental attention, but Elder Perry. We had to travel into Lima so that he could have the dentist check on his wisdom teeth. We were comforted by our knowledge that the dentist was a bishop in one of the Lima wards. After seeing him check Elder Perry, I concluded that I had been unduly arrogant in fearing all Peruvian dentists simply because I came from the United States. He was very competent, skillful, and friendly. I decided that if I had any dental problems while I was in Peru, I would look him up. One unpleasant part of going to the dentist was the hour-long bus ride it took to get there and the hour-long bus ride coming back.

I hated riding on buses in Lima. In their defense, they were not crammed as fully as the old rickety wooden buses in Iquitos, where it was not uncommon to be hanging out the door with three other people. The buses in Lima were more modern—large German buses seemed to be the norm. The drivers forced everyone to the back so that they could cram them as fully as possible. We usually ended up standing in the aisle trying to hold any bar, appurtenance, arm, or other body part when the bus came screeching to a stop, to avoid plowing into the people next to us, or landing on the lap of someone fortunate enough to be sitting down. The bus drivers had only one operational mode—foot full to the floor on the accelerator until it was time to stop and then full to the floor on the brake. By slamming on the brakes the drivers helped those getting off to spin down the aisle and careen out the door. It was not unusual to find ourselves next to a cholo lady making her way back from the marketplace, with a raw chicken barely covered in a bag, its neck and head hanging out, or large smelly onions or other foul-smelling or gross objects that managed to rub against our pants or find its way onto our suit coats as we were flung back and forth with the bus driver's spastic foot on the gas and brake. As if that was not bad enough, there were always people on the bus who had never heard of deodorants or were legitimately too poor to invest in them.

One of the reasons I initially distrusted Peruvian dentists was that I could see that many of the people in Peru had terrible tooth and gum decay. Many did not care for their teeth, or did not have access to dental care. This was due to differences in local economies and traditional hygiene habits. It was unfortunate, but too common, for us to walk down the street and see a very attractive young man or young woman who, when they smiled displayed a whole row of rotten teeth or teeth completely capped in gold. I had seen little kids in Iquitos actually take the caps off bottles of soda pop with their teeth. This must inevitably lead to a need for capped teeth. We had several health missionaries in our mission field who spent their time teaching people hygiene habits.

The biggest disappointments in the mission field came with seeing people we taught come close to the truth, and close to embracing it, but then backing away by failing to read, pray, and go to church to gain their own testimony. The truth and the way to salvation were at their fingertips, yet they would not lift them to learn for themselves the most important lesson we can learn on this Earth—the way back to our Father in Heaven. I was getting a taste of the frustration my parents felt in seeing me stray away from the gospel during my teenage years. One of my journal entries, after a particularly frustrating day, read:

> We tried as hard as we could to get a charla, "discussion," but nobody seemed to want to listen. It was always, "Otro dia"—"Some other day"—or, "I'm a Catholic." People down here can really be snotty and mean at the doors. I get so sick of their lies. I have to work hard on my temper, be-cause lately I've been losing it too much, but it makes you so mad when somebody treats you so ignorantly, when all you want to do is tell them about something that their salvation hangs on. If they'd only open their eyes and mind.

There was no air-conditioning in the houses in Lima, so we had two choices at night during the summer—sleep with our windows closed and sweat to death, or sleep with our windows open and get eaten alive by the mosquitoes. There were no screens on our windows, and I do not believe I saw screens on any windows in Maranga. We explored several possible remedies. One member told us we needed to burn eucalyptus leaves in a little pan during the night because the odor would drive away the mosquitoes. Unfortunately, we could not keep the leaves burning all night, and the smell was probably more offensive to us than to the mosquitoes. The mosquitoes came in waves anyway. Next, we asked Hermano Lee what we should do. He sold us what looked like long, coiled-up Fourth of July snakes, which we lit on one end, and left to slowly burn through the night. It gave off fumes that actually kept the mosquitoes away. These coils would last until four in the morning but then in the last two hours before we awoke we got eaten alive again.

As a missionary, I had an indescribable feeling of joy and warmth when I was able to bring happiness to some-one who actually appreciated it. We received a reference from Elder Donaldson for a little old lady in our area, and we went to visit her. She was confined to a wheelchair because of a disease in her legs and joints. As we arrived, she started to cry, happy at seeing the missionaries. We enjoyed visiting with her because she was so delighted at having our company, and she ate up the discussions. We called a taxi on Sunday and passed by to pick her up to take her to church. It thrilled us to see the joy our church brought to her.

We heard there were two young priests from the United States who lived in our area. We decided to go meet them. The one we met did not look like a Catholic priest. He was about thirty, well built, with a thick head of blond hair—and he looked like a Southern California. surfer. He came from New York, and decided to dedicate his life to working among the poor in Peru. He lived in a dirt adobe compound surrounded by the poorest huts on the coast, and seemed dedicated to his cause. He told us how he had to go bail out one of his young people for something they were falsely accused of. He kept a pretty close watch over his flock, and we later noted he kept a pretty close eye on us also. He made follow-up visits to people we were teaching, but he never said anything harsh about us. Several times, as we were walking in our area, he passed by in his old beat-up Volkswagen van and stopped to give us a lift.

Each week we looked forward to dropping by in a taxi to pick up our faithful little old lady and her daughter, who had also started coming to church. One Sunday morning before leaving for church, we felt a fairly strong earthquake. Everyone on the coast of Peru seemed even more accustomed to earthquakes than Californians, and nobody had much to say about the earthquake at our church. One night in Maranga, while we were on a bus, I looked up and to my surprise I saw the same secret policeman who had held Elder Brooks and myself captive in Iquitos. I think he recognized me and recalled the withering look I had given him, because at the next stop he hurriedly jumped off the bus. He hardly had anything to fear from me since he was the policeman. I did not dare open my mouth or say a word to him, for fear that I might get Elder Perry and myself in trouble, or collect another twenty-four hours locked up somewhere.

One afternoon as we were out knocking on doors, we heard some recordings of good rock-and-roll tunes wafting through the air from one of the houses—Led Zeppelin, and Emerson, Lake and Palmer. We just had to see who was listening to this music. It was a young man with one of the largest collections of good rock-and-roll albums I had seen. We didn't let ourselves stay too long, but we did enjoy listening to a few good tunes. We tried to slip a plug in here and there about why he should have us teach him the discussions. He enjoyed talking about music, but did not want to have anything to do with missionary discussions.

As my attitude became more positive, our teaching grew more effective. I committed myself to developing grew patience and more love for the people. I got to the point where I could shrug off rude or angry confrontations at the doorways. I found that when I had less anger and more patience and understanding, my whole attitude about our work and our teaching improved.

Early in February 1973, for our P-day we met with two of the other elders in our district and took a bus out to Pachacamac—the huge city of ruins south of Lima that Elder Adsero and I had traveled to with the Cartwrights, in their jeep, several months before. As we were walking around the ruins, I looked down and saw a bone. I thought it was the bone of a cow, but then I looked further and saw hundreds of the bones lying around and found out that we were standing in the middle of an Incan burial ground that had been pilfered by midnight diggers looking for the artifacts buried with the Incan dead. We saw jawbones with teeth, skulls with eye sockets intact, pieces of cloth that still showed designs and colors, and sun-bleached hair. We took a few pieces of the cloth and some of the bones back to our pension as souvenirs. Although there was a ban on digging at archeological ruins, there was nothing prohibiting us from picking up pieces lying on the ground, out in the open. In the center of the ancient city was a courtyard where several llamas and a couple of their smaller relatives—alpacas—roamed free. One of the elders with us, Elder Dowdle, contrary to our warnings, managed to get himself too close to one of the llamas and had his efforts rewarded with a stream of slimy green juice sprayed all over him by a spitting llama he managed to irritate. We all had belly laughs over the whole incident, but it did not make Elder Dowdle too happy, since the green slime didn't easily come off with water.

The family we had been living with planned to move back to a home they owned up north in Peru in Trujillo. They were going to lease the house we lived in to another couple. They arrived from up north and we were introduced. They brought a live turkey that screeched all throughout the night and kept us awake, so we lost the snoring bears but gained a turkey for a wake-up caller. Fortunately, the turkey was slaughtered later in the week and we had turkey dinners for weeks. To send off our hosts, who had been very warm, friendly, and generous with us, we bought cardboard and colored paper and made cards for them, with our pictures and signed notes inside. They seemed genuinely touched by the gesture, and said they planned to have the missionaries live with them in their home up north.

February was a month fraught with danger for the missionaries. The entire month was called "Carnavales," which was the equivalent of the Mardi Gras in New Orleans and Rio de Janeiro, Brazil. The entire month was dedicated to pranks like throwing water in buckets, or in water balloons, on anyone that came within range. Anytime we passed by a two-story house, we watched out for the windows and walked in the middle of the street. Elder Perry did have a small crisis—he bent over during one of his gas cramps and split the seat of his pants and broke the zipper. As a compassionate senior companion, I dutifully started laughing. He did look slightly ridiculous with his suit coat tied around his waist—a college preppy look with a suit coat instead of a sweater. He covered up like this until he could reach a friend of ours, a tailor. The tailor installed a new zipper and restitched the split seam. I kidded Elder Perry that whatever he had been eating, it sure had had a powerful effect on his pants!

We became friends with the youth that hung out in the park in front of our house. One afternoon, they were but there with a shot put, which had really been my forte in high school. It was a twelve pounder, and I think I astounded them when I was able to throw the thing over forty-four feet on my first attempt—that was done in suit pants and dress shoes!

We gave a blessing to our little old lady in a wheelchair, and she seemed to improve. She and her daughter had mounds of faith. They were both emotionally and spiritually affected by the priesthood blessing we gave them. It felt great to practice our Priesthood and give the blessing, especially in a home where so much faith abounded.

The shantytown where Hermana Ofelia lived is known as the *ciudad de papel,* or "city of paper," because of all its cardboard walls and flimsy structures. Most of our teaching opportunities were in this little town of huts, where the people were more humble, and interested in things of the Spirit, since they did not have many worldly possessions to weigh them down, or any other materialistic pursuits. We did get some skepticism from people in this area because of the pervasive traditional philosophy used over the centuries by the monarchies to hold the masses down, telling them they should sacrifice and devote themselves to building up the aristocracy since the masses would receive their reward in the next life. From this doctrine, which had been used as justification to exploit the people of South America for years, came the cynical view that all churches were simply a tool of the ruling class. As a result, even some of those in humble circumstances were cynical about all religions. We also found atheists who did not understand why, if there was a just God, there was so much injustice, poverty, sickness, crime, and general evil in the world and why he would allow it. We tried to explain, but they did not understand that we are placed in the world as free agents, and as men we bring many of the evils and problems in the world upon ourselves without there being any direct cause-and-effect relationship to God's will.

Elder Perry had to get another pair of pants fixed. This was the second blowout—doubling over with gas cramps and splitting them out. The poor guy cannot seem to adjust to the food, although it was better in our present house than it had been in almost any other area. I could only imagine the problems he was going to have in his future areas. One of my journal entries noted:

Elder Perry has been having trouble with gas lately; at times he just about blows me out of the house.

Elder Perry's indigestion soured his attitude a little in general. He got angry one afternoon because the maid came off the roof with the laundry and walked through our room, which was the only access to the roof. She happened to catch Elder Perry standing there in his garments. It was not her fault, but Elder Perry chewed her out, up and down, until I finally told him to "cool it." I had not been feeling well and we were staying in that afternoon, but he kept going on and on with his com-plaints until I reached the point where I told him to get dressed because we were going out to work. He told me he thought I did not feel like going out to work and I said, "Rather than hear you complain the rest of the day, we are going out to work." We stayed out knocking on doors until about 10:00 P.M. and I told him the next time he chose to complain, and keep on complaining, we would stay out even later. Well, fortunately, he didn't harbor any ill feelings and we started the next day on good terms again. I really cannot blame Elder Perry for getting sour at times, I was struggling myself to keep positive when we ran into so many people that treated us rudely during the day, and had only a handful of investigators to teach. It was important to patch things up quickly as companions. Letting feelings simmer hindered the joint receiving of Spirit to teach. Elder Perry and I always managed to work out our gripes and differences and then moved on.

There was dust everywhere in our area. They were trying to fix the road down on the main avenue and were also dumping dirt along the edge of the cliffs on the coastal road to try to stop the cliffs from being eaten away by the ocean. The dust billowed up in clouds over the road and into the neighborhoods. Our shoes were continually covered with a thick layer of dust. The mosquitoes also kept coming in clouds at night. Our burning coil would run out in the early morning and then, as we tried to sleep, we could hear legions of mosquitoes circling and moving in for a snack. We would flip on the light and try to smash them on the ceilings and walls. We thought we got them all and turned out the light, but they were all around us. We finally started burning two of the coils-whoever would wake up in the middle of the night would start another one.

I got arguing one morning with the son-in-law of the people we lived with about God. He told us that, as a materialist, he believed only in what he could see. I asked him if he believed what the Bible said about God and he said the Bible was just words and he did not believe it because he could not see it for himself. I told him I did not believe Peru ever split from Spain. He thought that was ridiculous and I said, "Prove it." He said, "Well, I can show you in any history book." I responded that from his own point of view, that would not prove it because it was just words in a book, like the Bible. Using his theory, we could not believe anything cited in a history book because we could not see it. That seemed to at least get him thinking, but arguing never really accomplished anything in the mission field. We never changed anyone's point of view by arguing. I would learn later in life, when I became a lawyer, that the same is generally true of judges. Most battles are won on the basis of briefs and paperwork, and little is accomplished by arguing to a judge who most the time has already made up his mind on the basis of what he has read.

One morning we switched companions so that Elder Donaldson could work with me in our area. We ran into a big jovial lady who was quite interested in us primarily because we were from the United States. She asked me where I was from and I said, "California." She said, "How nice," and then asked Elder Donaldson where he was from and he said, "Utah." She responded with, "What's that?" It got better as she asked me where in California I was from and I told her, "Near Disneyland," and then she looked at Elder Donaldson and said, "What part of California is Utah in?"

I thought most of the superstitions were held by people in Iquitos, but as I got back into playing the piano—we were fortunate enough to have one at the house we were living in—I found that superstitions existed everywhere. One evening, the lady of the house told me that once I finished playing the piano, I needed to close the key cover or else the piano would catch a cold!

There were groups of girls in our area who gathered and hissed like snakes at us when we went by. They looked like they would like to strike us, like a pack of hungry wolves. We ran into one of the "ringleaders" of this group one day while knocking on doors—Elder Perry was practicing his door approaches. He knocked the door: a sexy looking teenage girl in a tiny hot-pants outfit came to the door, and instead of reacting to the situation, Elder Perry proceeded with one of our standard door approaches—"Hello, we have come to visit you, can we come in?" I just about died as she smiled and put on a sexy expression and said, "Of course." Elder Perry started to go but I grabbed him and asked her if her parents were home. As I suspected, they were not. I told the girl we would come back when her parents were home. She looked disappointed. Just when we thought we had knocked on virtually every door in our area, one day we discovered a whole neighborhood we had not been in before. On the first day of working there, we found three good families to teach. It was a poorer area and once again, because of the more humble circumstances, we seemed to have more success finding people willing to listen. We worked on getting references from the members by having them pull out pictures of their family gatherings, parties, weddings and so forth. As we examined the pictures, we asked them about the pictures and their relatives. We got their names, addresses, and references from the members so that we could to send missionaries to their relatives, wherever they lived.

We went from being infested with mosquitoes to being assaulted by flies. I found that my little souvenir blow guns came in handy for more than shooting at noisy dogs. I attached a pamphlet to the end of one of them and turned it into a swatter. It looked ridiculous and we had a good laugh over it, but [it worked.

Missionary work is very hard on shoes. We went through many, many soles. Several times I took my shoes to little shoe-repair booths to have them retreaded. They used a regular tire tread sewn and nailed onto existing leather. I finally broke down and had a pair of my black shoes retreaded because I was getting dust and dirt through a hole in the bottom. The shoe-repair man used nails that were too long and I had stubs coming through the heel. I took them back to get the nails removed.

One day late in February 1973, I switched companions with the district leaders and went to work in their area. We spent most of the afternoon knocking on doors in a large apartment building where they had a later appointment scheduled with a lawyer. He turned out to be a real arrogant loudmouth whose proudest accomplishment, according to him, was spitting on then Vice President Richard Nixon when he had come to Peru and passed by him in a motorcade. I looked at him after he related this incident, and told him, "You must have been so proud."

It was always invigorating to walk along the coast from one appointment to another in our area. The coastal road was the most convenient way to get through our area anyway, and it always lifted my spirits and reanimated me when I walked beside the ocean. When it was calm, I could see a sharply contrasting green color ending in a deeper blue farther out. The whole effect was ruined near the shore, though, where the sewage emptied directly into the water and left a sharp, murky brown line. There were always schools of dolphins just off the coast, breaking the surface, blowing spray, submerging again, and frolicking. There were large groups of anchovies, close to the shore that the dolphins fed on. We saw thousands of birds—pelicans, seagulls, and cormorants—also feeding on these fish. The birds soared about one hundred feet above the water and then dropped straight down like rocks, plummeting into the water, and under it, to snatch the fish.

As we attempted to visit with a man we'd met earlier, a man with a big yellow dog and a little white one, who had been reading the Book of Mormon, this yellow, dog stuck his head through the metal framework gate dog tried to bite us. I reared back and kicked him in the jaw, but he grabbed ahold of my sock and ripped it, which made me really mad, so I let him have it with my ammonia bottle. He released his grip on my sock, which by this time had become smelly from more than my own perspiration, and he ran away, squinting and sneezing. He did not bother us for the rest of our visit with his owner but instead lurked in the shadows in the back room. I found another effective remedy for nuisance dogs as we were later walking down one of the dusty dirt roads and a dog came running out, barking and chasing us. I picked up a piece of gravel and let it fly just to scare it, but all of a sudden a "thunk," and the dog went whining back to its house. In some of my next areas, I became deadly accurate with rocks to avoid being bitten by the many stray dogs.

Unfortunately, on a typical day in Maranga, most of the discussions we'd set up the day before with the housewives fell through—either they forgot to tell their husbands, or their husbands were not interested. Because I happened to be in Peru on my mission and experiencing this frustration, my first reaction was to blame it on the culture and the country, judging that the people were not learning to follow through. After I returned from my mission and saw how the people in the United States re-acted to the missionary work, I realized it was the same reaction everywhere. People generally focus more on the pleasure of the moment—their worldly pursuits. It is difficult, regardless of their nationality, to interest people in the gospel. On the day of judgment, I do not believe that the excuse I hear, "But I was too busy to go to church or be a member of your church," will get very far.

Once I started to realize I was unfairly condemning an entire culture and country because of general attitudes that were pervasive everywhere, I was able to better my own attitude. Any missionary who starts to become negative about the culture or people he or she is working with, will lose his or her effectiveness as a missionary. Without nurturing a love for the culture and the people and praying for them, charity did not enter into the work, and without it, we could do nothing.

I learned to pray for others on my mission. I would pray out loud with my companions in the morning, before going to work, and after lunch, before going out again to work, and then again in the evening, as well as holding my own personal prayers almost as often. We would pray that we might meet people who'd be sincerely interested in learning about the gospel. We also prayed that those we were teaching would sincerely read and pray to discover the truth, and that they would progress on the road towards their baptism. We prayed for those afflicted with any physical ailments, and for the members. Before my mission, I had usually been too selfish to worry about others in my prayers. In the mission field I discovered that praying, with real intent for others, brought a warmth into my chest and soul that I had not experienced often before. It also focused my companions, and me, more on our work, and brought the assistance of the Spirit to it. This effective use of prayer also helped dissipate any negative feelings we developed during the course of a frustrating day, while attempting to talk to people and having discussions fall through.

It seemed easier to be bold while knocking on doors and talking to people in Peru than it would have been in the United States. It seemed easier to talk to somebody in a different country, culture, and language. This probably was just the phenomenon of acting as representatives of Jesus Christ in the field. We made a transition from timid civilians to "fearless" expounders of the gospel—this transition does not depend on where you go.

We had a good laugh after meeting with an older man one afternoon and discussing his beginning efforts at reading the Book of Mormon. He was getting a little confused, and asked us, "How come, in the Book of Mormon, Noah is called Nephi when he builds his ark, and it does not say anything about all the animals?" We explained that Lehi and his group came at a different time, and were not the same as Noah and his ark. The next family we went to from that discussion was even worse. The man of the house showed up at the door smelling like a brewery. He had definitely drunk his lunch. We wisely decided to reschedule him.

We had regularly scheduled interviews with President Driggs, which I always looked forward to. Although it ate into our workday, it was always motivating to meet with the president. He was a great man who exercised a tremendous influence in the lives of the missionaries. He mixed, in perfect proportions, spiritual motivation with a good sense of humor.

My overall attitude and demeanor toward missionary work was aided by an organized study schedule. I had been reading Mormon Doctrine and taking notes, then following up with a regular reading schedule for both the Old and New Testament. On the schedule I set, I would be able to finish both of them within nine months. Prior to my mission, I would never have envisioned myself actually thirsting after the scriptures and looking forward to the end of the workday, so I could read for one hour to two hours in the scriptures! As a missionary I ate the scriptures up. I looked forward more to reading my scriptures than to almost anything else we did during the day.

March brought the foggy season to Lima, especially near the coast. It made an eerie but interesting sight, in the evenings, to see the mist flowing by, illuminated in the streetlights. It also got colder at night, eliminating our mosquito enemies. We met a man on the police force, and just out of curiosity, I asked him about the most dangerous areas in Lima. I was astounded to hear him cite three of my previous areas—Callao, La Victoria, and El Augustino. I was glad I did not learn this while I was working in them.

It was always easy to tell when we were teaching a sincere family and actually getting through. The Spirit would be present with such great strength that not only would we feel it, but we would also describe it and bring it to the attention of the family, so they understood what they were also feeling. We met a new family in March and had this kind of experience with them in teaching the second discussion. The challenge was making that Spirit last through the remaining discussions so that they would be guided toward their baptism.

Once again in Maranga, I had to learn that we did not make progress through satisfying our own pride and egos by demonstrating our knowledge of the scriptures or arguing with those of other faiths. Bernie had shown me that in Iquitos, but once I became a senior companion in Maranga and, more or less, set the tone and control of our program, I had to learn this lesson as a senior companion. Elder Perry and I had started Bible "bashing" with some of the Jehovah's Witnesses, Seventh-day Adventists, and Catholics in our area. We began cross-referencing our Bibles with the use of color codes—a separate color for our refuting scriptures for each different religion we wanted to challenge. I had blue for Jehovah's Witnesses, red for Catholics, and yellow for Seventh—day Adventists. I could go to cross-referenced scriptures to "prove" that their beliefs were false—what a spiritual conversion process! We had even picked up a copy of the Jehovah's Witnesses' green Bible—the "Green Dragon," as we called it—and studied some of the scriptures in it that we knew we could refute. We were armed to the teeth with scriptural knowledge, brimming over, waiting to do battle with any one of these religions that chose to take us on. At one point we were so caught up in this ridiculousness that we actually enjoyed locating members of these various faiths who wished to argue with us.

We finally took stock of where we were going one day and realized that we had never had a spiritual experience or a warm feeling, or even a good feeling, about even one of these encounters with members of other religions. We also realized we never received an invitation to return and talk with people we had argued about the scriptures with. We did not see any investigators who had become interested in the gospel through this approach. We realized we were only satisfying our own egos and pride and we resolved that we would stop, cold turkey, bashing or otherwise presenting the gospel in an argumentative or contentious manner. In looking back at it, I believe it was one of the frustration points for us and the reason why our program had not been going better. With having chosen to satisfy our own ego and pride, instead of relying on the Spirit and teaching through testimony, the Lord left us on our own, to grapple with our own inadequacies. In listening to the stories of missionaries who have returned, I realized I was not alone in this experience. Many missionaries have gone through a similar conversion to teaching through testimony, instead of through book knowledge and argumentation or contention. Had I paid attention, I'd have known that the scriptures warn that the spirit of contention is the spirit of the Devil, and not of our Savior.

One P-day early in March, we decided to take in some of the sights of Lima. Lima had some historic areas built in a beautiful old-Spanish style. We went downtown to the University of Lima and took pictures of the peaceful courtyards, and the Spanish balconies, with their ornate Spanish woodwork. We walked downtown to the Palace of Justice. This sprawling stone building was the huge palace where the highest court of Peru sat. It had large fountains spraying water twenty feet high in front of it. We continued our tour to the top of one of the hotels downtown and to one of the large cathedrals, which had catacombs below it. As we descended a narrow stone staircase into the catacombs with our guide, and walked through the dusty, dark corridors illuminated only by his large torch flashlight, we saw rows and rows of skulls and bones organized for viewing by the tours. Our guide advised us that these were the bodies of those who had, over the past centuries, paid for the privilege of being buried beneath the church. Through reading the history of Peru, however, I learned that actually many of these were bodies of those burned or otherwise tortured to death as heretics during the holy Spanish Inquisition, imported to Peru from Spain during the Inquisition of the medieval times. It was eerie walking among so many dusty bones and skulls that seemed like they were staring at us in a dark hallway as we walked through the catacombs.

We ascended into daylight from the catacombs and walked three blocks to the principal Lima cathedral, right in the middle of the Plaza de Armas—Plaza of Arms. The front doors to this cathedral were over fifty feet high and had decorative door knockers up about twenty feet. It was the largest cathedral on the continent, and as we looked into its interior, it extended forever. It was almost one hundred yards long inside, with a ceiling close to a hundred feet high. Inside was the semi-preserved body of Franciso Pizarro, the Spanish conquistador who opened Peru up to the Spanish conquest and proceeded to     conquer the Incan Empire in the early 1500s. He had not weathered the centuries that well. His muscles had dissolved, and he looked like a skeleton wrapped in dried leather.

After our expedition downtown, we went to the mission office. On the way, we almost got run over. We were crossing an intersection with an island when a driver pulled up, cut right in front of us, almost running us over, and then slammed on his brakes to stop and wait for traffic. We walked right into his car and he sat there laughing at us until I kicked his fender, so then he got mad but we just laughed. The fender I kicked was already busted up and crinkled from his past driving experiences, which probably were no better than the one he imposed upon us. You have to be on your guard continually while walking in Lima or you will end up as road kill, just like many of the hundreds of dog carcasses we saw piled up, waiting to be burned by the local trash collectors working the roads.

Well, here is another old wives' tale from the people we lived with. They continued to monitor our saga with mosquitoes. Their new theory was that mosquitoes fly around only from 6:00 in the morning until 6:00 in the evening, and that if we kept our doors shut until 6:00 in the evening, we would not have any trouble the rest of the night. The problem was I didn't have any problem with mosquitoes except between 10:00 at night and 6:00 in the morning. The 6:00 A.M. to 6:00 P.M. mosquitoes didn't bother us. It was the night owls that really got us, at least before the winter weather reduced their forces.

We met one family that seemed very promising, but when we showed up to teach them, we found that they had invited the wife of the local Baptist minister to at-tend and that she in turn had invited some of her students over to argue with us. Our earlier inclinations, before we resolved not to argue or contend with people of other faiths, would have been to enjoy the confrontation. Since we had decided to take a different course, we tried to politely leave. I told the minister's wife that she did not really need to defend the people of the house. They could talk for themselves and think for themselves. We continued to run into these "ambushes."

After Elder Perry had been in Maranga for about four months, he started anticipating a change. I did a bad thing and started building his appetite about some exotic place like Iquitos. I told him Elder Lower had been in Iquitos for about four months and that it was about time he was transferred. Elder Perry, like all other missionaries in Peru, longed to see the Amazon, or some other exciting place. When we finally received word of his change, shortly after I started this process, we learned he was heading for Chimbote. Chimbote, an inside joke with many of the elders, was a small town up the coast, about one hundred miles from Lima, built completely around the fishing trade. It had a fleet for fishing, factories for cutting up, processing, and packaging fish, and trucking fleets to distribute the fish products. The place smelled bad from fishy odors, and it had a serious rat-infestatied problem. One elder who had been there told me you could get used to the smells after a while, but you never get used to having to wear cowboy boots into the bathroom in order to stomp on the rats while you are trying to go to the bathroom.

Three elders received changes at the same time, which left three senior companions to work together while we waited for our new companions. They would not arrive until the next day. I received a brand-new companion, fresh from the Language Training Mission— Elder Partridge, who came from Salt Lake City. He was tall, with black hair and was a little quiet at first, but soon demonstrated a dry, entertaining sense of humor. Once I collected him from the office, we went right to work, leaving his unpacking until after work on his first night. It was fun to go through the process of introducing a brand-new missionary to all of the cultural differences of being in Peru, along with all of the differences of actually being out in the mission field. Elder Partridge was excited about the whole process, and brought a good spirit to the mission work, as well as the humility needed to learn what it was all about. He also was not opposed to hard work and seemed to enjoy our long hours of knocking on doors and teaching. He had managed to memorize most of the discussions in the LTM, and I was able to work him right into our discussions, since we were averaging two to three a day. I also let him start taking on his own door approaches almost immediately, which rather unnerved him at first, but did not take him long to get used to. I provided a good laugh for some of the kids out playing soccer near our house one afternoon. They invited me and Elder Partridge to try to kick a few goals. I swung my leg back to make a big kick, and as I did so, my other foot slid on the gravel, and I fell on my knees in the dirt—ouch! I completely whiffed on the ball—strike one! Later that afternoon, we traveled into downtown Lima to try to process Elder Partridge's Peruvian visa papers. All of the new missionaries who had arrived the week before were down there. While they teamed up as companions to go through the administrative process together, Elder Dowdle, one of the other senior companions, and I left and went into the big cathedral and took pictures. The place was vacant, so we photographed each other as we sat in the archbishop's chairs, which looked like wooden thrones raised up above and behind the altars, and teased each other about being "Cardinal Dowdle," "Pope Hoyt," and so forth.

At our next mission conference in Lima with President Driggs, we received good advice on seeking a vision for the work, and why we were there. It was a good spiritual meeting, which ended on a high with testimonies. Missionary testimony meetings were indeed unique. At home my eyes were riveted at the clock as it came time to end a testimony meeting—I had hated long meetings. In mission conference testimony meetings we all lost track of time, it was not important. We were spiritually enveloped by the power of the testimonies and fed off the spirit of the meeting, recharging ourselves for the work. Some of these meetings went three, four, or five hours and we loved it!

I introduced Elder Partridge to our Friday night tradition of going for Chinese food. He took to it as well as I had. We looked forward to dinner on Friday evenings. I was getting more adventurous with my dinner choices. I had not really experienced Chinese food before my mission and I found the selection both intimidating and exciting. I tried to stay away from the really exotic choices, like bird nest soup, sweet and sour bird guts, and chicken feet soup, to name a few.

We were irritated by the bad press the United States received in Peru. Peru was led at that time by a military dictator who used leftist semi-communist rhetoric to further his own military agenda. Most of the newspapers took their cue from the government and dared not contradict the government to any degree. As a result, the daily headlines often talked about how the "Imperialists used their South American friends," how the "Imperialists badly treat the Indians and invade countries like Panama," and expressed a continuing stream of anti-Yankee dialogue. There were people who worked themselves up with this propaganda and yelled, "Go home, Yankees" or other "friendly" diatribes at us on the street or in the buses. We tried to ignore them since we didn't want to aggravate the situation. We were not in Peru as U.S. ambassadors. We were there as ambassadors of our international church and representatives of Jesus Christ. Patriotic defenses of U.S. foreign policy could accomplish very little and we stayed away from this topic for most of the time, although we discussed it occasionally with friends or people we lived with, on a friendly basis. It was difficult to ignore the insults about our country. We had to stifle our patriotism and our yearnings to "set the re-cord straight." Most Peruvians, however, were warm and friendly and more curious than angry about the United States.

About one week after Elder Partridge arrived, I startled him one evening as we were walking down the coastal road. As we passed a group of ten teenagers sitting on the wall, they called us obscene names in English. We proceeded a ways past them and I told Elder Partridge, "Watch this." I walked back to the teenagers. Elder Partridge looked at me like I was crazy—he thought I was going to get mugged. I approached the teenagers and asked them if they would like me to teach them some manners. They each pointed at the others to place the blame, out of fear I might get physical with them. Elder Partridge stood there dumbfounded, his jaw dropping, and asked me if I was determined to get us both killed. I explained I was only having a little fun. I knew I could count on the teenagers to be intimidated by our size and by the mystique about Americans and martial arts that came from the American and British films with Spanish subtitles, that played on Peruvian TV. Elder Partridge still just shook his head and thought I was crazy. It was a little childish of me, but I couldn't resist the urge to shock Elder Partridge.

We met the Cortez family, a sincere, receptive, and humble family in the barrio at the southern end of our area. They loved the discussions, and we were encouraged by their progress. Hermana Cortez could not read, so we spent hours teaching her, explaining gospel concepts out of the pamphlets about Joseph Smith and the First Vision, and the Book of Mormon. In the evenings I drew pictures for her to demonstrate various stories and principles from the Book of Mormon. Because of her sincerity and desire to learn, I felt the warmth of compassionate service in these pictures. It took a lot of patience to deal with some of these investigators, especially those that could not read, but we were rewarded with spiritual "good feelings" as we dedicated our time to helping them learn.

We started using the members more in our work, which proved helpful. We asked Hermano Lee, our big Chinese friend, to start visiting the Cortez family. We heard it was the members that really made the difference in the success of the work in Mexico, and we were determined to make more of an effort involving members.

It took us forty minutes to teach Hermana Cortez how to pray. Since she was illiterate, we had to take the home to explain and reinforce everything to her, lest she might forget it as soon as we left. Her devout desire to learn kept us going. We met another family, the Zanellis, and also started a fellowshiping program with them. We could immediately see the difference it made when the members were involved with the work. The Cortez family came to church with Hermano Lee and the Zanelli family came their very first Sunday with their member family. After church that Sunday—April 8, 1973,—we went to the Hubers to listen to the General Conference from Salt Lake City.

I had the greatest feast of my mission on our second P-day in April. Hermano Lee helped us plan an eight-course Chinese meal he agreed to prepare if we would purchase the ingredients. He made up his shopping list and while the rest of the elders helped in the kitchen at the Hubers—our restaurant for the day—following Hermano Lee's orders, Elder Donaldson and I traveled to Chinatown in Lima to buy the specialty ingredients needed. Going into Chinatown in Lima was like being transported into the middle of Hong Kong. All of the street signs and storefront signs were in Chinese. Everywhere we turned, there were Chinese people scurrying back and forth against a backdrop of open-air stalls, large burlap bags of different herbs stacked on sidewalks in front of the stores, hanging items of poultry in the windows, and incense burners wafting sweet aromas up through the air. It was an exotic place. We purchased what we needed, caught a bus back to the Hubers' house and proceeded to follow "Chef" Lee's orders. The kitchen began to emit the most indescribably spicy smells. We began to salivate in anticipation. Finally the meal was ready. We brought out one delicious dish after another—sweet and sour pork, sautéed strips of duck, spicy chicken, four-meat-flavored soup, fried rice, fried wontons with sweet and sour sauce, and on and on and on. We ate enough to last us for a week. At the end we were barely able to stand up to help clean up and wash the dishes.

It was only one week later that we had another big feast. Hermano Lee called and invited us to the Chifa for lunch. He picked us up in a taxicab and took us to China-town. We went through a small doorway and climbed the stairs to the second-floor restaurant—his favorite restaurant in Chinatown. Once again we stuffed ourselves with all kinds of Chinese delicacies.

Through prayer, involving the members more in missionary work, and by striving for a more positive attitude, I changed in Maranga to the point of actually enjoying knocking on doors, because of the different people I could get to meet and talk with. On these door-knocking expeditions, we enjoyed stopping in at Hermano Lee's store to get a cold soda pop and to chat. He had four dogs out behind the store that he had found wandering in the area. He took them in and fed them. They were like his little children, following him everywhere.

I saw how simple mistakes in the way I spoke my Spanish could cause a problem—for example, when the Zanellis stopped coming to church. We went to visit and to show them a filmstrip and ask why we had not seen them at church. They became reanimated about the gospel even though they had been falling away from it. We found they had grown cold because they had misunderstood me on our previous visit. When I invited them to church, they thought I was inviting them to become members and then come to the church. They thought they had to be members before they could come to church.

We could see a real transition in Hermana Cortez. Although she was illiterate, she worked hard at remembering what we taught her. Her husband spoke to her about our lessons, the Book of Mormon, and Joseph Smith. She actually started giving us answers and remembering details as our discussions progressed. We had four complete families come to church by mid-April and it seemed we were making real progress. With this success came another transfer.

Indeed it seemed a transfer was always my reward for seeing progress in our programs. I had only enough notice to go by briefly to say goodbye to the Hubers, Her. mana Ofelia, the Cortez and Zanelli families, and Hermano Lee. This change was as hard as the others— it was never easy to change when you felt like you had made great progress with investigator families and had grown to love the members.

# CHAPTER 9

## A Baptismal Jackpot, and the District Leader in Comas

I received a change to Comas, which consisted of a barrio of houses built up against the foothills about eight miles northeast of Lima. The shops and houses fronting the main road running out of Lima, through Comas, and on to the mountains were made of brick and plaster, but farther from the main road, up in the hills, the houses were more flimsy, less substantial, typically huts or card-board shanties. There were areas built up near the tops of the foothills that had no electricity or running water. Water trucks plowed up the dirt roads daily, delivering water to barrels kept covered with a piece of wood out in front of the houses.

Fortunately, the house that my new companion—Elder Larsen, from Blackfoot, Idaho—and I shared had running water and all the amenities, including a refrigerator. The home was vacant except for us. The owner lived elsewhere and was renting us the house. We had both stories to ourselves but lived in a room upstairs. The view from our window upstairs was of endless waves of houses and huts stretching as far as the eye could see up into the dusty foothills. There seemed to be no vegetation anywhere, just gray dirt and dust, with houses scattered all over it. Many of the houses were in a continual state of construction as the owners continued living in them.

Elder Larsen was about 6'6" and the people stood staring in awe of him as we walked our area. The little kids called him "Rascacielo," or scraper of the sky. My first item of business in working with Elder Larsen was to get to know the members in our area. I had learned, from

Maranga, that our program would not progress well until we used the members to lead us to investigators and help us friendship them.

We visited one member who was on the police force and we started playing around with his handcuffs. As we put the cuffs on, Elder Larson joked about how the *hermano* had probably lost his key. The *hermano* went into the back room to look for the key, but came out in a panic, stating, "I actually did lose my key, and I cannot believe it." I started laughing. It took twenty minutes for him to go down the street to a friend of his who was also on the police force, to borrow his key and uncuff Elder Larsen.

On my third day in Comas, we went to visit a shoemaker. He made shoes at sewing machines in his small adobe brick home. His home was partitioned with bamboo and tin. My perception at first was that he was, at best, moderately interested. Little did I realize that he would become the starting point for the baptisms of three families, including his own. On our first visit, he transformed from boredom to complete animation when I started talking about old Incan artifacts and legends and relating them to the Book of Mormon. He opened up and started sharing with me his interest in the legends. We scheduled a second discussion for the next day. He talked himself right into it since the discussion was on Christ in America.

We attended church services in Comas in a large house. The Sacrament meeting and Sunday school were held downstairs in what had been a fairly large living room. Walls had been knocked out to handle about fifty of us. Classes were held upstairs in former bedrooms. It was rather packed and noisy during the main meetings. Hermano Romero, our shoemaker investigator, came to church on my second Sunday in Comas. It was still hard to get a read on whether he was excited about the meetings. The next day, we crossed the main highway and walked the one block to the Romeros' house, to present our second discussion to him and his family. They lived just below the main highway, off of a dirt road that wound through adobe brick houses that were in a perpetual state of construction. We entered this neighborhood through a wooden doorway in a wall that continued along the road. Once we passed through the doorway, we were in a dirt compound that stretched toward the back of the Romeros' house, where their chickens and ducks wandered around. Another set of walls within the interior compound formed the house, which was roofed with bamboo mats and tin. Their common eating and living area had sewing machines, leather pieces, and shoe parts mixed in with the table and chairs. As we gathered to give them the second discussion, Hermano Romero's niece, Celia, and his sister, Hermana Pastrana, also gathered to listen. Hermano Romero seemed generally interested in our discussion about the Book of Mormon and about Christ in America, but his wife was reluctant to participate. When we invited all of them to come to church, she told us she was Catholic and she intended to stay that way.

I had been reading James Talmage's *The Great Apostasy*, and during the week I put together a lesson to focus on Hermana Romero and explain the apostasy. On our next visit, I briefly described the apostasy and how the priesthood power was lost from the Earth with the deaths of the apostles. I explained how her church arose out of the confusion and the lack of authority created by the vacuum left by the apostles' deaths. I also taught her how, according to Talmage, the office of Pope arose from prideful bickering between the Bishops of Rome and of Alexandria in regard to who was the lead the then already floundering church. The Bishop of Rome won the dispute and ultimately became the central authority and Pope.

I had prayed about this discussion and about how much detail to go into before teaching. I wanted to be able to work the fine line between offending Hermana Romero, and actually informing her of details that would help her find the truth. I went into some of the practices of her church that we found many people questioning, including infant baptism, and the philosophy that if an innocent child died without a baptism, it was condemned. I could tell, as the lesson unfolded, that Elder Larsen was a little embarrassed and skeptical about my frank discussion of the Catholic Church. At the end of our discussion I gave Hermana Romero a challenge. I asked her to come to our church Sunday—our fast and testimony day—to listen to the testimonies and feel the spirit, and then compare that with what she felt or didn't feel when she went to her church for mass on that same weekend. I then exhorted her to pray about two experiences, because I knew she would feel a spirit in our church that she had never felt before in her own. The lesson at least pricked her curiosity. She agreed to take up the challenge.

Our administrative duties as missionaries included submitting weekly reports of our teaching, tracting, and study hours for the week. On the report for each individual missionary, there was a section for comments or remarks to President Driggs. Elder Larsen happened to leave his report for our eventful week with the Romeros' lying open on our desk. As I glanced at it, I saw that Elder Larsen had indeed been skeptical about my apostasy lesson to Hermana Romero. He wrote to President Driggs that I had been too aggressive with investigators, possibly offending them with a discussion about their church. Although I became a little perturbed that Elder Larsen had chosen not to discuss his feelings with me, I also began to question the wisdom of my approach, and feared that Hermana Romero was offended and would not show up at our church. Sunday came, however, and the entire Romero family, including the niece, Celia, and the sister, Hermana Pastrana, came to church. They seemed to enjoy the experience. The members were very friendly and I felt the spirit of the meeting fill all of us in the room.

Monday, when we returned to the Romeros' house, Hermana Romero was aglow. She was enthused about her experience over the weekend. Before we could start a discussion, she blurted out that I had been correct—she had felt a spirit, a warmth, and a glow within her, when visiting our church. She had never felt this in all her years of attending mass. She had prayed about it, and felt that we were teaching the truth. Elder Larsen and I looked at each other and smiled. We were blown away. We had found a really golden investigator.

As we continued to teach the family, Hermana Romero became the stalwart She set an example for Hermano Romero, the Romeros' children, their niece, and their sister. I encouraged them all to read, to pray, and to attend church, and Hermana Romero reinforced my exhortations like a third missionary. Eventually we also started teaching Hermana Pastrana's husband. We looked forward to our visits and discussions with the families. Elder Larsen and I were floating with the thought that these families were quickly working their way toward baptism.

Elder Larsen and I became close friends with Elders Gray and Sayre, in our district of six missionaries. Elder Gray and Elder Sayre made quite a contrast. Elder Gray was tall, slender, blond, and light complexioned. He usually grinned but was somewhat reserved. Elder Sayre was short, stocky, with a very dark complexion, and I presumed he was of Hispanic ancestry. He grown up near the Texas/Mexico border, in El Paso. While Elder Gray was quiet, Elder Sayre was outgoing, with a continual borderline smile/giggle and a wacky sense of humor that kept us all laughing. He reminded me of Flip Wilson, the famous Afro-American comedian. Elder Sayre was truly a blast to be with. We spent one P-day going bowling in downtown Lima, where we were all laughing so hard that none of us had a good score. Elder Sayre ordered a basket of nacho chips that were supposed to be covered with cheese. When they arrived, they were covered with this bright orange oozing stuff. I joked with him about who had provided the nachos—the Revell model company? We started laughing because we all recalled building, in our younger years, model airplanes by Revell that had the same bright orange plastic look. We got into further hilarity after our district meeting that evening as we were sitting in the little Chinese restaurant we always went to—the Win Wah. It was a converted house. The kitchen was where the bathroom used to be. As we joked about the food coming out of the bathroom, a fly died up on the ceiling and suddenly spiraled downward, landing in Elder Sayre's wonton soup. This brought a tearful, red-faced, seizure of laughter from all of us. We gasped out further jokes about what other nice tidbits might be lurking in our wonton soup from prior spiraling deaths. We were the dummies, though, as we kept coming back to the same restaurant, and the food always tasted good to us.

About a block down the road from the Romeros' house, we found the house of President Lorenzo. It was a brick adobe hut with a bamboo mat roof, and a wooden door set right in the middle of it. After we knocked on the door, President Lorenzo opened it and, with a gold-capped, toothy grin, invited us in. He and his family indeed lived in extreme poverty, with a few chickens running around, and a dirt floor inside, with little if any makeshift furniture. The children were happy, but always running barefoot, with runny noses and dirty faces, Hermana Lorenzo often chasing after them with a good-natured grin. Hermano Lorenzo painted pictures on canvas for a living. He was quite talented at painting Peruvian pictures—scenes of the Lost City of the

Incas, Machu Picchu, and other postcard type scenes. Although poor in a worldly way, Hermano Lorenzo's family was very rich spiritually. They were very closely knit, always at church, and Hermano Lorenzo was a commanding presence as district president. He had a real air of authority about him and was a very good public speaker. He had the respect of all of the members and was extremely knowledgeable about the Gospel. He was proof to me that the humble and unlearned truly can become strong through reliance on our Father in Heaven.

At the end of the lots where the Romeros' and the Lorenzos lived, to the west of the main road, was a large dusty field that at one time had been planted. Across this field was another housing development where some members lived. Occasionally we walked across this dusty field to the other side of the valley, past a little airport for private planes. Once, as we crossed this field, a massive yellow dog followed us. After we finished meeting with the member family, the "beast" was still waiting for us and followed us on the trail back—at least someone enjoyed our company.

Later this same day, we visited a tailor's shop on the main street. Elder Larsen had heard the tailor was a member of the church. We started talking to him and he was very friendly. Elder Larsen asked his wife, "How long have you been baptized, Hermana?" She responded, "Oh about twenty-five years." Elder Larsen and I laughed and said, "Hermana, we didn't mean that baptism," referring to her Catholic baptism. We thought she was joking. We then asked the tailor which elders had baptized him. He seemed confused by the question. After more good-natured bantering for about ten minutes, he finally told us, "I don't belong to your church." He demonstrated a good sense of humor about it and we all laughed, realizing we had come to the wrong tailor.

I switched areas a couple of days later and worked with Elder Lloyd, companion to our district leader—Elder Madsen. We worked their area, which was farther north from ours but in a similar setting—barrio-type housing backed up into the hills. Up on the hill we witnessed a large fight. An organization called Sinamos was in charge of organizing and building government housing. Part of their responsibility was to take land away from wealthier landowners and give it to the poor for housing. A few representatives of Sinamos were telling the ladies of three families they would have to move and have their homes torn down because they were on government land. They had been given notice, over the period of one year, to move. Sinamos planned to build a park on the land where these people had built squatter housing. The three ladies went crazy as the Sinamos agents were talking to them. One lady grabbed a knife from her apron and charged after the agents. A policeman grabbed her and wrestled the knife from her hand, but then another lady grabbed a stick. Several people in the crowd grabbed her and the policeman wrestled her down to the ground, then hauled her off to his car to calm her down. Just when it looked like everything was calming down, another lady came out of the crowd, running, picked up a big rock, and tried to hit a Sinamos representative over the head. He ducked just in time, and others grabbed her and calmed her down. They were indeed losing their houses to make way for yet another dusty plaza devoid of vegetation. I could understand their anger and frustration, but the violence was startling.

We had a very closely knit branch in Comas, where we enjoyed activities together. One of these activities was a talent show on a Friday evening in April. Our district of missionaries organized and put on a shadow show behind a sheet for the branch—we conducted a mock operation, with a light from behind us illuminating our shadows on the sheet. I was the doctor and Elder Sayre was the patient. I used a machete, a hammer, and pruning shears as my surgical tools, and proceeded to pull a hose, an alarm clock, a boot, and a phony leg, made of a blanket and shoe, out of and off of him. The members had never seen such a show before and hooted, hollered, and laughed themselves silly.

While knocking on doors, we met a teenager who refused to get his parents for us but instead started yelling at us and calling us names. As we left, I told him "Okay, since you want to be so discourteous, tell your dad that he can come pick up the package himself." That got him real curious, but we refused to say anything more. I had no package but thought it might be a good way to get in the last tease.

We had an initial success with a family of fifteen we met in Comas. They came to church at least twice and we taught them with two discussions. They were progressing well until their neighbors found out they were having visits by us, whom they called "Los Mormones." The neighbors descended upon them in an effort to dispel all of the "ridiculous notions" the neighbors said were being taught by the Mormon missionaries. The family grew cold and seemed confused on our next visits. Their heads had been filled with lies and distortions. This experience was not unusual. The ridicule, persecution, and contentiousness that followed us, and confronted those we taught, were often stumbling blocks they could not overcome, much like the weeds choking out the good seed in the Savior's parable of the sower.

The Romeros, the Pastranas, and several of their nieces and nephews continued to attend church and progress through the discussions. We were also having success with a man who had received a few discussions before I arrived—Hermano Rivera. He had an intense interest in receiving the discussions, but his wife, staunchly Catholic, refused to listen. He was very enthusiastic; he had a large, toothy grin and a pleasant disposition. I had never met anyone more teachable and eager to learn the gospel. On my first visit, I was sure he would be baptized.

At the beginning of May 1973, we had a mission conference in Lima with Elder Loren C. Dunn of the First Council of the Seventy. He spoke on recommitting ourselves as missionaries and either getting all the way into it or getting out of it. He was a no-nonsense speaker and personality and really laid it on the line. He mentioned many things I needed to work on to get more committed to the work and increase my spirituality. It was easy in the mission field for a person to slip, getting lax at study habits, lax in disciplining thoughts outside of the work, and lax about 100 percent effort. Recommitting ourselves weekly seemed to be the best way to stay tuned up as an instrument for touching the lives of the people we came in contact with.

As we gave the third discussion on the Word of Wisdom to the Romeros, we had yet another spiritual experience. Hermana Romero, who, just two weeks before, was telling us she could not come to church because of her Catholic faith, had learned so much and changed so much, it was unbelievable. I noted the following in my journal:

She [Hermana Romero) was saying how none of the Protestant

or Catholic churches could be true because they do not have apostles. When I bore my testimony about the Word of Wisdom to them, I could really feel the Spirit present, so I mentioned, "What you are feeling now is the Spirit, which testifies to you of the truthfulness of my testimony." Hermana Romero said, "Yes" and started describing the feeling she felt inside.

The Romeros gave us their coffee cans to take away; they had no vices with drinking or smoking.

I worked with Elder Madsen, our zone leader, in my area the next day and we met with Hermano Rivera to answer some of his questions. Elder Madsen felt he was ready for his baptism. We planned to baptize him the next Saturday. After this meeting we dropped in on the Romeros and gave the second discussion to his sister and brother-in-law, the Pastranas. The discussion went smoothly. It was exciting to watch the gospel change the lives of these families. The Romeros were becoming a closer family through gospel study, family prayer, and Family Home Evenings.

By the middle of May we were up to the fourth discussion with the Romeros. They had consistently come to church as a family. On Mother's Day we ate dinner with them—they made one of their poor ducks walk the plank! After dinner we talked for a quite a while, just enjoying ourselves with their family. Later that day we always gave the sixth discussion to Hermano Rivera. This discussion dealt primarily with paying tithing, and I always felt nervous and a little uncomfortable giving it to investigators in Peru. This was a breaking point discussion for most. Due to the difference in economic conditions and lifestyles between the United States and Peru, many of those we taught made only about two dollars a day for the support of their family. Coming from my middle-class, comfortable lifestyle, I felt a little uneasy when challenging these humble people to pay 10 percent to the church, even though I knew it was the Lord's commandment and necessary for all of God's children, regardless of their circumstances. Hermano Rivera surprised us. Because of his great faith in the Lord and his belief that he would be blessed through sacrifice, he did not hesitate. He committed to pay tithing and to be baptized. We went to the church house in the middle of the week to clean out the baptismal font. It looked more like a big goldfish pond. We had to start filling it on Wednesday for the Saturday baptism, since the water came on in the morning only between 8:00 A.M. and 11:00 A.M. It took us three days to fill!

Two days before the baptism I traded companions, so I could work with Elder Madsen, who in turn would inter-view Hermano Rivera. Hermano Rivera passed the baptismal interview and would be baptized Saturday. The Romeros would follow close on his heels. The next day we switched: I worked with Elder Lloyd, and Elder Larsen worked with Elder Madsen. Elder Larsen was not very happy with us when he came back on Saturday because a lady member in our area, Hermana Celi, had invited him and I to celebrate his birthday and her daughter's birthday that Friday, but we had forgotten that Elder Larsen would be working out of our area. It didn't soothe him any when I told him not to worry because Elder Lloyd and I had gone over to Hermana Celi's to celebrate so that she would not be disappointed that the elders did not come to eat the two chickens she roasted. Hermana Celi had gotten a little upset when she thought none of the missionaries were coming, so we assured her at least the two of us would come over and celebrate with her and her daughter. It also didn't help Elder Larsen's reaction to the situation when I assured him we had had a good birthday celebration for him. I treated him to dinner the next night to make up for the missed party and all the ribbing.

Although we wanted a member to baptize Hermano Rivera—we believed this created a special bond between the members and the new converts—no one was home. I had the privilege of baptizing him. We had a spirit-filled baptismal service. I felt a special bond with this humble, faithful man as we entered the font and I recited the prayer, then baptized him. My heart filled with appreciation at being a part of his conversion. He bore a strong testimony after the service, saying he felt "like a new person."

The following week, we also reached the end of the discussions with the Romero family and set their baptismal date for the next Saturday. They were getting a little nervous, but we kept finding a pretext to drop by and visit them to reinforce their decision. We gave them a Family Home Evening on Monday night, and were out late, arriving home about 11:00 P.M. I was dead tired and I plopped on my bed, almost falling asleep before and during my prayer.

In Comas my ammonia squirt bottle was not sufficient to take care of the dog problem. In Maranga the dogs were usually on the roofs and off the street, but in Comas they roamed the streets. I needed a more long range remedy—accuracy with rocks. One afternoon we visited a member who lived up near the top of the hill in the barrio. While we were there, Elder Larsen walked down a path to buy one of the kids, who followed us, a corn-dough scone. As he was walking down the path, a dog from the house below the path came running up and nipped at him. At first I thought the dog had missed him, but when he returned, he showed me that the dog had ripped a hole in his pants. Both out of anger, and concern that the dog would come after both of us as we walked back down the path, I picked up a rock and nailed the dog in the side. He went off yelping and a woman came running out of the house, asking us why we were throwing rocks at her dog. I explained that the dog had just bit my companion. Her "sympathetic" response was that he bit Elder Larsen "because he did not know him." If that was the attitude of the owners of dogs that were allowed to roam free and bite people, I decided I'd better carry a rock in each pocket of my suit coat. I took this precaution while in Comas and in my next areas. I had to use these rocks, especially as we crossed the large field on the other side of the main road beyond the Romeros' neighborhood. Once, while we were crossing this field, a congregation of dogs chased us. This dog pack followed us to the other side of the field. While Elder Larsen's inclination was to run, I told him we'd be better off making a stand and letting a few of the dogs have it with rocks. As the pack surrounded us, I picked out a few of the dogs within our and let them have it. As soon as they started yelping, squealing, and running off, the rest of the pack decided the pursuit was not worth it and they dispersed.

I got so good with problem dogs that one of the members living on the other side of this field, after hearing of my marksmanship, casually mentioned he had had several run-ins with a Great Dane, a mongrel, just down the lane from his house. This beast had ripped the seat out of his pants as he rode by on his bike. I liked the challenge of dealing with such a large problem dog, especially if it would help out the *hermano*. I got the specifics on the house and the dog. The next time we crossed the field we made a point of walking down the lane by the Great Dane's house. Elder Larsen thought I was nuts, but I felt fairly confident. As we approached the house, a big yellow beast erupted in a howl. He was about twenty yards away starting to rise to his feet—no doubt, to come after us—when I whipped a rock, with a side-arm shot, in his direction. The rock glanced off the ground and smacked him on the top of the head. He collapsed back down on the ground, whining and squealing, without ever making it to his feet. Elder Larsen stood in awe, as did the *hermano*, when we reached his house and explained that this big bad hound from outer darkness had not even reached all fours before I shut him up and flopped him down. The *hermano* decided to carry a rock from that moment forward and I never heard him mention this dog again.

Only once in Comas did I fear I was going to lose a battle to the dogs. We were out one day in one of the barrios and it got dark. As we were standing there, looking for a house, one obnoxious dog started barking at us. Before we noticed it, twenty other dogs came running because of the commotion, and encircled us. I groped into the pockets of my suit and realized, with horror, that I had not restocked from my last episode, as I had no throwing rocks in my pockets that day. As I started to scan the dust that there were no rocks within reach. We stood there for a while, terrified that we might get bitten by these wandering mongrels carrying unimaginable diseases, when I  came up with the next best thing to a rock—the flannel board that we used to illustrate our discussions. It was folded up like a compact umbrella. I heaved it at the closest dog I could find, smacking him in the rib cage. His wheezing yelps dispersed the crowd long enough for us to slip away, and I grabbed my flannel board again as we left.

The same night we had this encounter, we saw there were other dangers on the streets of Comas. As we walked down the main avenue, past an empty lot, we saw a guy rising to his feet, with his pants ripped open and his face bruised. As several teenage boys darted away through the vacant lot, we realized they had just assaulted and robbed this man. We took off after them, but they were gone before we could even see which way they scattered. They had ripped open the sides of the man's pants, then had torn his pockets off, taking with them the cash receipts he had just emptied from the registers of his business, which he had closed only minutes before. Just as we thought we had seen all the crime and vicious dogs we wanted to see in one day, farther down the road, we ran across some kids sticking tools in their pants. We grabbed them and asked them where they had found the tools. They muttered a bunch of excuses and then slipped out of our grasp and ran away.

To top off a day that was otherwise filled with unseemly and disturbing events, we visited the Romero family and found them totally committed, ready, and willing to be baptized Saturday. They accepted the principle of tithing easily, and told us they had been praying often during the week to make sure of their commitment, to get ready for baptism, and to receive final confirmation that that was what they should do. Hermano Romero told us he had prayed the night before about whether to be baptized and that after his prayer, he sat there feeling like he was burning all over, and this sensation lasted until he ended his prayer.

Elder Madsen interviewed the Romeros. They were ready! The only thing holding us up was the "three-day" baptismal font. Somewhere between Wednesday and Friday, someone had pulled the hose out of the pit. We were determined to get them baptized even if we had to get a bucket of water out of the main tank to fill it.

Saturday, May 26, 1973, was a golden day for the Romeros, their niece Celia, and for us. After a spiritual baptismal service and their baptisms, each member of the family gave his or her testimony. I could really feel the Spirit as they testified to the truth of the gospel and their appreciation for baptism. I felt at that moment, as much as I had felt at any other moment on my mission, the importance of what I was doing. Being able to see the Romeros' progress and change through the gospel brought me great happiness. That evening, after the baptism, we went to an upscale Chinese restaurant downtown. I treated the Romeros, Hermano Rivera, Elder Larsen, and myself to the meal. It was a day I will always remember. Nothing could mar it, even the drunk on the bus as we headed downtown, who kept yelling toward the back, where we were sitting, "Why don't you Yankees go home." Hermano Romero came to our defense and shut the grizzly old man up, telling him that we were his friends, and that he should not insult us.

The next week we gave a fifth discussion to Flor, sister of Hermana

Romero, who was also progressing sister baptism. Hermano Romero, became the sower of many gospel seeds among his relatives.

On the day of my one-year anniversary in Peru—May 29, 1973—Elder Larsen and I attended a zone conference. We had workshops where we learned different approaches to first-time contacting and member work. We ended the conference with a testimony meeting. As usual, the entire chapel was filled with the Spirit. I got up to give my testimony and it hardly seemed like I was actually talking. I felt like I was burning up. My whole body was shaking.

Successful teaching and baptizing could turn even the most unpromising area into an exciting place to be in the mission field. Through our wonderful teaching experiences with Hermano Rivera and the Romero family and their other relatives, I grew to love Comas. When I had first arrived and looked at it, I thought, "What a hole." It was dusty, rocky, and desolate. Most of the people were destitute and lived in temporary huts built of bamboo, cardboard, and tin. Yet as I learned, it was not the living conditions, the beauty of the surroundings, or the material attractions that made an area enjoyable in the mission field. It was the attitude, faith, and spirituality of the missionaries and those they contacted. The members in this area contributed significantly to the work, and were a very closely knit group. On the birthday of each adult member in the ward, a group of the other members gathered outside the member's home at midnight with guitars. They lit candles and serenaded the member. Once the birthday member awoke, as if the person had ever really gone to sleep, knowing the tradition, the member invited the serenaders in for hot chocolate, and to visit. It was a bonding tradition that drew the members close to each other. Elder Larsen and I stayed up late enough one night to go to one of these serenadings to experience it firsthand. I took flash pictures of the gathering.

The district leaders changed branch presidents while I was in Comas. The new president was Hermano Fajardo. He was a good, humble man who would make a good president. It was a little humorous that he drove a beer delivery truck for a living.

Elder Larsen and I became disenchanted with our eating place. The lady who cooked lunches for us also did our laundry. One afternoon as we started to dig into our potatoes, I looked down and saw something white that was wiggling around in it. I pried out a large worm. Elder Larsen's had the same. We held the worms out to our cook and she shrugged it off, like it was no big deal. It was a big deal to us and we decided to change our eating place. We had been taking our chances on the street in the evenings, often going by a little street vendor, with a charcoal grill cart, who braised chunks of liver and beef over an open fire. He marinated them well and they were quite tasty. We had not yet gotten sick from them.

At this point we finally nailed our most hated dog, Gitano. He always barked at us and tried to sneak up and bite us on the backs of the legs as we walked by his house, down the street from the Romeros. After leaving the Romeros, we walked close to the walls, so he would not see us. He failed to see us until we were almost on top of him. After trying to bite us, he escaped to the door of his house, but the lady of the house had closed the door. As Gitano tried to run, Elder Larsen—who had taken lessons from me—hit Gitano with a rock, causing him to squeal, and teaching him a lesson I hoped he would not soon forget.

Flor Romero was next on the baptismal schedule. She was baptized on the third Saturday in June 1973. The day she committed to her baptism, I learned I was receiving another change. I was not going far, though, I would take Elder Sayre's place, with Elder Gray as my new companion. Elder Sayre was transferring to another area outside our zone. This was the easiest change in areas, in distance traveled, I would ever have in the mission field. I packed up my stuff, loaded it in a taxi, and traveled approximately two miles to my new pension.

My new pension was a nicely plastered house with two stories, fronting a little green park with real grass and trees! We lived on the ground floor in a bedroom toward the rear of the house, with a window looking out on a small grass-covered courtyard with more actual trees and bushes! In the small square park in front, children gathered in the afternoons and evenings to play soccer. The couple we lived with were in their fifties and very friendly, although they were not members. In Peru, as a general rule, the missionaries didn't live with members. This kept members from overindulging missionaries at the expense of their own finances, and also provided opportunities to teach the gospel to nonmembers.

Our pension was convenient in its proximity to the main highway for bus connections, and for eating. We ate right next door at the home of a lady who had been feeding the missionaries for several years. Elder Gray and I already were friends from being in the same district for a couple of months. We had done things together, along with our other companions. He was from Salt Lake but I did not hold that against him!

Many of the strongest members of the branch lived in my new area, which we called "Kilometro 11." It was approximately eleven kilometers outside central Lima. This area belonged to the same branch as the Comas area I'd worked in with Elder Larsen. Having the opportunity to work in two of the three areas that formed the branch meant I would get to know the members there better than any other previous missionaries in the area had. I was convinced this would give us success in finding and teaching investigators.

Elder Gray was astounded at my dexterity with rocks and picking off charging dogs. One of the first mornings he and I went tracting, a large, snarling beast came rocketing out at us from a dark doorway. Almost as a matter of reflex, I reached in my suit pocket, grabbed a rock, and fired a side-arm shot that caught him in the side and sent him whimpering right back into the doorway he had jumped out of. Elder Gray, who was still in the middle of getting ready to run from the dog, was flabbergasted. I could see I was going to have to teach him, as I had taught Elder Larsen, how to handle these dogs.

We were getting tremendous help from the members in fellowshiping and in gaining referrals. The members were very animated and excited about the gospel, and, having drawn very close together, they were looking for ways to increase their numbers. We had developed friendships with the members and they trusted us to teach their friends.

As missionaries we always tried to present a dignified image to the members. This was especially true on the night of the talent show, when I did my imitation of the famous Latin pop star—Rabito. I ratted my hair up into an afro, put on a phony beard with dark sunglasses, and then hummed through a comb with a piece of wax paper attached, to produce a kazoo sound, while I sang high notes, off-key, and sounded generally lousy. The branch members laughed loudly. I am sure they continued to have great confidence in my ability to teach their friends! Actually, our willingness to the wind and just have fun with the members furthered the bond among us.

Once again, we had to deal with the "three-day" baptismal font at the branch house, or the gold fish pond, as we began calling it. Flor Romero had passed her baptismal interview and we were trying to make sure there was water in which to baptize her. Yet again, when we arrived, we found the font half full and had to hand carry water in buckets to fill it up. Fortunately, Flor was very petite and we really did not need much water for her. We had a great baptismal service for her and once again we heard a very spiritual and committed testimony. It was also a special occasion because an *hermano* who had been inactive for a long time, but who had recently become reactivated, baptized her. It always made the occasion more special when members became involved in it, showing how much they cared about the new convert, and also creating a lasting bond between them.

The required quarterly gamma globulin shot was a scary ordeal. It was supposed to protect us from hepatitis. I found out, after I got back, that the vaccine we received from the United States worked just fine for the strain of hepatitis circulating in the United States, but really did nothing to combat the hepatitis strain in Peru. Fortunately, I never got hepatitis, but it was not because of the shots. While we were in Lima, we were able to go to the mission office to get our shots from one of the as-assistants, who had become fairly proficient at injecting the other elders. Those elders in the outlying provinces could either try and show how "macho" they were by stabbing themselves in the leg or some other accessible area and then injecting the vaccine, or they could take the chance that their companion could do it—usually an ordeal because of their timidity and the fear of pushing it in too fast or too hard. Generally, the first attempts were flesh-stabbing, half-hearted efforts that pricked the skin but did not go deep enough. While in Comas, I went to the office and had an assistant inject me. I remembered watching with horror, a few months before in Iquitos, as Elder Bernsten tried to inject himself in the thigh. He missed the muscle and injected the vaccine between the skin and the muscle, creating a big fluid sac that swelled up and took days to go away.

Two days before my birthday in June 1973, Elder Gray and I had an experience that left no doubt in our minds that prayers are heard and answered. We were nearing the end of a tiring and frustrating day, one which had seen us knock on many doors, with none thrown open with an invitation. As we were heading back along the main highway to try to find a snack for dinner, we ran into the Bordases, a member couple who looked nervous and harried. We asked them what was wrong. They told us their four-and-one-half-year-old daughter had never made it home from school at 12:00 in the afternoon when she was supposed to arrive. When we ran into the Bordases, it was 5:00 in the evening! They had asked at the school, but none of the teachers or school administrators had seen her. They also asked the little girl's friends who lived nearby but they could not recall seeing her. The Bordases had just come from the local radio and TV station after trying to convince them to announce over the air that their daughter was missing. The station managers said nothing could be done until the next day. We went with the Bordases to the police headquarters in Comas and asked if they could notify their officers and the other precincts. The police would do nothing for another twelve hours.

We hiked to the home of Hermano Fajardo, the new branch president, and told him about the situation. He bratacted Hermano Vega, who brought his van. We piled in and traveled to the branch house to meet several other *hermanos* from the branch. There were about eight of us at the church house. We all agreed it would be best to start our search with a prayer. As we knelt down on the cement floor, I looked at my watch and noticed that it was 8:15 P.M. Hermano Fajardo offered a heart-felt and pleading prayer that the little girl would be safe from harm and that we would find her. After the prayer we jumped in Hermano Vega's van and went to the Bordases house where we obtained a list of the little girl's friends. It was difficult for them to give us much information as by this point, they were both on the verge of hysteria. Hermana Bordas was crying uncontrollably and envisioning all of the bad things that could have happened to their daughter. Hermano Bordas was doing his best, with his arms around his wife, to console her, but was barely maintaining control himself.

In the van we went around to the houses of the other students at the little girl's school. Our efforts were fruitless. None of the children remembered seeing her. When it got to be eleven o'clock, all of the children and their parents were in bed. We decided we could accomplish nothing further but anger those we were trying to contact. We called off the search and agreed to meet back at the Bordases' house in the morning and then go by the school.

We met at the Bordases' house and ended up at the school at 8:30 the next morning. As we stood talking to some of the teachers from the little girl's class, suddenly, from down the street, a lady and a man were walking toward us with the little girl in front of them. The woman explained to us that the night before, she had felt a sudden urge to take a different route home from her job in Lima. She recalled that about 8:15 P.M., she passed an empty lot and saw a little girl that appeared to be lost, wandering. She stopped to see if she could help. This lady had stopped and taken the little girl from off the streets at exactly the same time we had been kneeling in prayer, praying for her safety! The little girl appeared to be fine. An older boy had apparently deceived her into accompanying him to Lima, telling her he was her cousin and was going to take her there to buy her a doll. We went with the Bordases to file a police report. Elder Gray and I, and the parents, were so grateful for the power of prayer and that our prayer had been answered in such an immediate and graphic way. It was a testimony of prayer I never forgot and I am sure that none of those in the prayer circle that anxious night ever forgot the experience.

Although we basked in the spiritual glow of this experience, we were also angry with the police. The lady told us she had notified the police headquarters where she lived and had given them the little girl's address from her lunch pail. Her local police had not even bothered to notify the headquarters in Comas, where we had filed a report about the missing little girl.

I celebrated my second anniversary in Peru by having lunch with the Romeros. All of the elders in the district were invited. We had roast duck—it was one of the poor little creatures that had previously wandered around their yard, mucking it up and quacking! The duck was much more enjoyable for eating than it had been as a general nuisance in the yard. The Romeros baked me a cake and put twenty-one candles on it. That night we went to the Chifa with the Rodriguez family, good members of the branch. We had a good time, even though when it came time for pictures, their teenage daughter made me rather uncomfortable when she leaned over, put her arm around me and pressed her cheek against mine for the photograph.

My best anniversary present was finding another golden family to teach—the Vila family. They were already familiar with the church from being friendshipped by another member family—the Olivareses. Using the promptings of the Spirit, and common sense, we started out with the fifth discussion, focusing on the importance of the family and adding in parts of the Plan of Salvation discussion to try and appeal to their interests, since they appeared to be a closely knit family.

The next day, I received another surprise when the Pastranas, including the *hermano*, came to church. Her-mano Pastrana appeared to be excited about the Gospel Doctrine class being taught by Hermano Lopez, who was no longer the district president. Hermana Pastrana had been desirous of baptism ever since the Romeros were baptized. It almost broke her heart to have the Romeros get baptized before her, but we convinced her to wait patiently for her husband, so they could be baptized as a family. It appeared the goal was in sight. The Vilas also came to church that day.

After church I stayed to play the piano for the choir. What a combination—my missed notes, the off-key choir, and the piano's dead notes and untuned sounds. The Mormon Choir we were not! All of us had a great time, though, and for a small rag tag group of sincere members, we did not sound all that bad.

The next week, we received tragic news. Lucho Celi, son of Hermana Celi, our friend in Comas, had been badly burned all over his neck, back, and legs, while heroically trying to put out a fire started at a neighbor's house, by an exploding kerosene kitchen stove. One of the neighbor's children had come running to Lucho, screaming that their kitchen was on fire. Lucho had run in and bravely removed the other children. As he turned to make an effort to put the fire out, the kerosene canister on the stove exploded and sprayed burning kerosene all over his body. We realized his burns were bad, but it seemed that he would be okay, because his family and other members had visited him in the hospital and found him sitting up and talking. Later in the week, as we were preparing to visit Lucho in the hospital, Elder Larsen arrived and I knew, from his quivering voice and ashen face, that the news was not good. Lucho had died the night before. It was a shock to us and a shock to all of the members in Comas.

We went to the funeral on the day we received word and saw a real contrast between religious funerals. On the one hand, we saw the doctrine of despair—Lucho and his family were the only members of the church among all the relatives there. All these relatives came in black and cried and howled pitifully during the viewing and the Catholic portion of the ceremony. It seemed they had no real concept of the Plan of Salvation, and could take no comfort in a testimony about life after death and all of its glory. We traveled to a cemetery, where a Catholic priest sprinkled water on the casket, and pronounced Catholic rites over it while Lucho's grandmother, veiled in black, screamed and wailed uncontrollably. On the other hand, President Fajardo spoke at the cemetery and gave a message of hope in the plan of salvation. This was well received by Hermana Celi and those members of the branch who were there. All of us were devastated by the loss of Lucho, who had been an outgoing, fun-loving boy, but we took comfort in our testimonies about the glory that awaited him, especially after his brave sacrifice. Lucho's death and funeral brought home to me how close at hand death is to everyone. It comes when you least expect it, and to many people when they are least prepared. I began to see the importance of living the gospel every day as if it were my last, because one day it would be my last day, and I really do not know which day it would be or when. We visited with Hermana Celi several times over the next few weeks to try to bolster her spirits. She proudly showed us a newspaper article on Lucho's heroic efforts to save the neighbors' children and house.

On our first P-day in July we traveled, as a district, by bus out to Ancon, a little resort city about forty kilometers up the coast from Lima. It was a farewell party for Elder Madsen, who had received a change the night before. As we arrived at the road, passing through the tops of the sand dunes, to the coast, we looked down on the city. It was beautiful, spread around an emerald-colored, clear-water bay, with big hotels built up right on the beachfront, like a miniature Acapulco. We walked through the town and saw fishermen and their sons paddling and pulling nets with floats out into the bay like a huge curtain. Two boats moved together after floating the net in a big circle, sealing off the enclosure, which they then manually pulled to the shore with long ropes. The net corraled all of the fish, which had the misfortune of being trapped within the curtained enclosure. As we watched the net draw closer to the shore, we could see strange and interesting sea life caught within the nets, including skates, rays, bottom-dwelling fish, and smaller bass and herring. One of the little barefoot boys grabbed a skate by its tail and swung it around, smiling like an imp for my camera. We had a great seafood lunch at the restaurant in one of the hotels, then went up onto one of the sand dunes above the city to light off skyrockets. We engaged in a furious fireworks battle using fireworks we had purchased in Comas the night before. We found a large dune and went running and sailing off the top of it to see how far down its face we could land and tumble, covering ourselves from head to foot with sand. It was a great time. It was a kickoff for our Fourth of July, which was coming on Wednesday.

On Tuesday we helped a member family celebrate their little boy's birthday, teaching them several games they had never seen before, including pin the tail on the donkey and musical chairs. After work I took an eight-foot-hot-air tissue balloon we purchased, and some poster paints, and painted the U.S. flag on the balloon in the good old red, white, and blue. I planned to fill the balloon with hot air and send it up on the Fourth of July, creating a surprise for whichever Peruvian found the balloon descending with the U.S. flag on it. On the Fourth we awoke early to hold a 7:00 A.M. discussion. Like many discussions, it fell through, and we took off for a Lima Zone Conference at the Magdalena chapel. We had another great inspirational conference with President Driggs, came back and had lunch, and then went out into the cornfield a block from our pension to send up our hot-air balloon. What a disappointment! It was so windy, the flames from the little self-burning lamp, which was to hang below the balloon, caught the side of the balloon in a blaze of fire. The flames spread over the balloon as it took off, burning it in a blaze within thirty seconds from the takeoff. The balloon lasted only long enough for me to get a picture of a flash in the sky over the cornfield.

We continued to teach the Vila family, and hoped to get them more excited than the last time they'd gone through the discussions, some months before, with other missionaries. They were a close family that did everything together, and we felt that if we could focus them on the eternal family and the Plan of Salvation, we had a good chance of getting them in the water.

To continue our good relationship with the members, we started a study program for them. We picked a subject and brought them a list of scriptures and questions for them to study on the subject for several weeks. Later we returned and discussed the scriptures and the subject together with them. This helped them increase their gospel knowledge and drew them closer to us, further enabling them to trust us to teach the gospel to their friends. This trust was the key to effective missionary work.

In Comas we tried many creative missionary ideas. One new approach we started in July was that of looking up references of newly married folks in the public records at the city hall. Once we found the listings, we would visit them and offer them congratulations on their recent marriage and then ask them if they wished to learn about a marriage that lasted beyond this lifetime. We found several good references this way. Another idea we pursued was that of visiting the mayor and discussing our teachings with him. He became animated about the family principles we taught, and we received his permission to use his business cards when we walked through his city. We were allowed to use the cards as an introduction to hopefully open doors to us. The mayor also helped us organize a meeting at the local theater to show "Man's Search for Happiness" for those in town who wished to see it. This turned out to be a successful afternoon, with quite a few curious townspeople attending. Although we did not receive numerous references, it did expose our beliefs to the people of the town and perhaps laid the seeds for opening doors in the future.

There were many bad accidents in the areas we worked in Peru, especially on the main highway through Comas. These accidents were the result of a combination of factors, including: old, antiquated vehicles on the road; poor maintenance because of the inability to pay for up-keep and replacement parts; inexperienced drivers who did not have the opportunity to receive the same kind of driver training we had been accustomed to; and poor traffic control because of insufficient funds. In some areas of Lima, instead of actual traffic lights, there were policemen mounted on pedestals in boxes lit up at night, enabling them to direct traffic with their white-gloved hands, even in the dark. There was not enough technology to track down vehicles and drivers by license-plate numbers, registration numbers, and driver's license numbers. As a result, most accidents of any consequence were hit-and-run incidents.

Elder Gray and I saw the tragic consequences of these factors one day in early July on the main highway that led north out of Lima, through Comas, and then veered northeast up into the Andes. Because Comas was on a hill sloping from the west and going uphill to the east, the two lanes of the four-lane road going north were butted by a large concrete wall, with steps placed every fifty yards, leading up to the frontage road above it, where shops lay stretched out as far as the eye could see. The two lanes going south were also butted by a wall, but a wall which lay below it to accommodate the slope below it. Our pension was about two blocks below the road to the west of it. As we left our pension and walked up to the road on this memorable morning, we saw a crowd gathered around a bus that appeared to have crashed into the wall adjoining the northbound lanes. It did not appear to be anything serious until we approached the crowd and saw a horrible sight. Where the bumper of the bus had smashed into the wall, there was an arm sticking up bent at a completely unnatural angle. When the bus crashed, it had pinned a lady who'd been walking unawares along the highway toward the steps, with her groceries from her morning trip to the market. It had killed her instantly. This was only half the tragedy. The bus driver had been traveling too fast and had swerved, trying to miss another lady who had crossed the street without leaving herself enough distance. As the bus swerved, it slammed into her with its tail end, sending her flying and killing her before it rammed the wall, pinning and killing another lady against the wall. As with most serious accidents we heard of, the bus driver had fled, running up into the hills. Whether it could be shown he was at fault or not, or whether any of the drivers who hit, and then ran, were at fault, was a moot issue since it was unlikely they would ever be caught.

Elder Gray battled tonsillitis for several weeks in July. We traveled to Lima to visit a doctor at the clinic. He told Elder Gray that if his condition didn't clear up soon, the tonsils would have to be taken out. Now that was a scary thought—having your tonsils cut out in Peru in a clinic located in a barrio on the outskirts of Lima! Actually, if his tonsils had to be taken out, we would coordinate with the mission home to find a doctor they recommended. Elder Gray battled more than his tonsils in Comas. Probably because of his fair complexion, and his dry skin, the fleas found him a very savory target. I had no problems with the fleas, but Elder Gray constantly had his lower legs and ankles peppered with fiery red marks—flea feasting sites. With all the dust in our area, the fleas would find their way onto his socks as we were out tracting, and then would proceed to do a number on him.

We were up to the second discussion with the Vila family, but we sensed they were less than enthused since it was the second time they had been through the discussions. Elder Gray and I fasted and prayed for direction on how to excite them about the gospel. We were still working with Hermano Pastrana. Hermana Pastrana had wanted for months to be baptized, but we were trying to teach them and baptize them as a complete family. We found this provided the best chance of continued activity in the church. Hermano Pastrana was up and down, at times excited and at other times skeptical and almost hostile.

Two sister missionaries, whose focus was on health and hygiene, came to our district. They would be working with the members in Comas to try to raise their health standards. They could also teach discussions to investigators more receptive to sister missionaries. There were many who preferred visits by the sisters. They greatly enhanced our district's ability to teach the people of Co-mas.

We enjoyed the family we lived with. I played soccer with the *hermano* and his son on P-days or after work. He and his wife took us to a restaurant one evening to help them celebrate their anniversary. He had a good job, which enabled him to have a car, a very rare commodity in Peru. He drove us to an Argentine steakhouse on the cliff running along the coast of Lima. It was called the Rincon Gaucho—meaning something like "Cowboy Corner." We had a feast of thick steaks imported from Argentina.

All missionaries—in particular, those serving outside the United States—hunger for good entertainment. Occasionally we were allowed to see a good, upbeat movie, but they were rare, even when we were able to go. In July the Young Ambassadors from BYU arrived in Peru. All of the missionaries were able to go to their concert in Lima. It was fantastic. They provided great dancing, great singing, great comedy, and special effects. They filmed the program to play it on Peruvian television.

In Comas I started reading books on Peruvian archeology and ancient legends. We decided to build a discussion around the correlation between Peruvian prehistory and legends and the Book of Mormon. We presented this discussion to the Vila family and to the Pastranas. They both seemed interested. It was exciting to be teaching the actual descendants of the Book of Mormon people, especially when, through my reading, I'd found so many rich legends of ancient Peru that coincided with the teachings in the Book of Mormon.

Only a few weeks after the bus accident, we saw the results of another serious accident on the main road—the crumpled remains of a car, sitting in front of the police station, which, the night before, had run into the rear end of a jacked-up car on the main road. Everything above hood level, including the windshield and roof, was pushed back behind the rear seat. The car had gone completely underneath the jacked-up car and the driver's seat was bent back and completely covered with dried blood. A police officer, standing by the car, told us the driver had been drunk and had swerved into the car. He lost his head in the accident.

We attended a mission conference in downtown Lima on July 24—Pioneer Day. President Driggs asked me to arrive early. We did and he told me I was to be the district leader for the newly combined district of missionaries in both areas in Comas and the area in Tuahuantinsuyo, next to Comas. That was a shock, but I felt I could do a good job since I had really grown to love the people in our area. I had drawn close to the branch members and gained their trust and respect through cooperation with referrals and friendshiping. I also had a good relationship with each of the missionaries in the district. That evening

I was immediately tested to see if I was mature enough and patient enough to handle my new responsibilities. As we were walking toward the main road, two kids threw rocks at me, hitting me in the shoulder, and making me very, very angry. As I turned, I could see fear in the eyes of these kids. They could see steam coming out of my ears and lightning from my eyes. I must have matured at least a touch, though, since I did not throw a rock back at them—I knew I could peg them from my experience with throwing rocks at dogs. My only reaction was a withering look. Later that same evening, we knocked on the door of a young family, which a member had found and perceived to be interested. The father-in-law came to the door and told us, "Nobody's home and they told me they do not want to listen to your religion anyway." We could tell he was lying, so we went out of his store and knocked on the door adjoining it, which led to his son-in-law's house. The old man came running out, yelling, "Get away from that door." Before we could turn to leave, he pushed me. This was the second provocation of the evening, and I was starting to burn with anger. I gave my books to Elder Gray and told the old man he had better be careful, but fortunately, once again I restrained myself and the mother-in-law came out and calmed her husband down. Hopefully, the next day would be better!

As a district leader, I continued with the same work responsibilities in our own area but in addition, had administrative duties for all areas in our district, including regularly interviewing each missionary in the district and working with them from time to time. This involved "splitting," or sending other companions to work in our area with Elder Gray while I worked with one of the missionaries in his area.

We finally reached the point of giving Hermano Pastrana a challenge and set a baptismal date for August. We were at least encouraged that he did not reject it immediately, giving us a glimmer of hope he might make it.

For the Peruvian Independence Celebration days—July 28 and 29—the city blocked off the main highway, Tupac Amaru, named after a freedom fighter against the Spaniards, and conducted a huge parade. All the school kids, marching bands, military bands, military formations, and even a tank passed by. In anticipation of the Independence Days, everyone had been out painting the fronts of their houses bright colors. Most of the men, except our members, had stockpiled cases of beer to assist them in getting comfortably plastered on Friday night the twenty-seventh. We had a good vantage point for the parade. We climbed up on the roof of the bookstore fronting the Tupac Amaru Highway. We knew the owner of the store and he let us sit up on the roof. That evening we had a branch party at our church meetinghouse. To our surprise the Vila family came and seemed to have an enjoyable time intermingling with and laughing with the members.

We were working with three partly active families, trying to activate one spouse or the other. It was rewarding from a teaching standpoint, since there was always at least one enthused member of the family present at the discussions. President Driggs told us that reactivating an inactive family was as good as bringing in a nonmember, since we were reconverting members to the church who had strayed or fallen away.

Our constant hunger had us always looking for good snacks. We found a little old man with a pushcart containing a propane stove and all the ingredients for hot scones smothered with butter and honey. Elder Gray and I bought several of these scones and decided we had really found something. We frequented that cart until I left the area. We attended a baptism for President Fajardo's daughter and ended up at his house afterward for goodies—we were always receptive to snack opportunities! For once we went through a day without hunger. Later that night we gave the Word of Wisdom—a third discussion to the Vila family. It was a challenge because they liked their coffee. By the end of the discussion, though, they were receptive and we walked away with their coffee cans.

As district leader, I notified elders of their changes. Early in August I received changes for Elders Larsen and Gray, but had to hold on to them for a couple of days before they were to be informed. That Sunday we had another discussion with the Pastranas, but he seemed insincere and probably would not make his baptismal date in August. He would not accept our challenge to pray and ask God if he should be baptized, or if the Book of Mormon was true. We felt he was afraid of the answer. It was discouraging since we had been on a roller coaster with Hermano Pastrana for several months, and now it appeared he had completely bombed out.

Tuesday night I gave Elder Gray the envelope containing his change. He was shocked, he was going to Arequipa, a pretty town located in southern Peru at the base of a large volcano. We then delivered Elder Larsen's envelope. He was heading to my old area, La Victoria. That evening we made the traditional visits to the members, friends, and investigators so that Elder Gray could take some pictures and say his farewells. The next morning we arrived at the office early. I saw Elder Gray off and then picked up my new companion, Elder Garner, whom I had known when he was in my district in Maranga. He was a really "cool" elder and I knew we would get along great. Our first day together we visited with the mayor of Comas. He was always very friendly and he invited us to his home that night to teach his family the concept of the Family Home Evening. We held a Family Home Evening with his family. They were enthused and invited us back to present the first discussion.

The second Sunday in August we went to a district conference in Callao. Approximately eight-hundred members attended. President Driggs conducted the meeting and spoke. It was so rewarding to see the Suarez family there, whom I had taught in Callao but had not had the opportunity to see baptized. It was gratifying to see them progressing in learning the gospel. Hermano Suarez had held many responsible callings and, at the time of the conference, was working as a district missionary working with the full-time missionaries to find and teach investigators. The entire Vila, Pastrana, and Romero families attended the conference.

We took a taxi to the conference. On the way, the driver stopped to pick up what at first appeared to be a homely girl with long hair, a dress, a purse, and all the fixings. When "she" spoke to give directions to the driver, we suddenly realized "she" was actually a man. It reminded me of the cross dresser who lived next door to Elder Adsero and one in my first area—Callao. I did not dare look at Elder Garner because I knew he was barely containing the laughter I also felt building up and pushing for release. We grinned and gritted our teeth to hold it in until he/she was dropped off. The cab driver then joined us in belly laughs. There was nothing like a mission to open the eyes of naive nineteen and twenty-year-olds who had spent most of their lives in conservative places like Orange County, California.

I had another opportunity in Comas to experience, as President Driggs described it, smells I had never experienced before arriving in the mission field. The combination storm-sewer drain flooded over near the Tupac Amaru Highway, releasing torrents of filthy water that streamed down the street and through the lot by our pension, where we played soccer. It was hard to tell which was thicker, the water or the fumes and odors following the gooey, slimy mess which settled over the entire area. To divert the filth from the front of the house, we built a little dam we dubbed "Little Hoover." The dam succeeded in blocking the filthy water from the doorsteps, but at the same time, it created a fetid, stinky lake in the park. The little dam finally gave way that night, allowing dirty water to rip down through the lot, carrying dirt, and other debris that did not invite or warrant closer inspection, all over the street.

Elder Garner and I continued the creative streak we had going in Comas, with novel approaches to missionary work. We tried a new twist on the use of the municipal records, finding those with new babies, and going by their houses to visit, to discuss the concept of the eternal family. We also met with the director of a large school in our area, who invited us to give a presentation on the Family Home Evening to the parents of his schoolchildren. While on the "brainstorm," we met the chief of police in Comas and scheduled a meeting for all of his officers and their wives, to show them "Man's Search for Happiness." It was challenging and stimulating to be creative with the work and thus to avoid spinning our wheels with the same old door-knocking approaches. We enjoyed the school presentation and received good references. To pursue the idea, over the next few days we met with the directors of other schools and set up similar meetings with the mothers of the students in one school, and the teachers and parents at another. If these meetings accomplished nothing more than helping us diffuse the myths and lies circulating about the Mormons, they were a success.

Visits to the hospital in Comas also gave us missionary opportunities. We visited members and investigators—in addition to giving us a chance to practice our priesthood and give healing blessings, we also spoke about the gospel with those in the surrounding beds and rooms. Since there were no television sets or other entertainment in the hospital, we usually found a captive audience hungry for any diversion or conversation to take their minds off their illnesses and boredom. Tremendous teaching opportunities arose with those who witnessed the priesthood blessings we gave. Some wondered if perhaps they might benefit from a blessing and we explained that with faith they could indeed benefit.

At one of the school meetings we used a huge presentation board we created to show the concept of a Family Home Evening. We passed around a sign-up list with a place for addresses. This list provided us with a few good references after the meeting. At one of these school meetings we obtained seventeen good references. This was topped off the same night by a great fifth discussion with the Vila family, whose members accepted a baptismal challenge for September 1. They had finally become excited about the gospel, primarily because of the friendships and associations they had developed with the members in Comas.

I had managed to interest Elder Garner in ancient Peruvian archeology and legends by discussing with him what I was reading in the books I had purchased on these subjects. To pursue our interest, we learned from one of the brothers at church that there were ruins spread throughout the valley, just a few miles north of our area. We hopped a bus one P-day in August and traveled up the Tupac Amaru Highway until we could see hills in the distance rising up out of cornfields. We were dropped off on the deserted road and walked across the cornfields, heading toward what, from a distance appeared to be natural dusty gray hills. On our way through the fields, we could see telltale signs of ruins—broken-down old adobe walls put together with hand-shaped adobes formed into thick walls shaped like large stones. As we closed in on some of the hills, we could see that their base was surrounded at one time by huge fortress walls built in the same way. We had seen pictures of the ruins of the Incas and the pre-Inca people up in the Andes and highland areas, where granite had been available. It appeared that down on the coast, where rock was unavailable, the Incas had utilized a similar architectural style, only in adobe. The adobe had been put together and creased every so often to make it appear like seams in giant rocks.

We found a passageway through the huge wall at the base of one of the hills and climbed to the top of it, looking out over the valley. As we climbed, we passed areas where treasure hunters had dug into the pyramid and left leg bones, arm bones, and skulls strewn all over the hill, scattered between pieces of burial cloth and pottery that had been interred with the mummies. At the top of the first pyramid, we found a hole excavated by the grave robbers. A mummified forearm and hand protruded from one side of the hole. It was completely intact, with dried leather skin and all of the fingers, down to the finger. nails. Upon closer examination, we saw a mummified calf and foot in the same condition, sticking out, as well as a complete skull with all its teeth.

With the mummy, there was an ancient bag containing fossilized cocaine leaves that had been buried with the dead pre-Incan people for their use in the afterlife. These sites dated back well before the Incas into the 800—1000 A.D. time period. Also surrounding the mummy were pieces of cloth still showing stylized birds and other motifs in different colors, preserved by the lack of any moisture or rain in this part of Peru. There were also pieces of pottery with different-colored designs. It was quite an adventure to walk over these pyramids, then go to the next hill in the distance, in some farmer's cornfield, rising up out of the stocks of surrounding corn, and finding other comparable bits of ancient Peruvian history lying around. We found one site with huge walls, multiple steps and doorways, and internal rooms. We were careful not to disturb the sites, and did no digging of our own, but simply observed what had been uncovered by those that had been less reverential toward the past.

This trip definitely put the archeology bug into Elder Garner and me. We spent the next two P-days on similar expeditions. From reading in my books, I learned of one site that dated back 2,000 years before Christ. The pictures of it showed a restored, beautiful stone temple that we wanted to find. We asked members and investigators if they had heard of it. It was called "El Paraiso," or the Paradise. No one had heard of it. Much like people every-where who take for granted the attractions close to them, many of the people we encountered in Peru had really not taken much interest in the fabulous archeological sites close to them. Of course it was hard to find fault with them, when for the most part these people were mostly concerned with simply eking out a living and providing food for their families.

We took buses to the desolate hills where I expected to find El Paraiso, and ran into a farmer who had seen it. We hitched a ride with him in the back of his pickup through the cornfields to the base of a hill between Co-mas and the coast. He told us the ruins lay somewhere around the hill to the side of us. As we walked up and crested the hill, there in the fog, standing alone at the base of the hill on the other side, nestled between the hill and corn fields, was the beautiful stone temple, completely restored. We walked through it, taking it in and taking good pictures. There were two ceremonial fonts in the main room near the front stairways, which appeared to be baptismal fonts. Since the site had been restored, there had been no damage done to it or the surrounding area by grave robbers, and there were no artifacts like cloth or bones in the area.

On our next P-day, we left early again by bus and traveled up the main highway, north of Comas, on the way into the Andes. We traveled farther north than we had before, until we could see what appeared in the distance to be an entirely uninhabited city at the base of the mountain. We walked across a valley, heading toward the base of the mountain. As we approached, we grew more excited, because we could see an entire ancient city, largely intact, with walls, rooms, walkways, steps, and burial grounds. A river flowed close by and probably provided water to the city when it was in its glory, some 1,000 years before. Remnants of the main walls were twenty feet high in parts, built with rock and mortar. We were the only people within miles of this site. It was desolate, making it eerie to walk through doorways, into rooms and down streets in a ghost town from 1000 A.D.!

As we looked into burial tombs, through narrow passageways underneath the remains of houses, mummies with emergent skulls and teeth leered at us in silence with that macabre death grin that only skeletons possess. Pots, vases, potter shards, and pieces of cloth were strewn throughout. We did not dig or excavate but we looked through the holes in the floors of the houses and observed. We collected pieces of pottery lying loose and exposed because of grave robbers, and also gathered a few of the better fragments of cloth that had not been completely sun bleached. I found a skullcap with a tie string woven from llama fur, and a throwing stick that had been used as a weapon. This was quite an adventure! We killed a snake with rocks when it slithered in upon us in one of the houses, and Elder Garner found a young falcon that had an injured wing.

Our afternoon slipped away much too fast. When it came time to leave, we gathered our artifacts and the falcon and headed toward the main road. We had to wait a while for a bus heading back to Comas, making us late for a district meeting. We decided to go directly to the meeting as we did not have time to change. As we paraded in with the falcon on a shoulder, a mummified forearm with a hand raised up in a grotesque claw, pieces of pottery in hand, cloth hung over our arms, and a full skull with a jawbone and teeth, we created a scene which, in hind-sight, was akin to an "Indiana Jones" entrance. The other elders in the district looked at us in wide-eyed amazement. Several murmured, "I don't know where they've been, and I don't know where they're going next P-day, but one thing's for sure, we're following them." After the distraction took its toll and things quieted down, we finished the district meeting, then headed, with our archeological entourage, back to our pension. There, superstition awaited us. The lady of the house refused to let the falcon in on grounds that it was bad luck. If she thought that was bad luck, I can only imagine what went through her mind when I scared the living daylights out of her by putting on my black trench coat and reaching around the corner with the mummified forearm and grotesque fingers sticking out of the sleeve of the trench coat, the skull and jawbone following close behind at head level. I probably should have checked how sound her heart was before I pulled this stunt, but we got a serious laugh out of it, and she did not hold it against us. We let the falcon go in the cornfield next to our house and wished it good luck.

Shortly after our "Indiana Jones" expedition, we received a wondrous surprise. All of the seventeen references from our last school demonstration proved to be actual addresses, and actual people who had attended the presentation. There was not a single false listing! We set up at least ten discussions from these references.

We gave special attention to the two teenage boys of the Vila family, Jaime and Miguel, since they seemed to be the most reluctant. We worked hard to help them make their baptismal goal of the first of September. About a week after the family set this goal, we passed the *big* hurdle with them—they accepted and agreed to pay tithing and to keep the Sabbath day holy. Sabbath-day observance was difficult in Peru since Sundays seemed to revolve around soccer playing and socializing at parties.

I worked with Elder Shelton, from Corona, California, (about 20 minutes from my home), in his area—Tahuantinsuyo. He was one of the missionaries in my district, and it was my responsibility to occasionally work with all the other missionaries. I found he hated Peruvian dogs more than I did. At least I had the great restraint to only throw at dogs who were threatening me. Elder Shelton threw at sleeping dogs on the theory he would teach them a lesson before they had a chance to bother him!

The members in Comas were unbelievable. To assist us in helping the Vila family feel welcome and to keep their baptismal commitment, they found out it was Hermano Vila's birthday. They gathered at midnight and performed a guitar and singing serenade for him outside his window. He came to the door with tears in his eyes, unable to believe the warmth and camaraderie among the group of friends he had made at the church. I knew that at that moment we had them.

Through our friendship with the mayor of Comas, we were allowed to go into the town hall and show the movie "Man's Search for Happiness" to all members of the administrative staff at City Hall. The mayor was so cooperative, he gave us a list of employees, so we could go talk to those unable to see the movie. Later that night I had my first baptismal interviews, as a district leader, with two children of members. It seemed a bit strange to be sitting and interviewing them about their worthiness. I guess that was natural for my first interview. I taught the investigator class, which I found enjoyable since I was able to think well on my feet and was starting to develop as a teacher. Comas brought out such a vision of the missionary work in me. I was brimming with joy, and as I look back in my journal, I found this entry:

I am really starting to get a better vision of the work as a missionary, I really do love these Peruvian people, and when I look at the Romero family, I feel great joy at having been able to help them receive the gospel.

One surprise to a missionary is how much his family changes, and the fact that life goes on at home without him or her. I received the shocking news that my little sister was now engaged. I could not believe this; it made me feel old. She and her fiancée decided to set the date shortly after I would arrive home after my mission, so I could be there to see it. I was indeed happy I would be there for the wedding.

Elder Perry and I were reunited when he transferred into my district, coming to Tahuantinsuyo as Elder Shel-ton's companion. I had an opportunity to work with him again for a day and found he was now much better adapted to the mission field and seemed to be enjoying his mission.

We went down the home stretch with the Vila family, setting up a member party for their baptism, and stopping by and having them bear their testimonies. It was a wonderful experience. Each of them bore a testimony of the truthfulness of the gospel, based on the answers they had received to their prayers about the Book of Mormon, Joseph Smith, and the church. Elder Garner and I were deeply moved and felt humbled to be a part of their conversion.

But unfortunately, now that we were near to a rewarding moment with this family, I received another change. I was to head to Arequipa, a beautiful city in the mountains of southern Peru at the base of a volcano, where I would be a zone leader with Elder Costley—what a shock! Fortunately, however, I did not have to report to the office until after the weekend when the Vilas were to be baptized. Once again, we continued to check on the "three-day" baptismal font at the Comas meetinghouse to make sure it filled up, and that Saturday we had the baptismal service, which culminated again on a high point when each of the Vilas bore his or her testimonies at the meeting. I knew I would greatly miss Comas, with the warmth of its members, and the deep relationships I had developed with those we had taught and seen enter the waters of baptism. I also knew these were eternal friends. As my last Sunday in Comas arrived, I was a little down, sad about leaving the wonderful members and friends in Comas, but also looking forward to Arequipa. I hoped that the new Elder coming in would be able to play the piano, since I had provided accompaniment for the choir, the sacrament meeting, Sunday school, primary, and just about every other activity in the district. The Vilas and Romeros were upset to hear I was leaving but they, and the other families I had taught and grown close to, came over to wish me a farewell on Sunday evening—I was leaving on Wednesday. On P-day we spent much of the time visiting members and friends. There were many hugs and many tears shed. We were fed so much on my last day in Comas that I really felt uncomfortably full, but didn't have the heart to turn anything down since the members were so eager to give.

We woke up early Wednesday morning to head to the mission home. The mission home was in the same neighborhood as the Chilean Embassy, and it happened to be September 12, either the day that President Allende of Chile was killed by the Chilean military in a coup, or the day after. The Chilean Embassy was swarming with high-ranking officials of the Allende government who had escaped from Chile as the military junta took control.

It was a pleasure to talk to President Driggs about my new assignment before I had to leave for the airport. After a pleasant one-hour flight, I arrived in beautiful Arequipa, with the sun shining through its crystal blue skies on the snow-capped volcano—Misti—which sits above the city as a constant beacon.

# Chapter 10
## Leading a Zone and Chasing Ancient Legends in Arequipa

Arequipa is in the high desert surrounded with beautiful, arid, clear mountain air. The city sits at the base of a volcano that goes up to about twenty-thousand feet and usually has a snowcap. The volcano's name is Misti, and much of the white lava stonework in the old section of the city was cut by the Spaniards out of lava flows from Misti. They used it to make beautiful white archways, buildings, and cobblestones that gave the city a real Spanish flavor. I could tell, flying over it, I would grow to love the city. Streams and irrigation meandered around the city, creating a dark verdant green patchwork. Mountain streams cascaded down from the nearby twenty-thousand-foot-plus mountain range, and cattle and sheep grazed on the outskirts of the city. I could also tell it would be easy to work with and enjoy Elder Costley. He had blond, thinning hair, smiling blue eyes, and a sunny disposition to match his surfer's good looks. He met me at the airport and we took a taxi to our pension.

I immediately began to enjoy our pension and the Fuentes family, whom we lived with. Jaime, the father/husband, who was short, a bit paunchy, with a black mustache, and a mischievous childlike grin, had a great sense of humor and a desire to tease the missionaries. His wife, Maria, was larger than Jaime, both taller and heavier set, but she was an attractive lady with a good sense of humor to match Jaime's. Their son, Pavel, about five years old, had received more attention than any child I knew. They enjoyed having the missionaries living with them, and we grew to love the family. We lived in a small one-room apartment atop their garage behind the house, but ate our meals with them in the main dining room. They had a piano, which enabled me to practice on a daily basis.

On my first day in Arequipa, while out tracting, I mentally wandered back to BYU. Everywhere we looked in the valley we were surrounded by mountains with snow caps, green fields, and a beautiful clear blue sky. I also thought I was dreaming when I took my first shower at the pension. It was the first working shower I had encountered, one which actually rinsed off all the soap with a strong stream of hot water, so that I didn't itch and dance like a man with hives afterward. The Fuentes family appeared to have adopted the missionaries. They treated us more like sons. They became so attached that Hermano Jaime refused to ever go to the airport to see the missionaries off since he got too emotional.

I finally met a couple of dogs I liked on my second day in Arequipa. Elder Costley took me to meet a member couple and their two boxers, Rex and Kaiser. After our visit, we left and apparently Rex and Kaiser slipped out of the gate, inadvertently left open, and followed us all the way back to our pension, a couple of blocks away. We tried to ditch them but they kept chasing us. We started down one road while they were not looking, then ran back up the street and around to our pension. They must have spotted us because when we looked out from the curtain, they were sitting out in front of the house! As we visited this member family over the course of my stay in Arequipa, it became a regular routine to have Rex, the bigger of the two boxers, jump the fence after we left, to follow us as we tracted. Kaiser was smaller and could not jump the fence, but because of the jealousy between the two and their affection for us, once Rex made it back from his missionary outings, Kaiser would attack him. They would get into angry battles, with Kaiser taking out his frustration at being unable to follow us. It got to the point where we could not show affection to one or the other when we visited with the family, because out of jealousy, they would attack each other.

At first we thought Rex was a wimp, although, to look at him, he was one of the sturdiest dogs I had ever seen, standing three feet high at the head, two and a half at the back, and every inch of him was solid, beige muscle—he indeed bulged with well-defined brawn. However, as he followed us one day, we passed a yard with a small mongrel dog sitting in it. This little nuisance came charging out at us. Without as much as a whimper, let alone a battle, Rex went dashing off. We thought, "What a wimp." We soon learned differently as we rounded a corner and Rex saw a German shepherd that he must have had some bad history with. Without any hesitation, Rex charged the much bigger German shepherd, pinned him on the ground, and grabbed his head between his jaws. He might well have suffocated him, had a car not almost run over the two of them, causing them to break apart. The German shepherd fled for his life.

Rex's fighting prowess would come in handy later. His boldness at times became an embarrassment. Once, while we were knocking on doors, a lady opened her door and Rex strutted in as if he had an open invitation. The startled woman asked, "Is this your dog?" We answered honestly, albeit somewhat misleadingly, "No." We did state, however, "We will be happy to try and help you get him out of your house, though." It actually worked out to be quite a good door opener and led to further discussions with this family.

I was reunited with Elder Gray again, after having sent him up to Arequipa, from my district in Comas, a month before. I was also reunited with Elder Partridge, who had been my companion in Maranga over four months earlier. Shortly after I arrived in Arequipa, President Driggs visited to present the same district conference I had attended in Lima. The president traveled throughout the various church districts, conducting conferences on a regular schedule.

At times I still had Comas on my mind. I had really enjoyed it there. The Comas Branch was one of the best I had ever experienced. Of course, I also missed my family and my girlfriend as well, and there were times at night, after we got in bed, that my mind wandered, and I shed a few tears from the heartache of missing loved ones, both at home and in past areas I had worked in. This just came with mission work, and I seldom let it get me down, but as a missionary, you never quite get completely used to the separation it creates. I suppose that is good, because I certainly appreciated my family more when I returned.

I encountered a whole different stratum of society where we lived and worked in Arequipa. Unlike Comas, the people in our area in

Arequipa were of the upper class, living in nicely laid-out plaster-covered homes with green landscaped yards. Many in the area had automobiles. We were just on the outskirts of downtown, where there were cobblestone streets, and most of the buildings were constructed of white, carved volcanic stone, giving them a clean appearance. Because of the upper-class nature of the people in our area, it was tough to get into their homes, or even to strike up a conversation. Many of the people were proud and lacked the humility, of those in Comas, to have an open mind to our message. I carried over a few of the teaching approaches from Comas. Shortly after I arrived, Elder Costley and I arranged to show "Man's Search for Happiness" to the teachers at a school near our pension.

I worked with Elder Partridge's companion, Elder Magelby, in their area for a day. Their area was on the far side of town, toward the mountains, and was filled with large farms and a beautiful valley that we traveled to via a cobblestone road in the countryside. It was a beautiful scene. Elder Magelby was a very aggressive, outgoing, and somewhat dominating senior companion, not because of any ill motive, but simply because he was so enthused about the work. My guess was, Elder Partridge did not get many words in edgewise in their door approaches or teaching situations. It was hard, in missionary work, to find the right balance between companions and their contributions toward discussions, door approaches, and teaching. There were as many types of companionships as there were individuals.

There were companionships in which senior companions dominated everything, others where a senior companion did nothing, leaving everything for the junior companion, and yet others where both were too lazy to do anything. Then there were those where the combination worked magic. Stories about lazy elders circulated through the mission. One of the most famous tales involved the son of a general authority. He was stationed in an outlying area and he and his companion had the habit of sleeping until about 9:00 A.M., casually rolling out of bed to do a little work, then generally "goofing around" between lunch and dinner, and coming back in at an early hour for pleasure reading. Apparently, his father found out about his lazy approach to missionary work and made a surprise visit to Peru while he was in South America for church business. He dropped by his son's area and knocked on his door about 9:00 in the morning. One of the elders yelled out "What do you want, we're in bed, go away." When the general authority said who he was, there was an immediate scurrying around until the door was opened by a tousle-haired, sleepy-eyed, stunned elder. As the story went, he got his act together after this surprise visit and finished an honorable mission.

The main road between our pension's neighborhood and the downtown area was just down a block from our pension. Across the main road from us was the hospital and the adjoining morgue. Occasionally, we would see hospital staff members wheeling a body from the hospital, down the sidewalk, and up to the morgue. This led to the inevitable joke that we really didn't like the recovery rate in the hospital. If we had to be hospitalized, we joked that we wouldn't want to be there. It led to an additional joke that although no one else seemed to want to listen to us, we could probably find a captive audience for our discussions in the morgue. It was more difficult to find open-minded people in the provinces, like in Arequipa-traditions were more deep-rooted outside the metropolitan Lima area.

Two weeks after I arrived in Arequipa, Elder Costley received a change in the package. He would be heading north to Chiclayo. We were joking that night with Hermano Fuentes about his cousin and his cousin's wife—the "Mooches." Hermano Fuentes said, "Watch and see, they will drop in about dinnertime tonight, I will guarantee it, and they will act like it is an accident that they drop in at dinnertime." In fact, they did drop by and waited for an invitation, responding, "Well if you are going to insist, we won't offend you by refusing to eat with you." Elder Costley and I both tired of this same routine over the course of several weeks.

We had a compassionate service opportunity with one of the sisters in the branch, who was in the hospital and needed blood. We spent most of one morning searching for members who could donate, then organized the group at the hospital to provide the blood she needed. I much preferred getting out and serving, rather than the administrative chores. Being a zone leader involved a lot more paper shuffling. I had to gather reports from the district leaders, as well as filling out our own zone-leader reports, and then assemble the package to messenger it to the mission home.

On the Friday that Elder Costley was to leave, the Fuentes family took us to lunch. We went to a fancy restaurant downtown, where they served us an Argentine feast. We had little portable barbecue pits on our table grilling a variety of meats and steaks. We gorged! Afterward, Hermano Fuentes drove us up into the valley for Elder Costley to take beautiful pictures of Arequipa and its famous volcano, Misti. He took us to a fabulous dream house up on the bluff, overlooking a beautiful green valley with a river running through it. This house was cantilevered over the edge of the cliff and had a man-made canal running from the backyard of the house, down the mountain and to the river. There were small boats at the house that the owner could ride down into the valley, from which he'd thereafter be towed back up by cable.

My new companion was Elder Shelton, who had been in my district in Comas. He and I were both strong willed, outspoken, and opinionated. We decided, through the course of our companionship in Arequipa and thereafter, that we were better friends when we were not companions. We had a few "rocky" times, but usually smoothed these over. Our senses of humor and interests in the Book of Mormon, missionary work, and basketball helped us find a common ground for working as a team. One of the greatest opportunities of a mission, as I noted earlier, was the chance to live with different personalities, learning tolerance and patience, adapting to their annoying habits and traits while they adapted to mine. Looking back, I realize this give-and-take better prepared me for the personality trials of school and the workplace. Missionaries who did not loosen up and learn to accommodate their companions had a miserable mission experience.

In Comas it took three days to fill the baptismal font and then it was only half full, requiring contortions to get the person underwater. In contrast, in Arequipa our first baptismal service caused a flood. Not only was the font full, but someone let the sink in the chapel overflow, and so we had to push over two inches of water out of the hall and kitchen and into the drain in the ladies' bathroom.

This distraction was followed by yet another, as a sparrow flew into the chapel through an open window during the service. It was flying around during the meeting, trying to find its way out of the building.

Everyone soon diverted their attention from the speakers to this poor sparrow that was doing loops and other maneuvers above the pulpit, trying to find an opening. Once the distractions subsided—the bird hid in the rafters—the service ended on a spiritual high.

Our zone included Tacna, a small town in the coast-al desert near the border of Chile. As zone leader, my responsibility was to travel to Tacna on a regular basis to work with the missionaries there. After four weeks in Arequipa I left for my first visit to Tacna. It took a six-and-a-half-hour ride on a bus that was completely uncomfortable. It had seats that reclined, but the shocks didn't seem to work that well as we bounced along. The bus did not have a bathroom and we made only one stop during the six-and-a-half-hour trip, at a little "hole-in-the-wall" cafe that had a hole in the floor for a bathroom. The room was filthy and I was overpowered by the stench created by previous users with poor aim. Just another one of those smells and sights that President Driggs had warned me about!

The first half of the trip was scenic. We traveled alongside the river that flowed from the Andes into Arequipa and then south. The valley was green and beautiful. After three hours we reached the desert. There was nothing to see, except sand dunes, as far as I could see. I managed to sleep most of the way and arrived at 2:00 in the afternoon. The elders in Tacna were surprised to see me. They had not received my telegram. Tacna was a quaint little town with narrow cobblestone streets. Desert fir trees fronted the main roads and the houses appeared old but well maintained. Tacna was an outpost to protect Peru's border with Chile. Murals of military scenes, made from colored rock, in the hillside surrounded the town. The district leader in Tacna, Elder Farnsworth, introduced me to the president of the branch and the mission leader, so I could help them coordinate with the radio station that would carry the General Conference in October. We visited the radio station to confirm they would be carrying the conference.

During my first evening in Tacna, Elder Farnsworth and I met a man from Chile who told us about a war Chile had won with Peru. I was surprised he was living in Peru, in view of his Chilean nationalistic attitude. I worked with Elder Farnsworth to help inject a little enthusiasm into his approach in door knocking and teaching. He was quite capable and knowledgeable, but seemed a little shy when meeting potential investigators. There were Chifas—Chinese restaurants—everywhere in Peru. Elder Farnsworth, Elder Martin, and I went to one after work on my second night in Tacna. I spent three days in Tacna then boarded the bus for an uneventful trip back to Arequipa.

Elder Shelton and I met one Saturday with President Gonzales, the branch president in Arequipa, to discuss branch problems. The branch seemed torn with strife because of gossip, backbiting, and pride. A few old time members felt they had been in the church long enough to know how it worked and the new members didn't. There was also some insensitivity in planning socials. Some required contributions for bands and refreshments, which meant that many of the members could not afford to participate. We tried to work with President Gonzales to overcome some of these problems.

We felt the wrath of the Fuentes one morning. The night before, Rex, our boxer companion, followed us home as he usually did after jumping his wall. He forced his way into the house and scared the little girl of the people renting upstairs half to death. We grabbed him and pulled him through the back, up the stairs, and into our room to take pictures of him. It was quite comical. As we were leaving, he further ingratiated himself with the Fuentes by rounding the corner ahead of us and making Hermana Fuentes chalk white with his ugly pug face. We were scared the next day—we were afraid to go out and work because it was "National Dignity Day." This was the fifth anniversary of the event in which the government of Peru kicked the U.S. oil companies out of Peru. A great celebration for a couple of U.S. missionaries! I decided it would be best to keep a low profile that day.

After the "celebration" I switched companions to work with Elder Gray. He had scheduled a meeting with various businessmen downtown, including bankers, lawyers, and salespeople. I found it interesting that we were both at ease and comfortable while talking with these men. I could not envision myself as a twenty-year-old in the United States trying to talk to comparable business. men. Being a representative of Jesus Christ in the mission field gave us courage to handle situations for which we would otherwise feel inadequate.

I found it difficult to stay enthused about the work in Arequipa, having come from Comas, where we had been in the process of teaching and baptizing on a regular basis, with the enthusiastic support of all the members. Al-though I loved the beauty of Arequipa and the warmth we felt with the Fuentes family, the work was definitely harder and we were not teaching on a regular basis. Areas in Peru I would have chosen because of geographic beauty or exotic flavor, such as Iquitos, with the Amazon River and the jungle, or Arequipa, with its beautiful mountains, volcano, and lush green valleys, were not the areas where I had the most success. Comas, with its dusty, boring roads and adobe, wood, and bamboo hovels, was nothing to look at or get excited about for scenery or location, but it was great for missionary work. I realized if I wanted to get out of my "funk," I had to get over looking back, and had to make my experience in Arequipa as meaningful as my experience in Comas.

Elder Shelton and I talked to the public relations manager in a large bank downtown and received an invitation to show his family a film on the Family Home Evening, as kind of a preview to giving the presentation to the employees at his bank. We started visiting more frequently with the members to gain their confidence as I had done in Comas, in order to involve them more in providing references and friendshiping those we were teaching. We held a baptismal service for a young man I had interviewed for two of the other elders in Arequipa. In looking at what he had gone through to get to the point of baptism, I realized how much I had taken the gospel for granted, having grown up with it. His family ostracized him and his fiancée dropped him, because she wanted to be married in the Catholic church.

Halfway through my mission, I started a practice I wished I had started at the beginning—meditating and writing down my thoughts in a diary after my morning prayers. This period of contemplation helped me sort out my feelings and focus on the missionary work as well as understanding different principles of the gospel I chose to focus on. It also provided listening time to the Spirit to receive answers, instead of quickly shutting off communication at the end of my prayers before I received a response. I received many missionary ideas this way.

By the time I reached Arequipa, I had been away from home long enough that friends and acquaintances seemed to be strange memories.

It was hard to picture my local ward, school, friends, and all others, except my family and my girlfriend, from whom I continued to receive correspondence, tapes, and photographs.

We gave the Family Home Evening presentation at the bank of the public relations man, but got very little response. He tried to be helpful, providing us with a list of his employees' addresses, so we could visit them individually.

Elder Farnsworth and his companion journeyed up from Tacna for a Zone Conference, and I saw how well I had taught Elder Farnsworth how to protect himself from the canines. We were out knocking on doors and he pegged two dogs that always came charging out at us, before I had my rocks halfway out of my pockets! One of these dogs got what was coming to him later that week. This midsize black, pantherlike creature lived in a housing tract we frequented when we went door knocking. He always waited until we were just past his house and then he slinked out furtively from an opening between the side fence and the house in an effort to ambush and bite us on the backs of our legs. We were usually prepared for him, and would scare him back, but we tired of the routine and worried that eventually he would catch us. We were determined to teach him a lesson. We packed our pockets with a few rocks and developed a plan—Elder Shelton would lag back, I would go forward as the bait, and as the dog came running out, Elder Shelton would cut off his path of retreat by standing next to the gap in the fence. The plan unfolded beautifully. As we approached, the sneaky dog came out, trying to get me, but panicked when he saw Elder Shelton blocking his escape route. He took off at full speed, running away from us as we threw a few rocks in his general direction. The rocks didn't come close to him, but as he was in a full speed panic run, his back legs tightened up. It was perplexing. He was running hard without getting anywhere. He dragged his back legs for a few seconds, then his front legs tightened up and he fell on his side, sliding to a stop in convulsions. Our postmortem conclusion was that he died of a heart attack or a stroke. We really felt bad, we had only wanted to scare him. We hid out at the corner store to see what the reaction would be. Apparently, "Rover" was not well thought of even by his family. One of the kids walked over to see if the mutt was alive. The kid reared back and gave the corpse a solid soccer kick right in the head! A very gentle and grieving way to find out! If not before, the dog was most certainly dead at that point. We felt a little vindicated—perhaps the dog's owners felt he had been a menace also. There was now one less nuisance to us. We felt sorry but later jokingly called each other a "dog killer," even though neither of us had had any real intention of hurting the dog.

In Arequipa I had the "privilege" of learning a whole new set of discussions. The church was going from the rigid discussions using flannel board presentations—which required investigators to give correct answers to ordered concepts before moving to the next—to a more free-flowing inspiration-based set of discussions out of a loose-leaf notebook. The new discussions were easier to pick up because they allowed the missionaries more opportunities to elaborate and expound upon the gospel. They were flexible and more open to relying on the Spirit to focus on a gospel issue that appeared to be important to the family. But, no matter how I looked at it, it meant I had to learn twice as many discussions as did missionaries just coming out or those who had gone home. I would not miss the rigidity of the older "Law of Moses" discussions. Because as a rule we were not to move on to another gospel teaching until the investigator correctly answered questions about the prior teaching, I remembered per-forming ridiculous clue-prompting machinations in order to solicit correct answers. One example involved waving two fingers in their faces as we asked, "How many di-vine personages appeared to Joseph Smith in the Sacred Grove?" It was like an elementary-school quiz, with the teacher helping the class cheat! There was one time when our audience got the number of personages right, but not their identities. After carefully going over the First Vision, we asked, "Who appeared to Joseph Smith?" With. out hesitation, they replied, "Mary and Joseph." The real value of the new discussions was in taking us to a higher level. We had to teach more with the Spirit and less with rote memorized presentations.

October 18 was called "Senor de los Milagros," or Lord of the Miracles Day. We saw huge processions of people marching up the cobblestone streets toward the cathedrals in central Arequipa, carrying huge images of Christ, Mary, and saints on poles. Thousands followed the images, carrying candles. Some in the crowd flagellated themselves with whips while others walked barefoot or on their knees on the cobblestones in the cold weather. Knees and feet became bloodied and bruised. These victims of self-abuse believed they could grow closer to God through inflicting pain. It was a complete misconception of the gospel and the Lord's message.

One P-day in October, Hermano Fuentes took us to a small town, thirty minutes outside of Arequipa, where we sat in the thermal baths. The baths were huge concrete spas filled with hot mineral water flowing out of the ground from underneath the volcano, Misti. The water was heated naturally by underground steam and heat generated within the volcano. It was soothing and enjoyable. Hermano Fuentes enjoyed our company. He had a lot of fun with us and we had fun with him.

In Arequipa, as in every other area I had been in, the mornings seemed fruitless. We knocked on doors and looked up references but because the men were not home, the women were reluctant to talk with us or to schedule anything without the husband's approval. We often visited with members in the morning hours, always finding a welcome reception there. A major enjoyment in the mission field involved drawing close to the members and becoming a part of their lives. One of the hermanas was about to have a baby and asked for a blessing. We gave her a blessing before she went to the hospital to deliver. I saw all aspects of life among the members in the mission field, everything from the death of our friend Lucho in Comas, and his funeral, to the blessing of this hermana for her to deliver a healthy baby and start a new life. A few days later we dropped by to see her new baby boy. Both were in good health. We tried to help the members where we could. We noticed the hermano of one family stopped coming to church, so we stopped by to visit his wife. She told us he was rejoining bad friends to go out drinking. We scheduled a Family Home Evening to draw closer to them and reactivate the hermano.

One Sunday in October, Elder Shelton and I had an argument over how to get to church. As we were zone leaders, I felt we should set a proper example of promptness and since we were running late, I flagged down a taxi.

Elder Shelton figured we should go by bus because it was cheaper. He complained all the way to the church, which drove me crazy. My philosophy was that complaining only spawned negative attitudes and bitterness among companions. As we arrived, I reacted badly. I snapped in anger, saying, that I would pay for the whole taxi ride, and I then wadded up the bill, threw it at Elder Shelton, and told him to pay the cab driver as I stormed out of the cab. It was not uncommon to have a few squabbles in the mission field with companions, but it did not pay to let a squabble drag on because of the negative impact it had on the work. We needed the Spirit to be effective missionaries. We could not kneel in prayer together as companions and sincerely ask for help with our investigators if we felt unkindly toward each other. Elder Shelton and I were able to put this conflict behind us after church.

Downtown, by the post office, where we mailed and received the package with the zone's mail, a beggar was wearing an old grease-stained suit. He had long, unkempt, matted whiskers, and greasy hair covered in part by an old felt hat, whose dark color contrasted with his long, white, goat-hair mustache. He had gone barefoot so long, his feet were all dried, callused, and cracked. He was a fixture at the post office, always standing there with an old wooden cane and with his hand out. He got to know us well because every time we passed his outstretched hand we would shake it and greet him with a friendly grin. This always started him giggling. Occasionally, we also dropped change in his hand while shaking it. We became friends.

For our big event for October we put on a good old-fashioned American spook alley for the Peruvian members, at a party at the church the day after All Saints Day. Not that we were celebrating All Saints Day in our church, but it was a national holiday. The day after was in essence Halloween, although in Peru it was called the "Day of the Witches." This went back to the ancient origins of Halloween when people believed the spirits of those who had died were allowed to come out of the cemeteries for All Saints Day, to be revered and honored. After coming out, they grew angry in the evening—"Hallowed Eve"—about returning to their graves. Because of their anger, on "Hallowed Eve" the spirits played pranks on people and scared them. Thus evolved "Hallowed Eve," or Halloween, and the "Day of the Witches," following All Saints Day. On All Saints Day everyone went to the cemetery to celebrate and leave flowers on the graves.

We prepared mightily for our spook alley, gathering everything from an actual skeleton to a coffin—we were teaching a mortician. We set a few of the more creative missionaries to work with their science skills, creating "Jacob's ladders"—electrical generating boxes with diverging wires on top, which sent up a steady stream of electrical arcs like something out of a Frankenstein movie. We put together an elaborate spook alley. We started the members out in a room, blindfolded and standing on a levered plank, with their hands on the shoulders of one of the missionaries. As they stood there, someone would stand on the other end of the plank, lifting them up off the ground by the use of leverage. The missionary would then sink to his knees, giving the "victims" the sensation they were traveling ever higher and higher until they bumped into the ceiling—a piece of wood we touched their head with. We then screamed that they were falling and we pushed them off the beam. Instead of their expected six or seven-foot fall, they dropped a total of four inches. From this room, still blindfolded, they were led into another room, where, after taking off their shoes, we walked them through noodles and jello and put their hands into pig guts and other miscellaneous remnants from the town's slaughterhouse. We wondered about the origin of the horrible odor coming from this room, and realized, to our horror, that the elders assigned to collect miscellaneous cow parts from the slaughterhouse, had gathered guts full of partially digested and fully digested fecal material. These were thrown in, along with everything else that the members were grabbing and spreading their hands around!

We walked the victims, still blindfolded, into the next "parlor." There, in the closet, hung a real skeleton in a trench coat. He had pig eyes in his sockets and a pig tongue, with ketchup hanging out between the teeth of the skull. For special effects, the skeleton's bony fingers held a flickering candle. We pointed our "sacrificial lamb" toward this horrendous image, then removed the blindfold. They victims screamed and then, in horror, burned from this macabre scene to the coffin, flanked by the Jacob's ladders giving off eerie electrical effects. Out of the coffin arose a member with a white-painted face and darkened eyes to grab them as they tried to escape. To escape to their final destination, they had to crawl through a cardboard tunnel lined with threads hanging down in the dark like spider webs. The tunnel opened to a darkened room where they were blinded temporarily by the filmstrip projector light. As their eyes struggled to adjust, we lit up another ugly skull with pig eyes in its sockets, using a flashlight. We illuminated this horrendous image off and on while moving it so that it seemed to appear from nowhere in the dark. Camera flashes were also going off and the piano was pounded to emit eerie high and low notes.

We had as much fun as the members had, or even more fun, while putting on this spook show. It received great reviews by all who attended. If the spook alley wasn't bizarre enough, the members could view my ghastly costume. I became a "beastly" monster with a black trench coat, wiry hair ratted straight up on top of my head, black makeup around my eyes and nostrils, and white makeup for contrast over the rest of my face. Artificial blood dripped down my mouth. I was ready to go tracting, either in Transylvania or the mental asylum. I was the "missionary from Hell."

Missions are indeed full of contrasts. The day after our monster bash at the church, we had a very uplifting and spiritual baptism with two young men who had been receiving the discussions for a year. Their parents and family came to the baptism, which was encouraging since they had refused to participate in the discussions.

Meanwhile, I corresponded with the Romeros, Celia, the Pastranas, and the Vilas in Comas. I welcomed news from Comas.

In November we saw firsthand some of the differences in freedoms we enjoyed as compared to Peruvians. The teachers of Peru were paid so little, they could barely live off their salaries. The government passed a law prohibiting them from having other jobs. As part of the law, teacher unions and syndicates were outlawed. This led to protests, and many teachers were imprisoned for pro-testing. We encountered part of the nationwide protests in Arequipa on our first P-day in November. Students at the university, a block from where we lived, started throwing rocks at cars and smashing the windows. They blocked off the main road by lifting up cobblestones and making a rock barrier they supplemented with burning logs across the road. As we turned to leave, I caught the vision of a rock hurdling toward us and bouncing off the road. I ducked but Elder Shelton didn't move in time and it glanced off the side of his head, giving him a nice bump and bruise—fortunately it was not more serious. The next day, as we were working downtown, we got caught up in the middle of a huge demonstration and protest and felt like we were in the middle of a swarm of fish, being unable to turn in any direction. We felt very conspicuous because of our height and obvious nationality. As a couple of students marched by, they looked at us and started chanting, "Yankees, go home." We were worried at that point, thinking there was a possibility the entire crowd could turn on us. We sheepishly grinned and made the "peace" sign, which caused the students to break up in laughter and dissipated any ill will they felt toward us. As we moved to get out of the swarm of students, we heard a small explosion down at the end of the street and saw a projectile whiz by our heads, trailing a stream of white mist. The overwhelming stench and burning sensation that followed left no doubt that it was tear gas. The crowd panicked and started to run away, pulling us with them. We were caught in the middle, choking, wheezing, and rubbing our burning eyes. Government censorship was apparent in the newspapers. The huge protests and riots occurring around the city were not mentioned.

The military brought in a tank that shot water, and started blowing people off the streets with a steady jet of high-powered water. This worked fine until students, on the roof of a building fronting one of the narrow streets the tank was cruising down, dropped huge cobblestones on the revolving turret with the water gun and bent it. Emboldened, the students then made stone barricades out of the cobblestones, stopped the tank, then turned it over on its side. The driver and gunner fled for their lives. We were trying to stay invisible during these demonstrations. The government imposed martial law and prohibited anyone from going out on the street after dark. The curfew began each night with machine gun fire into the air to intimidate everyone, to make people stay indoors. Everything closed down, including banks, schools, businesses, and even the trains, until the government brought the military in to try to take over the transportation. The strike was still continuing several weeks after it had begun at the university, near where we lived, the students had blocked off the street again with cobblestones, throwing rocks at cars that tried to pass. A lady got a flat tire from the tacks and nails the students had thrown into the road, so we helped her change her tire and she gave us a lift to an area we were tracting, as well as a reference for us to teach her. Sometimes, all it takes is a good deed to make a good reference and contact. Elder Shelton escaped the strike and disturbances via a change to Puno, a city on the shores of Lake Titicaca, high up in the Andes. At 14,000 feet, it is the highest navigable lake in the world. Elder Shelton became the branch president in Puno. He later told me he tried to play basketball at that altitude and just about collapsed in a wheezing pile of spent flesh. The cholos living at that elevation had developed large barrel chests, increasing their lung and oxygen capacity.

My new zone leader companion was Elder Magelby, who transferred over from Elder Partridge in the adjoining area. He and I shared an avid interest in archeology and ancient legends. We were both enthused about using these subjects to interest investigators in the Book of Mormon.

We were always looking for fun games to play with families when we presented a Family Home Evening lesson. At the end of one Family Home Evening we filled a glass with flour, then turned it over on the table to make a mound of flour, and dropped a marble on the very top of the white pyramid. One at a time, we took turns cutting away the flour with a knife until one of us was unlucky enough to cause the marble to fall. Punishment involved picking the marble out of the flour with our teeth, powdering our faces in the process, and emerging with a white, clownlike image, holding the marble in our mouth. The kids squealed with laughter as we played.

On a couple of our P-days, we took Rex and Kaiser out to the campo, or open country, just blocks from where we lived. They had fun romping and roaming with us as we walked through the agricultural fields. On one of these outings, Rex battled a dog, much bigger than himself, who came charging after us. Rex jumped on his back and pulled him down, which ended the problem rather abruptly. As we continued our walk, Kaiser suddenly dropped from view. We hurried to the spot where he had disappeared and found he had fallen into a little stream covered over by weeds, which ran through the field. We laughed uncontrollably when this big pug-face burst out of the weeds ten feet downstream, smiling at us with his tongue hanging out, thoroughly soaked. Later that evening we visited our member mission leader in the branch, Hermano Cordora. Rex escaped and followed us. Herma-no Cordora, who was proficient on the accordion, played for us, with his daughter accompanying on the piano. The music was going great until Rex started with a whine, building to a howl outside the door. It disrupted the mu-sic but we all got a laugh out of it. We good-naturedly asked the Hermano, "What can we do? Rex thinks he is as much a part of this companionship as each of us."

We met an old university professor—Pierre Zam-petti. He was an Italian who spoke fluent Spanish, and English, and taught Latin, Old Greek, and Italian at the university. The professor was an eccentric, fascinating old man who had written numerous books. His two-room apartment was covered with memorabilia from his college years in Italy. Rotund, bald, with a crooked Roman/Greek nose, he typically wore an old European golf cap and old sweaters. His old tomcat had about the same disposition as the professor. The orange, mangy cat man-aged to find living space among the books and clutter in the apartment. We struck up a friendship with the professor. He did not really want to talk about the gospel. He preferred talking about the United States and practicing his English. Occasionally he liked to shock us by throwing out one of the most vulgar words in English he could come up with. When he saw the shocked look on our faces he would follow up with a comment like, "I find that to be a very fascinating word in the English language, for which we have no comparable counterpart in Italian or Spanish."

We became such good friends with the professor that Hermano Fuentes decided he would like to meet him. The professor had a reputation in the city, and Hermano Fuentes invited him to dinner. We had a very pleasant meal and Hermano Fuentes and the professor hit it off quite well and carried their conversation well into the evening. After he heard of our interest in ancient Peruvian legends, especially as they correlated with the Book of Mormon, the professor invited us to the campus of the university, where there was a vault holding many original historical accounts written by Spaniards who had come to Peru in the 1500s and 1600s. He got us access to the vault for a couple of hours. Elder Magelby and I entered the vault like two kids in a candy shop, using handheld Dictaphones to record, as fast as we could, the fascinating legends we found in the ancient manuscripts. These accounts ranged from those describing the visit of the great white bearded God to the ancient Peruvians, to those relating Old Testament beliefs recorded in the Peruvian legends, including the flood, the creation, and many different sacrifices identical to those required under the Mosaic Law. These legends were fascinating, especially to anyone who had read the Book of Mormon. They were so fascinating that we later put together a ninety-page book on the legends of Peru, as they correlated with the Book of Mormon, for use in tracting. The members were interested in it, as was the mission home, which ended up publishing it to distribute it to the missionaries for use in proselytizing. (The next chapter of this book describes a few of the highlights of the incredible legends of the ancient Peruvians.)

The strikes we witnessed culminated in violence to-ward the end of November 1973, when the police stormed the university to take it back from the students holding it. At least twelve students were shot and killed. In retaliation the students attacked police stations downtown. Martial law was again enforced with a curfew from 10:00 P.M. until 6:00 A.M. and all judicial rights were suspended. The following night, we saw many students outside, breaking streetlights and windows with rocks. The army came out to patrol after dark and take control of the city. Across the street from our pension, tanks and armored cars guarded the morgue to prevent anyone from gaining access to the bodies of those killed in the battles the day before. Apparently, in past student/ government confrontations, a student had been killed and his friends had carried the body around the streets to incite the people to further anger and violence. When we finally ventured out a few days later, we could see that every window in the government buildings downtown was smashed out. Glass was lying in shards all over the streets. It looked like a ghost town, with little happening except an occasional military jeep speeding by. Thanks to the strike, we grew extremely tired from having to walk everywhere for eight days. All transportation was shut down because of the citywide strikes.

The strikes finally ended when union-syndicate leaders sat down with the general in charge of the city and signed an agreement. We got back buses and peace and calm again.

The end of the strike brought us immediate relief from our teaching drought. The night it ended, we showed "Man's Search for Happiness" to a young family and some of their relatives. At the end of the filmstrip, the man told us, with a strident tone, that we were imposing our political views by showing such a movie. In his opinion, we were teaching poor people to subject themselves to Yankee exploitation, leading them to believe that after this life, they would go to paradise if they were willing to sacrifice for American imperialism during this life. What a genius! It never would have occurred to me to see such a profound underlying message in what appeared to be a beautiful filmstrip about the plan of salvation. We had no further visits with this family.

Whenever we needed to lift our spirits, we went to see Hermano Paredes, a member who looked a lot like José Jiménez, and was just about as funny. He spoke good English and usually regaled us with numerous jokes and funny stories. He was of great assistance when Elder Magelby and I printed our book on the ancient legends of Peru. He took our notes, typed them at his office, and then edited and corrected our Spanish.

We visited the professor to introduce the other missionaries to him during Thanksgiving week. Thanksgiving is an unknown holiday in Peru. Except for our visit with the professor, the day passed without any special recognition by us. The more we chatted with the professor, the more interesting he seemed. He had lived in Italy, England, the Philippines, Venezuela, and, finally, Peru. He left the Philippines after being warned by General MacArthur that the Japanese were about to take the islands.

As a zone leader giving baptismal interviews, I found myself in unique situations, including having to counsel an investigator, much older than myself, about how to repent and get his life in order for a baptism, after having indulged in serious immorality. It seemed incongruous for a twenty-year-old young man living a life of celibacy for two years, to give sage advice, but I felt with prayer I was able to provide counsel the Lord would approve of.

President Driggs and one of his counselors, President Souza, arrived in Arequipa on Saturday, December 8, to conduct a mission conference on Sunday, December 9. They helped animate us about the new discussions and brought us a movie, "Meet the Mormons," to introduce investigators to the church. We were enjoying the movie, when suddenly President Driggs appeared in the movie, walking through Temple Square! All the missionaries started laughing and saying, "That's why he is showing us this movie."

We found a lawyer downtown while asking general questions. President Driggs gave us his address and we dropped by to give him a discussion. It had to be a night when Rex leaped over the fence and followed us! He often scaled the fence and came to our pension about the time he knew we would be leaving from lunch to go out to work. He would wait in ambush and come running up, with his tongue hanging out, and his pug-faced slobbery, joviality, anxious to get at the missionary work. He followed us to the lawyer's. The lawyer suggested we lock Rex up in the backyard until we were done with the discussion. This worked out well until Rex once again started howling and whining during the middle of the discussion.

I found a better solution to our dog problem than rocks. Rex usually protected us, but as "insurance" we bought cracker balls—small round balls filled with gun-powder that blow up on contact when thrown. When landed on or next to the culprit they effectively scared away dogs and drunks.

In December we saw signs of success, primarily through the efforts of the members. We started teaching the parents of one member family and the wife of another member—Hermano Paredes. With the support of their members relatives, the discussions were going well.

Elder Magelby and I completed our book of ancient legends during our companion study time each day by studying numerous authors on the Inca and pre-Inca legends of Peru. We became legend and archeology fanatics. At the same time we got a taste of what it must have been like to be missionaries in Mexico. One of the young men we were teaching rented a room from a lady who did not like the Mormons, so he made appointments to come to our apartment to receive the discussions. We decided that was the way to go—wait until our investigators arrive and then come downstairs to give them a discussion right there in our home.

As Christmas approached, the cholo vendors lined the streets of downtown with so many booths and shops, there was barely room for the buses to cut their way through the crowds. I had one of my most memorable Christmases in Arequipa. Like everywhere else I had worked in Peru, there were areas where the poverty was so heart-rending, it brought me to the verge of tears. At least fifteen families we knew of lived under these conditions, with dirt, adobe, cardboard, and tin hobo huts that they called home. Their children generally had one set of clothes, or two sets that were ragged, torn, and dirty all the time. Elder Magelby and I realized that we could organize and provide the only Christmas these families would have. We collected the names of the parents and children in each of the families, then prepared a list of the types of gifts that would be appropriate for girls, boys, and adults. Included on the list were homemade dolls, clowns, candy, fruit, shoes, sweaters, and blankets. We involved member families in the preparation of the family Christmas baskets. The participating members were excited about these true acts of charity for other members of their branch. Some sisters made dolls, others clowns, and others gathered or prepared food items, while we provided the financing for purchasing goods like candy and fruit. We also collected used pairs of shoes, blankets, and sweaters.

On the Sunday evening before Christmas we met the members involved in this project at the church and made up the baskets, putting name tags on individual subpack-ages for each child. We then assembled the baskets, complete with these packages, clothes, and food. After the Sacrament meeting we divided into three groups and left, in two cars per group, to deliver the packages while singing Christmas carols. It was hard not to get emotional, and I confess I did as we watched these families with tears streaming down their faces from gratitude because of our Christmas charity. I felt warm all over and tingled with excitement, Christmas spirit, and the true love of Christ. Christmas in the mission field was a true celebration of Christ's birth. We served him with little regard for presents or any other commercialism usually associated with Christmas back in the United States.

We met, as a zone, Christmas Eve for a jovial yet spirit-filled Christmas party. We read aloud excerpts from *A Christmas Carol*, by Charles Dickens. His writing is so full of good old English humor, and hilarious descriptions of Scrooge, that we started giggling. It built up, and up, into outright laughter until we were having one of the best laughs ever by the time we finished with Scrooge. After we calmed down to taped Christmas mu-sic by the Mormon Tabernacle Choir, we read prophecies of Christ's birth in the Bible and the Book of Mormon, and ended the meeting with our testimonies. This was the most spiritual and literal Christmas commemoration I had experienced. We returned home and stayed up until two in the morning, celebrating with the Fuentes family. Hermano Fuentes gave us gag gifts, baby bottles, and other items he told us were of necessity in the mission work. We gave them each a gift, and had a good time visiting, laughing, and talking about our own Christmas traditions in the United States.

On Christmas Day we journeyed to the countryside, looking for ruins to satisfy our mutual archeology "bug." We found no ruins but discovered beautiful vistas of the mountains, agricultural fields, and an old granary. On Christmas evening we walked downtown and saw the movie "Lost Horizon."

Elder Magelby and I were immersing ourselves ever deeper in ancient legends of Peru. We visited a museum on P-day to view ancient artifacts including pre-Inca pottery with painted images of both white men and red men! Contrary to the skepticism of critics, here was evidence that there had been an ancient race of white people on the American continent.

Shocking news arrived: that Prophet Harold B. Lee, of the Mormon Church, had passed away. He had seemed so young compared to the other prophets and we had assumed he would be a prophet for many, many years. I had a very special place for him in my heart after listening to him in the Salt Lake Temple while I was in the mission home.

I found someone with yet another approach to handling obnoxious dogs. Walking up a narrow cobblestone street, heading toward a Catholic cathedral in one of the outlying areas of Arequipa, we encountered a drunk shuffling down the street in the opposite direction. When he saw us, his eyes lit up almost as if he recognized us. He stumbled over and told us, in a slurred, salivary whisper, that he knew a lot about the church. To prove his point, he pulled Joseph Smith pamphlets out of his greasy over. coat. As we talked, a Great Dane came charging toward us. He appeared friendly—tail wagging—but I never took chances. As I started to pull out a rock, the drunk stuck one arm straight out, with his fingers extended, and raised the other arm as if he were going to perform an exorcism. In this stance he stared the dog down, and started yelling at him, "Joseph Smith," "Nephi," "Lehi," and on and on with a barrage of prophets' names. The dog, perhaps as amused and puzzled as we were, cocked his head first to one side and then the other, wondering what this nut was up to. The dog seemed the more intelligent of the two at that moment. The Great Dane sat there taking it in and the drunk calmly turned around with a grin on his face and told us, "You should know that the priesthood and power of our prophets can subdue wild beasts."

We spent New Year's Day picnicking in the countryside with the Fuentes family. After picnicking, rock-throwing and jumping contests, and eating ice cream downtown, I took off for another visit to the elders in Tacna. This time I traveled on a new Volvo bus that smoothly cruised the road, especially compared to the old beat up contraption I had ridden to Tacna in before. The bus stopped for breakfast at the same little café between the cities of Tacna and Arequipa that I remembered from my prior trip. I did not feel like risking it, so I stood out back by a ravine, throwing pebbles at swarms of birds as they sailed up and down the gully. It was good to see Elder Farnsworth again when I arrived in Tacna. Things got a little lively my first night there. As we stood out on the balcony of the elder's apartment, a drunk stood down below, yelling at us, telling us "The Gringos and the Yankees should go home" and other taunts. We teased him and chuckled about his inebriated condition. As he left, Elder Farnsworth lit a firecracker and landed it behind the drunk helping him pick up his pace! I had the pleasure of receiving my last gamma globulin injection in Tacna at the hands of one of the other elders—what an experience! It took him only two stabs to get it right! Once done with the needle, we melted wax and pulled it up inside the needle with the plunger. After it hardened, we unscrewed the needle tip until it was loose, then had a dart-shooting contest by forcing the plunger of the injector and sending the needle flying like a missile toward the cardboard target.

As I worked with one of the elders in Tacna, cars with megaphones and trucks with speakers cruised all over the city, screaming out propaganda for a meeting at the plaza to celebrate the government's takeover of a large U.S. copper mine a couple of years before. The military government was always trying to focus people's attention away from the misery and poverty created by government overspending on outdated military equipment. Apparently, their theory was that if they focused attention on hatred for the Yankee imperialists, there would be less civil unrest. The military government kept telling the people they were in a "progressive revolution." From what I could see, a military dictatorship, spending most of the nation's resources on military equipment, was not much of a revolution.

An alarm clock was unnecessary in Tacna. The newspaper boys started their rounds at 5:15 in the morning, yelling and moaning with voices that sounded like corpses in the grave, *"Correo, Correo, Correo"*—the name of the newspaper they were peddling. It did no good to cover my ears with a pillow, it was enough to drive me crazy. We met a Catholic priest in Tacna who let me borrow a book discussing the legends of the Incas' Great White Bearded God. He also showed us around the little plantation where he and his mother lived. It was beautiful with grapevines spread all over, growing higher than the house. They also grew onions, corn, and other crops.

I spent the Fast Sunday in January in Tacna. The members asked me to play the piano for the meeting. It was a beautiful piano that came from the former Toquepala Branch. The town and the piano had at one time been owned by a Utah mining company that employed many members of the church. This had been one of the first branches in Peru but was closed due to difficulties with the government's nationalization program—seizing of mines and other U.S. assets. After returning from Tacna, I found the assistants who had come up from Lima to work with us until our mission conference a few days later. Elder Corbridge, whom I had met in Callao, was one of the assistants. We enjoyed working together again. We tried contacting lawyers downtown and I could see why they'd been criticized heavily by Joseph Smith and the prophets in the Book of Mormon. Most of them seemed closed-minded—they already knew everything, just like teenagers. (Little did I know, I would become one of them—not closed-minded, but a lawyer.) We met a few who were receptive. We left copies of the Book of Mormon with them and gave most of a first discussion to another.

One morning, an article in the newspaper caught our attention. It was accompanied by a picture showing a statue of a little bearded man reading an open book in his hands. The statue was from Cuzco. It was significant because the Incas had no writing system, but they re-corded their traditions with a system of knots on small woven ropes called *quipus*. These were maintained only by the priests. Further, the Incas, like North American Indians, did not have facial hair. The significance of the little bearded man was not lost on us because of our familiarity with the Nephites and those before the Incas that did have reading and writing and grew beards like the other Israelites.

I spoke for ten minutes to kick off our mission conference in January 1974. We enjoyed hearing from President Driggs. We rented a banquet room at the hotel were President Driggs always stayed, and after the conference the zone members ate dinner together. Elder Magelby and I stayed for an hour after dinner to talk with the president. I had grown really close to him and always enjoyed his company, advice, and counsel.

We reached the point with some investigators where we had to see them get off the fence and make a commitment or stop using our time. One investigator refused to read or come to church, but he always enjoyed visiting with us. We decided we might occasionally visit with him, but we were not going to spend substantial time with him that might be spent in a more meaningful manner, seeking other, more sincere investigators.

We had been trying to get Hermano Paredes to give us advice on our paper on the Book of Mormon and on ancient legends of Peru, but he was difficult to get a hold of. One evening, we knew he was home, but he would not come downstairs to get the door, so we played the old trick I learned in Callao, stuffing the buzzer with paper to keep it ringing until someone pulled out the paper. He had a good laugh over that one. A few days later he agreed to start typing our paper.

My experience in Arequipa reinforced my earlier belief—that you don't often find good scenery together with productive missionary work. Arequipa was geographically a beautiful location, with spectacular vistas of verdant valleys backdropped with snowcapped mountain ranges and the volcano, Misti. The town itself was beautiful with its white volcanic stone architecture. The missionary work, though, was slow. It was difficult to find open-minded people interested in hearing our message. This difficulty with the work, combined with the bad weather we had in January—every afternoon brought clouds and heavy rains—drove us to a "January depression." The rains created large puddles that assaulted my holey shoes and unprotected suits—I had given my overcoat to Hermano Fuentes in exchange for having an alpaca sport coat tailored.

Hermano Paredes finished our paper on the ancient legends of Peru and the Book of Mormon. We felt it was quite impressive. We made copies and circulated them first to the elders in our zone, because they were anxious to use the paper in discussions with investigators.[2] Just when missionary life started to get boring, there was always some exciting new event during the day that would lend a bit of either humor or diversion. As an example, as we were traveling on the bus to distribute our paper to elders on the other side of our zone, a drunk started causing a scene on the bus, yelling incoherently and acting like he was angry at everyone on the bus. He rattled off streams of slurred swear words, a mile a minute, and screamed at the money collector as he walked down the aisle. It was quite a show.

I soon received my final change: to go back to Lima as a zone leader in Ingenieria. I received it with mixed feelings. I had made good friends in Arequipa with the Fuentes family, the members, a few investigators, and of course Rex and Kaiser—our tagalong boxers—but the prospect of going back to an area where missionary work was moving at a faster pace excited me. A few days before I had to leave, Professor Zampetti took us to the university and introduced us to history professors anxious to discuss the legends of Peru that we had digested from the ancient writings in the university's vault. It was a dream discussion. We had become experts even in the eyes of these professors.

The Fuentes family was shocked when I told them I was leaving. They took us out to dinner for a feast. It was difficult to go around on my last day to say good-bye to all those who had become special to me. The night before I left, Rex jumped the fence and followed us for the last time, at least for me. It was a fitting send-off. I hoped my clothes would survive the last couple months of my mission because they seemed to be reaching the end of their road. My green suit was

---

2.   I discuss some of the highlights of these legends in the next chapter of this book.

starting to shred at the pant legs, and my shoes were falling apart. I looked like a missionary hobo!

After an emotional send-off by Hermano Fuentes at the airport—he made an exception to his general rule of not going to the airport—I had a beautiful flight down the mountain range to the coast of Peru and arrived for another visit with President Driggs. He was interested in the paper Elder Magelby and I had authored and took a copy that was later printed by the mission home for use throughout the mission. I was assigned as a co-zone leader with Elder Naylor in Ingenieria, a zone encompassing my favorite place—Comas. I would be able to see some of my favorite people again.

# CHAPTER 11
## Ancient Legends of Peru and the Book of Mormon

"The statue was of a man of large stature with a long beard and wearing a long tunic. It was thought to be Saint Bartholomew, who might have come to Peru to teach the gentiles."

Written in 1600, this description was given by the Inca Garcilaso de La Vega, a half-Spanish, half-Incan historian, about a statue the Spaniards found in a temple outside of Cuzco, near the center of the once flourishing Incan Empire. They destroyed the statue early in the 1500s, hoping to find a cache of gold underneath it. It might seem strange, to those not familiar with the Book of Mormon, that the Indians of this continent, who were dark-skinned and beardless, had a myth and legend of a white-skinned bearded God, especially since the common belief is that the aborigines had never seen a white-skinned bearded man until the arrival of the Spaniards. It is not a mystery to those of us who have read the Book of Mormon.

Just as the visit of Jesus Christ to the ancient Americas is the center point of the Book of Mormon, the legends about the Great White Bearded God, and his visit to the ancestors of the Incas, provide the central theme of ancient Peruvian history. This legend was deeply entrenched in the religion of the Incas, whose main deity and, according to the foremost authorities their only deity, was "Viracocha," who became incarnate as a white-bearded half man/half God. This legend is found in a similar form among the Mayans and Aztecs, and the various other ancient cultures that predated them—Teotihuacanos, Toltecs, Olmecs, Zapotecs, etc. The Mayas of the highlands called this

God "Cucumatz." The Mayas of the lowlands and the Yucatan called him "Kukulcan," as I noted previously, while the Mexican civilizations called him "Quetzalcoatl."

I already described how Elder Magelby and I were shocked to see a headlined story in the paper one morning in Arequipa, titled "Was Jesus Christ in Ancient Peru?" We read the article eagerly, finding it had been written by Franklin Pease, a noted Peruvian expert on the ancient civilizations of Peru. It was based in part on the Inca Garcilaso de La Vega's description of the godlike statue. When I got to Lima and looked up Mr. Pease, I tried to interest him in the Book of Mormon but to no avail.

The ancient legends of Peru were preserved in the accounts of Spanish clerics and historians derived from their conversations with the Incas during the "conquest." The clerics and historians learned Quechua—the dialect and language of the Incas—and spoke to the Incas about their religion and legends. Although they wrote these histories in the 1500s and 1600s, the records were not available to the public until the late 1800s. They were suppressed in storage in the Library of Madrid, in Spain, and released only at the turn of the century, so none of these legends or accounts were available to Joseph Smith.

After my mission, I took an archeology class from a peculiar professor who had an eye problem that made him appear to be looking directly into the opposite corner as he was talking to me. In his class I wrote a paper titled "Did Jesus Christ Visit Ancient America?" (I discuss many of the legends and sources in this chapter.) Although he gave me an A on the paper, the professor told me he questioned my premise, although he could not question my sources, which were impeccable. He believed the Spanish clerics interjected Catholicism and other Christian slants to the legends. I responded that, to the contrary, the accounts showed the Spanish clerics firmly believed the Incas were heathens who had been misled by the Devil into idol worship and other unchristian acts. They believed the "savages" had to be converted to Christianity. Because of this bias, if anything, the legends as recounted by the Spanish clerics were slanted away from Christianity and toward heathenism. Ironically, it was probably because those clerics did not understand true gospel principles that we are still able to find bits and pieces of them in the legends.

We know from the Book of Mormon that the ancient Peruvians, like the other ancient civilizations on this continent, had the gospel of Jesus Christ and knew of God the Father, his son Jesus Christ, and the Holy Ghost. Like us, they received the gospel to help guide them through this life to return to our Father in Heaven through the intercession and atonement of Jesus Christ, with the testimony and influence of the Holy Ghost. They were familiar with all of the saving ordinances of the gospel and the fundamental steppingstones of the Law of Moses contained in the brass plates Nephi took from Laban. Thus, it is no surprise, but very interesting, to find many true gospel principles embodied in the legends of the Incas and their ancestors, starting with their conception of Jesus Christ.

For many years the "experts" thought the Incas had numerous gods representing different aspects of nature, although the chief God was always called "Con Ticci Viracocha." Through our study, we learned it has become generally accepted that at least the Incas in the upper levels of their society did not worship many Gods but worshiped only Viracocha. When they showed adoration for the different objects of nature—rivers, trees, mountains, the Moon, and the Sun—they were not honoring a deity inherent in the objects, but were showing respect because they believed the Great God Viracocha had created them, placed them here, and impressed upon them some mark of distinction beyond other objects of their class. Thus, they felt these objects of creation were appropriate spots for worshiping the maker of all things. This concept was demonstrated by the fact that the Incas did not address their prayers to objects of nature, but only to Viracocha.[3]

The Incas knew Viracocha as the creator of all things in Heaven and earth—the Sun, the Moon, stars, and Earth. This belief was recorded by Pedro Cieza de Leon, a noted Spanish historian writing in 1553, in his *La Cronica del Peru* (Ediciones Peisa, Biblioteca Peruana, Lima, 1973).

Viracocha had a pre-Earth life. "The natives of this land [Peru] say

---

3. "Relacion Anonyma do los Costumbres Antiquos de los Naturales del Peru." p. 138 (1675), published in Madrid in 1879, and also "Culto entre los Inkas." pp. 1-8.

that in the beginning before the world was created, there was a God called Viracocha."[4] Franklin Pease explained that the ancient legends and histories of the Incas showed "the creation was a type of organizing and stratifying material which already existed in one form or another. The creator of the universe [Viracocha] is the organizer that dominates chaos." Further, "The word is the creating power. Viracocha creates by words."[5]

According to the Incan legends, Viracocha first created the world in darkness, without the Sun, the Moon, or stars. After creating the world, he formed a generation of deformed giants to see if it would be good to have men that big. He then decided it was not good that they be bigger than himself, so he created man in his own image, but they continued to live in darkness. He ordered them to know and worship him and gave them precepts, warning them that if they violated these precepts, he would confuse them. These people fell into transgression and an indignant Viracocha confused and dammed them. He later converted them into stone and caused a huge flood, called "un pachacuti," meaning that "water that covered the earth" destroyed all creations. After the flood, Viracocha populated the world again, this time illuminating it with lights. He created man in a great lagoon in Collao, an island in Lake Titicaca. He commanded the Sun, the Moon, and stars to shine forth giving light to the world. He then commanded those he had created to go forth and populate the Earth.[6]

Viracocha later came to Earth to visit the men he had created and appeared to them as half God and half man. He was described by the Incas in their legends as a "beautiful man, white and with a flowing beard, and a face of not much age," and "with blue eyes."[7]

---

4.   Sarmiento de Gamboa, Pedro, Historia de los Incas, p. 101 (1572; Emece Editores, Buenos Aires, 1943).

5.   Pease, Creador, p. 84, citing Juan Diez de Betanzos, Suma y Nar-   racion de los Incas (1551; San Marti y C. Lima 1924).

6.   Betanzos, pp. 206-208; Sarmiento de Gamboa, pp. 101-102 and 106; Molina, Cristobal de, Ritos y Fabulas de los Incas. p. 15 (1572; Editorial Futuro S.R.L., Buenos Aires, 1959); Urteaga, Horacio H., Historia de los Incas y Conquista del Peru (1533-1552), p. 82 (Lima 1924).

7.   Calancha, Antonio de la, Cronica Morlizada del Orden de San Augustinn en el Peru. (1639; Pedro la Cavalleria, Calle de la Li-breria, Barcelona, 1939).

This visit by Viracocha was the central focus of the ancient legends. About it, Pedro Cieza de Leon stated:

> After being without the sun for a long time, and after making pleas to their God for light... the sun rose... and later towards midday, there came a white man of large stature in whose manner was manifested great authority, and this man had such power as to make plains into mountains and mountains into plains, as well as fountains of water out of rock. With such power, they called him creator of all things created, first of all things, Father of the sun, because they say he gave life to men and animals.... In many places he ordered men to live in peace, and he treated them with love and charity, teaching them to be good to one another and have charity....They generally called him Ticci Viracocha and wherever he went he ...healed the sick, giving sight to the blind with just words.[8]

In this beautiful account of the visit of Viracocha—Jesus Christ—we find in great detail an account that complements the Book of Mormon's description of the visit in the Third Nephi. These legendary details include: the darkness that preceded the visit; Christ's appearance at midday; Christ's stature—large; the destruction that preceded the visit—plains were changed into mountains, and mountains into plains, and fountains of water out of rock; his power and recognition as the creator of all things; his status as life giver to men and animals; his teachings on charity and love; and the healings he performed, including giving sight to the blind by words.[9]

"At the end of his visit, Viracocha went by way of the Andes, visiting the people, and he descended below all things of this earth, and then he ascended to Heaven."[10] He took abrupt leave of the people in Peru, and left for the West, promising that he would return from the East.[11]

---

8.   Cieza de Leon, Pedro, El Senorio de los Incas, (1555; Lima 1948).

9.   See Book of Mormon, 3 Nephi, chaps. 8-28.

10.  Brinton, Daniel G., American Hero Myths. pp. 188-189 (Philadel-phia: H.C. Watts and Company, 1882).

11.  Brinton, Myths, 188-189.

The Spaniards found Greek-style crosses in Peru, which the ancients associated with Viracocha and used as symbols of him. Antonio de Calancha, in his chronicle, noted that "the people say that a beautiful white man passed through and brought a cross to Guatulco; then he entered the ocean and walked on the water like the earth."[12]

A summary of the characteristics and qualities of Viracocha, listed below, when compared with those describing Christ in the Book of Mormon, easily shows they were one and the same being. These qualities that were derived from the legends include:

1. He had a pre-Earth existence.

2. He created Earth, man, and all things.

3. He created by organizing already existent matter.

4. He created by the power of his words.

5. He experimented in creating man several times and destroyed the first men with a huge flood, after turning a few to stone (the pillar of salt—Lot's wife).

6. He first created the Earth in darkness.

7. He became incarnate, half man and half God.

8. He was white, bearded, of large stature, and wore a long white tunic and sandals.

9. He was a great teacher, teaching peace, charity, and love.

10. He had power over nature—causing plains to rise to mountains and mountains to flatten to plains and water to come from rock.

11. He ascended above all and descended below all.

12. He healed the sick, including the blind.

13. He walked on water.

14. He left for the West, promising to return from the East.

15. He was associated with the symbol of the Greek cross.

The pre-Incan legend of Viracocha became firmly entrenched in the Incan religion after one of the Incan princes, Prince Ripak, defeated a

12. Calancha, 316.

warring tribe called the Chankas. He credited the victory to a visitation from Viracocha warning him of the impending battle.[13] The legend became so dominant to Incan religion and beliefs that it facilitated the Spanish conquest. The conquistadors arrived on the coast of Peru while the powerful Incan nation was in a civil war. The ruler of the north, inland from the coast where the Spaniards landed, was Atahualpa. His brother, Huascar, ruled the south from Cuzco. Atahualpa was so curious about the appearance of the white bearded man, remembering that Viracocha had promised to return from the East, that he allowed the conquistadors to travel through easily defensible canyons unmolested, to appear at his capital. Instead of treating him like a returning god, they promptly captured Atahualpa and held him as ransom, thereby decapitating the central leadership of the Incan army, which otherwise could have easily suppressed the Spaniards.

The Incan religion preserved numerous remnants of the true gospel of Jesus Christ. Their conception of the universe was limited to dividing the earth into three distinct parts: the upper world, the middle world (this world), and the interior or lower world. "Hanan Pacha"— the upper world—was a sublime transposition of life on Earth. Those who never died lived there. It was graced with trees, plants, rivers and animals like in this earth life. Heaven was reflected in this life. It was an abstraction of life on Earth but outside limits of time and space. The Incas believed that all species of plants, animals and men had their progenitors in the upper world. The middle world, or this life, was called "Cay Pacha." Cuzco, the capital of the Incas, was also the center of this world. The lower world, called "Oco Pacha," was a place of mysterious powers. The Incas feared this world because it was the home of "Supay," who, according to Bartolome de las Casas—a noted Spanish priest who wrote about the ancient civilizations of America— had contravened Viracocha's desires. An angry Viracocha threw Supay out of the upper world and into the ocean, for him to die. Instead of dying, he took over the lower world.[14]

---

13. Vega, Inca Garcilaso de, Los Comentarios Reales (1609; Editoriale Mercurio S.A., Lima, 1970).

14. De las Casas, Bartolome, Historia de las Indias (1555, Mexico). See also, Cieza, Cronica p. 163, and Cieza, Senorio, p. 23.

Those with vices in this life went to the lower world to work without rest and suffer for their bad deeds. All gods lived in the upper world with the exception of Viracocha, who lived above them all.

As shown in this "eternal plan," the Incas believed in the existence of the soul after life on Earth. They believed in the resurrection. The seed was a symbol to them of eternal restoration and the circle of life.[15] Pedro Cieza de Leon said that "they believed in the immortality of the soul and said that those who had been obedient in this life would go to a delightful place and those who had dis-obeyed would go to a dark fearful place. "[16] Further, "This people believed that there was more inside man than just a corporal body and they believed that their bodies ... would resurrect."[17]

It was because of their belief in the resurrection that the Incas buried the dead with their eating utensils, plates, silver goods, and food. When nobles died, their favorite wives and children were sacrificed and buried with them. The Incas did not want to journey to the life beyond without the necessary commodities and good company. By violating burial grounds and disturbing bones while looking for treasures, the Spaniards distressed the Incas. Because of their belief in the resurrection, the Incas wanted all remains undisturbed in one place. So literal was their belief in a complete resurrection that they would even save hairs that fell from their heads while they were combing, and fingernails, in order to bury them with their body to await the resurrection.[18]

We were astounded to find, among the ancient legends of Peru, a prehistoric account that revealed a large tree symbol cut into the slope outside Nazca, Peru. The ancient Peruvians called this symbol the "Tree of Life." The "Tree of Life" was found in the upper world. This legend of Lehi's dream was also found among the Mayas.

---

15. Valcarcel, Luis E., Ruta Cultural del Peru (Lima, 1972).

16. Cieza, Senorio, at 14.

17. Cieza, Cronica, at 73.

18. Garcilaso, Book 2, at 142.

Incan society revolved around a large priesthood presided over by High Priests in each district acting under the direction of one central supreme High Priest. These priests managed provincial temples.[19] The priests conducted rituals and ordinances at the temples and directed all religious ceremonies. To assist the priests with these duties, the Incas established an institution similar to the Catholic monasteries. Young virgins were chosen to dedicate their services to Viracocha, their god. These "Virgins of the Sun," lived within walled structures or convents and were supervised by elderly matrons called *mamaconas*. Under their direction the Virgins of the Sun learned their religious duties and learned to weave the temple garments of the priests and the clothing of the Royal Incan king and his family. As one of their duties, the Virgins of the Sun protected the holy flame which burned continually near the sacrificial altars.

Incan priests performed different types of sacrifices. Many of these sacrifices coincided in numerous details with those described in the Books of Moses in the Old Testament. Animal sacrifices, performed on altars, usually involved yearling llamas, white and unblemished. Additionally, the priests conducted a variety of food-and-wine-offering sacrifices. As in the Law of Moses, Incan priests performed a penitent offering. Penitents prepared by fasting for several days, then confessed to the priest, who would place the ashes of a burned offering—a yearling, unblemished, white llama—on the altar. He then blew the ashes, scattering them to the wind, to eliminate the sins of the confessor.[20] In the temples, by the altars, burned "perpetual flames" like those in the holy sanctuaries used by Moses and the Israelites. These flames were protected and kept burning at all times by the Virgins of the Sun. To prepare for these sacrifices and ceremonies, the priests would fast and abstain from sexual relations for many days.

---

19. Prescott, William, p. 81, chap. 3, Historia de la Conquista del Peru (1847; Editorial del Universo Lima, 1972), and Garcilaso, supra. Book 2, at 146.

20. Gerol, Harry, Dioses, Templos Ruinas (Buenos Aires, 1961); Leviticus 24 (describing the perpetual flame); Numbers 29 (concerning sin offerings and the use of yearling lambs without a blemish).

Other rituals performed by the Incas included baptism, confession, and the sacrament. Jose de Acosta re-corded the fact that "the Incas did not confess their sins to any man, but rather to the sun, so he would tell them to Viracocha that he might forgive them.... After confessing, the Incas would go to a certain washing font to wash themselves clean from their faults.... Placing themselves in this font or a river, they said, 'I have told my faults to the sun and you are to receive them and wash them to the sea."[21] Acosta also noticed, among the Incas, a form of the Sacrament. He relates: "After concluding the ceremonies and dances, the pieces [corn dough] which were consecrated were parted into many pieces and starting with the oldest, the Virgins of the Sun gave them to all those present, who received it with great reverence saying that they were eating the body of their God.... Upon ending the solemn communion, an elderly man of great authority would get up and preach to the people."[22] This appears to be an account of a Sacrament meeting with an attending High Council speaker!

The feast of the Passover was replicated by the Incase in a ceremony they called "Inti Raymi." They held this festival once a year in our month of December. The Incas prepared for this ceremony by fasting, praying, and abstaining from sex. The night before the ceremony they gathered at the house of their oldest brother. Before dawn they would wash themselves, then smear corn dough, mixed with llama blood, over their heads, faces, legs. The oldest brother spread this blood mixture over the doorways of the house as a sign that those within the house had washed and purified themselves.[23] The next day this "passover" ceremony started with a multitude of sacrifices. The sacrament was passed to all and the congregation made covenants to obey the mandates of the sun—from Viracocha and the Royal Inca.[24] This festival correlated in many ways with the Israelites' Passover feast to commemorate the last deadliest plague—the deaths of the Egyptians' eldest-born sons—and to escape from destruction by the angel of death as he passed over the homes of the Israelites who had smeared lamb blood over their doorways.

---

21. Acosta, Jose de, Historia Natural y Moral de las Indias. (1590; Mexico 1940).

22. Acosta, 1415. See also, Garcilaso, supra, Book 7, p. 18, and Prescott, chap.3, p. 84.

23. Garcilaso, Book 7, p. 18.

24. Acosta, at 411.

There are many more details of Incan religion that coincide with the gospel of Jesus Christ, as written by the ancient prophets in the Book of Mormon. I have presented only a few of those I consider to be significant. Elder Magelby and I realized these legends would not give us a testimony for the Book of Mormon, but it gratified us to find additional accounts of the visit of Jesus Christ, and of his gospel, among the ancient Americans. It further strengthened our already strong testimonies of the truthfulness of the Book of Mormon.

# CHAPTER 12
## My Final Assignment—Ingenieria

Ingenieria ("In hen yur eeah") is a part of the sprawling suburb surrounding downtown Lima. It is situated between the downtown area and Comas. In appearance, it is like Callao, mostly flat land covered by streets and thousands of houses sharing common walls and fronting the sidewalks with multicolored plaster facades, and roofs covered with discarded tidbits of the occupants' history. We lived in the converted garage of a one-story small house on a busy street that ended in an intersection a block away. Next to the intersection was a field adorned with an old mound from pre-Incan ruins. How convenient for me! At the other end of the street was a military base and the main road leading out to Comas. There was less open space than in Comas because we were closer to downtown. It seemed like the town had lost its own identity after being gobbled up in the spread of downtown Lima—much like the towns around Los Angeles.

In Ingenieria, Elder Naylor was a good-natured, rosy-cheeked elder from, of all places, Utah—most companions were. He had a good sense of humor and developed an interest in archeology after listening to me de-scribe my expeditions with Elder Garner in Comas; he read the paper on legends that Elder Magelby and I had worked on.

In February, a summer month in Peru, Ingenieria was hot. I began to feel sticky and sweaty again even at night. Shortly after I arrived, there was a meeting in Callao for all branch leaders in the district. At this meeting I saw many friends from Comas, including the Pastranas and Hermano Vila. It was great to see them again, especially at a leadership meeting. Not only had they maintained their activity, but they had also progressed into leadership roles in the church. This was significant in view of the high attrition rate of members in Peru. It felt like a homecoming after being away from these friends for five months.

My passion for archeology rubbed off immediately on Elder Naylor. On our first P-day, we walked down the street to the ruins in the fields at the head of the road running by our pension. There were large mounds, but the details were almost completely wiped out. We found the typical digging spots from night-time black-market robbers, and the usual debris left in their wake—bits of ancient cloth and pieces of pottery.

The work in my new area contrasted greatly with that in Arequipa. We were teaching eight families, most of whom were also attending church. It was a great program for the end of my mission. The time was going so fast toward the end that it seemed as though the complete experience—all of my memories of faces, members, converts, even dogs—was slipping through my fingers. I could not imagine returning home and not being a missionary.

Elder Naylor introduced me to the Bravo family. Hermano Bravo was a shoe repairman with eight children. Their home was a bamboo mat hut with dirt floors and a wood roof and little in the way of any furniture except that pieced together by scraps of wood. Hermano Bravo eked out a living from a small portable—a stand on wheels— shoe-repair business in town. Since it was so difficult to obtain a divorce in Peru because of bureaucracy and tradition, Hermano Bravo and his family had not been baptized because of his inability to officially end his prior marriage with a divorce. He had been in this predicament for over eight years! He had attended church faithfully and paid tithing for five years as a nonmember. I was astounded by this, especially in view of the dire financial situation of his family, as they were scratching to survive. I asked him how he could afford to pay tithing. He responded, "We have been so blessed, because of paying tithing, that we would not survive if we had not been paying." He taught me a lesson. By their example, with the law of tithing, the Bravos, the Romeros—also the family of a shoemaker, and the Lorenzos—showed me you cannot judge the strength of a man's character by his social class. Most of the good leaders of the church in Comas were in economically stressed circumstances. Their humility gave them great strength as leaders and great compassion and empathy for those they led. They also showed faith to a degree I had not often seen in the United States.

We were teaching another family, the Nunez family, who accepted the baptismal challenge after I had been in Ingenieria a couple of weeks. We were not sure that Hermana Nunez understood everything we were teaching—every time we asked her a question she answered it with the same answer, "We have to have faith." But, she was interested, and felt good about the discussions. We took a little longer to explain the discussions to her. The Chavez family, another investigator couple, had the most comical pair of pets I had ever seen—a green parrot and a small black copper-marked dachshund-wiener dog. This bird/canine couple were good friends. The dog walked around with the parrot perched on his shoulders riding like a ship captain in the crow's nest.

In the La Florida Branch that we attended, the members were helpful. We jointly planned an open house to help members introduce friends to the church and to have them mingle with our investigators.

Elder Naylor and I took another "archeology expedition" into the valley of Chuquitanta. This valley was north of our area and according to the books I had read, it contained a restored ancient temple. It was about thirty-five hundred years old and made of rock. As we arrived in the farmland off the Pan American Highway, we could see ruins overgrown by cornfields. We crossed huge walls twenty feet high and made of mud, as we clawed our way through six-foot cornstalks. We found the stone ruins at the base of a hill. It appeared out of the mist as we parted the final curtain of corn with a green field spread before it and yellow-gray fogged-out sand dunes as a backdrop. We walked through the doorways and explored each room, soaking in the antiquity of the site.

As the zone leader in Ingenieria, I had the opportunity to work with the district leaders in Comas and, in the process, visit the Romeros, Pastranas, Vilas and others. I exchanged bear hugs with all my friends, as it was great to see them again. We planned a final banquet for my return visit. Elder Ebbert, the district leader in Comas, had to learn how to take care of threatening dogs. We were surrounded by a pack of dogs when I picked up a rock and nailed the lead mongrel on the top of the head. This sent him off in a screaming fit. Instead of trying to bite us, the rest of the pack took off after the "squealer," biting at his haunches. This show of force converted Elder Ebbert to my "rabid-dog-bite-avoidance" technique.

I went through my second "Carnavales," or Mardi Gras, in Ingenieria. The goal of Carnavales revelers was to throw water on every person within range on every Sunday of the month of February. On Sunday we walked down the streets like army lookouts checking for snipers. When we came to two-story houses, we walked in the middle of the street to avoid a water ambush from roofs. While we were walking on a street one Sunday, a teen-ager came from behind us and threw water all over me. Unbeknownst to him, I had a small rock in my hand and I let it go in a Sandy Koufax type of delivery that caught him right in the rump!

On our third P-day in February we left early and collected Elders Ebbert and Lambert in Comas, on our way to visit ruins we had read about. We found pieces of cloth, an Inca skullcap, a throwing stick, and a ceremonial shaker. The other missionaries were catching my archeology addiction.

One effective way to ask golden questions in Ingenieria was to "pick on" men walking their children on the weekend. They appeared to be good family fathers. We conversed with them about the gospel as it related to their families.

Toward the end of February we met a family that was every missionary's dream. The husband—father of the Castillo family—had been working up in the Andes near Junin, in the mines. Somehow he came across a Book of Mormon, either through coworkers or friends. Because he had little else to do in his off hours at the mines, he read the entire book and came to believe it was true, though he had had no contact with Mormons or missionaries. When we met the Castillos in Ingenieria, he was excited to have the missionaries because he knew the Book of Mormon was true and had wanted to get baptized! His wife was interested also and we challenged to accept baptism. They accepted during our first meeting. We gave them a discussion every other day for meet weeks and they were baptized just before I left to go home. They were a truly golden family! I was really finishing my mission on a high.

We had two other families preparing for baptism before I would leave. The Bravo family finally received the paperwork necessary to process Hermano Bravo's divorce from his prior marriage. This would enable them to be baptized as well.

Hermana Alvarez, from one of our districts, helped us expedite the Bravos' paperwork through the city government, so we could get them ready for baptism. It took connections to get anything through the bureaucracy. Hermano Bravo saved all the money needed out of his meager earnings to pay for their marriage, which would take place the same day the divorce papers were processed. The faith of this family astounded me. Not only had they been paying tithing for years, but they also walked two miles to church every Sunday as an entire family so that they could save the money otherwise spent on bus fare.

We shared a good laugh with the Bravos—both in their fifties— over instructions received from Hermana Alvarez, who helped us process their divorce and marriage papers. She said "the *newlyweds* have to be there at nine in the morning." We kept teasing them about their newlywed status and what they would do for their honeymoon.

As I got closer to my time for leaving the mission field, certain things would take me back home, like receiving my BYU schedule to fill out for the spring term. I suppose I was getting "trunky," the term applied to all missionaries who have their trunk packed both physically and mentally in their efforts to ready to leave. I started collecting souvenirs and old books and other memorabilia from Peru that I would bring back with me.

Early in March I had a final banquet with the Romeros and the Pastranas while I was trading off and working in their area with Elder Ebbert. We shared favorite memories of their conversion process, joked together, and took some pictures of all of us together. We made plans for them all to come to the airport with Hermano Fajardo in the back of his pickup, along with other families I had worked with, to see me off in a couple of weeks. That night we baptized the Castillos after teaching them for only two weeks—the quickest start-to-finish conversion I had seen. Of course, they had both converted before we even met them. It was a great service. They both bore burning testimonies afterward.

I scheduled an appointment to talk to the director of the Museum of History who had written a number of books on the Great White God of the Incas and the pre-Incan people. I had spoken to him on the phone earlier about his books, and their correlation with the Book of Mormon, which he was not familiar with.

My phone call had been precipitated by an article we saw in the newspaper in Arequipa. The lead article one morning asked, in bold letters, "Did Christ Visit Peru?" We did a double take at the stack of newspapers we passed that showed this article on top. At first, I thought President Driggs had invested big bucks to advertise on the front page, but on reading the article, we learned that the author—the Museum of History director and the foremost authority on the Incas— theorized, based on the ancient legends and accounts of the bearded, apostle like statue, that Christ may have visited the pre-Incan people. When we arrived at the museum, the director, unfortunately, for us, was preparing for a trip to Cuzco. We talked with his assistant, who gave me a book on the religion of the pre-Incan people and told me of other books on the subject. I left him with the Book of Mormon, which he seemed to be developing a keen interest in as I discussed its description of the appearance of Jesus Christ on the continent and how it would explain the legends of the Great White God among the Incas and pre-Incan people.

My last mission conference, in the middle of March, brought me mixed feelings. It was my last opportunity to see missionaries I had grown to love as friends in the mission field. A tremendous camaraderie and team spirit indeed develops in the mission field, and you realize, as you leave to go home, that you will probably never again achieve the same level of camaraderie. No friendships were so intense, and so rooted in the gospel, as those developed in the mission field between companions, district members, zone members, and missionaries in general. We stopped by to say goodbye to the mayor of Comas. I gave him one of my ties—one that had survived in a respectable condition— as a present. In return I asked for one last favor—his help in obtaining a birth certificate for one of the investigators' little girls who was about to be baptized. He agreed to obtain the certificate and was very pleased I had stopped in to say goodbye.

Almost my entire mission had passed without any run-ins with the notorious criminal elements in Lima. Then my luck just about ended one evening as we walked back to our pension. Suddenly, a shadowy figure darted across my peripheral vision from the left, grabbing my wrist in an effort to yank off my watch. I jerked my wrist away with force. The effort knocked me on my back and I slid downward while the shadowy figure escaped. I crawled to my feet and tried to run after him. He disappeared but I still had my watch and was unhurt.

The Vila family also prepared a farewell luncheon. As Hermana Vila tearfully brought me an embroidered tablecloth and napkins that she had made, we all choked up with emotion. I left them my Bible as a *requerdo*—remembrance. We showed our last filmstrip to the Bravo family. Before we got to the spiritual part of our discussion, I projected the light on the ground, which drove their dog nutty while he was trying to chase the light as I maneuvered it around in circles. He started doing loops until he was so dizzy, he fell over while trying to walk. We were in tears with laughter.

The branch president found out I was leaving and invited me to speak to the La Florida Branch on my last Sunday in Peru. It seemed a fitting way to end my mission. I was in the office the first thing the next morning, after packing for Cuzco, as four of us who had finished our missions were traveling to Cuzco for a few days to see Macchu Picchu—the Lost City of the Incas.

# CHAPTER 13
## The Lost City of the Incas, and Homeward Bound

Our trip to Cuzco was an archeological smorgasbord. Cuz-co had been the capital of the Incan Empire. We stayed there two nights. Walking the ancient streets laid out by the Incas and built upon by the Spaniards after the conquest in the 1500s, we admired the accomplishments of the Incan civilization. The foundations for the buildings with Spanish roofs and sides were granite stones beautifully pieced together by the Incas. The stones had snug seams too tight to admit a knife blade. Spectacular stone walls, built by the Incas, dominated the Spanish cathedral. When the Spaniards came and were unable to convince the Incas to worship in the Catholic cathedral, they tore off the top of the Incan temple and rebuilt the cathedral on top of it, thereby ensuring that the Incas would attend the church. Of course, the Incas were only returning to their traditional place of worship.

We paid a taxi driver twenty-dollars for an all-day excursion for four of us outside the city. We wound our way up through the Andes—Cuzco is already at eight-thousand feet—past small alpine thatched-roof villages reminiscent of pictures of Switzerland, until we reached a valley surrounded by high peaks lined with hundreds of terraces that had been built by the Incas. We hiked for two hours straight up one of these peaks, passing terraces and waterfalls, until we reached the top. Situated on the ridge was the ancient city of Pisac. Built of perfectly square, carved red granite stones, the city had a vantage point that was breathtaking—a panoramic view of three valleys converging thousands of feet below. It had been a strategic lookout for the Incan Empire.

That same memorable afternoon we visited the ancient walled fortress of Sacsayhuaman, just outside Cuz-co. With its massive—at times, over twelve-foot—boulders pieced together with perfect seams, the fortress had guarded the entrance to the Incas' ancient capital. We mingled with the alpacas and llamas that were roaming freely through the grasses and ruins. Later our cab driver/guide took us up the valley to the site of the royal Incas' bath. The water spilling out of the stone terraces had traveled sixty miles down a perfectly carved stone conduit before emerging at the baths where the Incan kings came to bathe and wash.

We were off by train the next morning for Machu Pic-chu—The Lost City of the Incas. It was situated in the jungle on the eastern side of the Andes, where the Incas had fled from Cuzco after the Spanish conquest. The Spaniards never found Machu Picchu. The inhabitants lived there for several hundred years, dying off naturally without outside interference. The jungle reclaimed the city, covering it completely. The city was not uncovered again until 1918. Hiram Bingham, an explorer, had arrived in Cuzco that year, like many others who over the years had heard of The Lost City of the Incas, but he could not find it. A small cholo boy told Hiram Bingham he had seen The Lost City. Hyrum paid him as a guide to lead an expedition to the city. They traveled for weeks into the Andes, until they came upon The Lost City. It was hard to see more than a few carved stones glaring through the greenery until the jungle foliage was cut away. As the foliage was peeled away, a spectacular scene unfolded—a beautifully crafted stone city, backdropped by a huge green spire peak shooting straight up three-thousand feet, out of riverbeds running on both sides of the mountain saddle that cradled the city at the base of the spire.

Traveling on the vintage wooden car train toward Machu Picchu, we passed monstrous glacial ice flows in the white mountains surrounding us, as we wound our way first up through the western face of the Andes and then down the eastern back side, until we arrived at the base of Machu Picchu. We climbed into old beat up Volkswagen vans, then proceeded, at breakneck pace, up a small one-lane dirt road that made a series of switchback hairpin turns on the sheer mountain face, before reaching the top of the ridge holding the city. Our van was one of the last to leave, and those vans that had arrived first would be coming back down, yet our driver seemed un-concerned as he raced around blind corners without even honking his horn. Finally, as I expected, we rounded one corner and skidded to a stop, head-on with the van coming from the other direction. After an eternity of grinding dirt, gravel, and brakes, we stopped a few inches from each other's bumpers. There were no guardrails and any plunge off the side of the dirt road would have been a free fall of hundreds of feet, so I closed my eyes and cringed as we made it to the top.

As we crested the top, I was in wonderland. We climbed over the city and took pictures from hundreds of different camera angles. The ancient city was beautiful with its granite stonework, terraced layout, and the backdrop of the huge spire looming above the city. The spire had its own terraces and temple at the very top—viewable only through my telephoto lens. The temple in the middle of the city was built with eight-foot-by-twelve-foot stones quarried over sixty miles away and carried through the Andes over suspension bridges built by the Incas with hemp rope. Some of the stones had been carved uniformly in a tremendous feat of stonework. One huge altar stone was eight feet across, perfectly smooth, carved flat on the top with a small section at its head, carved into a triangular point. One of the guides told us it was a sacrificial stone. From my reading, I believed it had probably been a mummification stone where the Incas freeze-dried the bodies of their ancestors. They froze the bodies overnight, worked the body fluids out during the day, refroze them the next night, and repeated the process until the bodies were freeze-dried, perfectly preserved to be stored away in a vault within the city.

Small aqueducts and other freshwater channels wound through the town. These provided drinking water and a sanitation system. The Incas had been an advanced civilization. They used communal storehouses to feed the needy, the handicapped, widows, orphans, and any others in need. These storehouses were administered by the Incan priesthood. We also discovered a meeting area carved into a massive stone. Seats were carved in the face of the rock. Little channels ran through the arms of the chairs, down to the chairs below, providing drinking water during the meetings. This would have worked well until a child at the top decided to spit into the water basin! Underneath this meeting area was an altar, leading me to conclude that this meeting area had been the site of Sacrament meetings. One of the legends associated with it was that after a Sacrament meeting, maize dough balls had been passed among the congregation, in remembrance of the body of their god, and a wise old man would stand up and speak for hours. This must have been an account of a Sacrament meeting attended by a high Council speaker!

Through the course of my trip to Cuzco, I learned much about the Incas. I had already been studying them as a result of my passion for archeology. I learned that no one could explain their tremendous stonework ability, although it was suspected they had developed some kind of enzyme that softened the rock. Their knowledge of alloys—they could combine copper and tin to create a metal stronger than any steel we can put together—helped provide the tools for stone working. Incan doctors also performed a crude form of brain surgery, carving into skulls with copper-alloy surgical instruments. Modern doctors still seek these surgical tools because they never lose their edge. Incan brain surgery appears to have been designed to release evil spirits and ease pressure on the skull. Seeing that the bones around the carved section of the skulls had grown back together, archeologists deter-mined that patients survived and lived years after the surgery. The "doctors" performed this surgery by carving and folding back a flap of skin, then cutting a square section of bone out of the skull. A plate was inserted over the hole and the flap of skin was sewn shut.

Our trip to Cuzco was a fitting end for a great mission—we were overwhelmed by the splendor of what we had seen. We arrived back in Lima in the afternoon, made some final preparations, and went out to eat Chinese food that evening. We would be leaving for the airport in the early-morning hours.

About midnight, my stomach grew rebellious. Surging, rolling cramps rocked my abdomen and I reluctantly admitted to myself, on the way to the bathroom, that I had a case of food poisoning from the Chinese restaurant. I didn't think I would survive the taxi ride to the airport. I sweated out the ride but while at the airport, I had to make trips every minute to the bathroom, while at the same time trying to say my farewells to over ten families who had come to see me off. There were families there from my days in Comas, Callao, and other areas in Lima where I had worked. It was a very emotional farewell, as I realized I would never see these people again in this life. We shared a strong bond in the gospel. I had taught, and witnessed the baptism of, many of those present. We all embraced—in between my runs to the bathroom—and I boarded the plane, hoping I could make it into the air before I had to run to the bathroom on the plane.

I was literally drained, physically, mentally, and emotionally, by the time the eleven-hour flight ended and we landed in Los Angeles. I went through Customs with some trepidation—I had heard stories of missionaries' luggage having been inspected in minute detail because of drug problems in South America. One missionary, who had unknowingly returned with a gourd with fossil cocaine leaves in it, was accosted by customs agents who seized the gourd and grilled him about the leaves. It took me two hours to get through, and then, with screams of glee, my family and I simultaneously spotted each other and ran together. It was like a taste of reaching Heaven and rejoining relatives who had passed on. I ran into my mother's arms, with my father embracing both of us. Our big warm family embrace was soon joined by my two younger brothers and my sister, grandparents, aunts, uncles, and cousins. It was great to be home!

# CHAPTER 14
## Readjustment to Civilian Life

It seemed awkward, at first, to leave the ranks of missionaries and join those of regular civilian life. I reported back to the High Council and the Stake Presidency on my first Sunday back. The girl I had been writing to while on my mission had moved to Utah and could not fly down to see me for a couple of weeks. We talked on the telephone. It was a strained conversation—we did not just resume where we had left off.

The richest blessing of my life came immediately on the heels of the service I had performed during my mission. I am convinced I received this blessing as a direct result of my mission. My father asked a Mormon business associate if he knew of any sharp girls for me to date after just returning from my mission. This associate told my father of one girl, in particular, who was "as sharp as they come," and he called her mother to see if this girl would go out on a blind date. This was all proceeding unknown to me at the time. The "matchmaker" told my father the girl—Gaylene—might consider it, so my father got her phone number and called me at a friend's, interrupting a showing of my mission slides to tell me about this "hot prospect." I agonized over whether to call a girl, whom I had never seen, about a date—most of the blind dates I had been on before had failed. I finally decided, if I could ask golden questions on the streets of Peru, among complete strangers, I could at least call this girl. So I called Gaylene and we had an easy-flowing, interesting conversation for about a half hour and set a date for that weekend.

When I arrived to meet Gaylene, her older sister answered the door. The older sister had just had a baby and had been up all night with the baby. She had just awakened, was in her robe, had not put on makeup yet, and, needless to say, was not ready to put her best face forward for the day. Erroneously assuming it was Gaylene, I was not too enthused about my prospects. Gaylene's mother then appeared and told me Gaylene was getting ready and would be down the stairs momentarily. As she descended the stairs, I was blown away. She was beautiful, poised, and had a wonderful smile, which she flashed in my direction. As she approached, I made a fool of my-self by sticking out my hand for a good missionary handshake! We laughingly concluded that missionary habits die hard. We had a wonderful date at the zoo and later at the beach. Each of us had a date with someone else that evening, but afterward, we thought only of our earlier date with each other. I brought Gaylene home to meet my parents the next day, Sunday. I took her to our meetings and showed her my mission slide presentation—she still liked me after the slides! We dated every day for the next three and a half weeks, and we got engaged before I went up to BYU for the spring term. I hated to leave her but I needed to capitalize on my opportunity to get a semester's worth of Spanish units by taking one Spanish class. After missing each other for two and a half months and running up expensive phone bills, I finished my term at BYU and returned. We were married in the Los Angeles Temple one month later. Gaylene is the greatest blessing of my life. She is a blessing I would not have received but for my faithful missionary service. As an eternal team, we passed through many years of school, I developed my legal career, and we had our greatest mutual blessings, our six children.

The mission experience prepared me for life as a husband, father, family man, and professional. It prepared me to magnify—expand— my priesthood by strengthening my testimony and rooting me more deeply in the gospel. It prepared me to live with someone twenty-four hours a day, giving and taking, communicating, ironing out problems, and cooperating in a companionship. It also taught me empathy and compassion, opening my eyes to the blessings I had received, and to the difficulties and hardships of life for many people in the world.

I learned discipline, how to keep a calendar, how to study, how to work hard, and how, after doing all I could do, to put faith and trust in my Father in Heaven through prayer. These tools became invaluable as

I sought a legal career through rigorous schooling.

In addition to all of these skills and tools acquired through missionary service, my mission provided a rich source of fond memories and great stories to use in teaching seminary, priesthood quorums, and Sunday school. Not a day goes by that I don't have a fond memory of my mission float through my mind. Every member should prepare to go and serve, and then, I would say, simply, "Do it!"

# EPILOGUE:
## The Joy of Saving Even One Soul

One evening in October 1992, over eighteen years after I had returned home from Peru, I received a mysterious telephone call. The woman's voice on the other end carried a trace of a Hispanic accent and asked, with some timidity, whether I was Scott Hoyt, the missionary who had been in Peru, serving a mission, almost two decades before. With growing excitement and curiosity, I answered, "Yes," and immediately went into Spanish and asked who she was. It was Celia, the niece of the Romeros who we had baptized with the Romeros in Co-mas, over nineteen years before. She explained she had moved to the United States a few years back and was now living in New York, but happened to be in South-ern California, visiting friends, and mentioned to them, "Wouldn't it be great if I could locate the missionary that baptized me, Elder Hoyt, he lived here near Disneyland." The family she was visiting suggested, "Why don't we look in the phone book?" They easily found my number in the phone book. We had a fantastic reunion the next day when Celia's friends brought her by for a visit. I pulled out my scrapbook, my slides, and my missionary journal and we recounted our times in Comas and friends from years past. I was most gratified to hear her explain how the Romeros, the Pastranas and the Vilas had continued faithful in the gospel and many of their children had served, or were serving, missions in various parts of South America and Spain! I felt the reward promised in the Doctrine and the Covenants, the great joy of bringing one soul back to our Father in Heaven, and the increasing joy with each additional soul. I could also see how the impact of baptizing one family expanded proportionally over the generations, with their children in turn serving missions and becoming church leaders. Through Celia, I also found the phone number of Hermana Pastrana and called her while I was back in New York on business. I later received a call from Hermana Oliveras, also of Comas, who had moved to the United States, and I met with Celia after our reunion. The joy at renewing these old acquaintances was indescribable.